The Penn State
Blue Band

The Penn State Blue Band

A CENTURY OF PRIDE AND PRECISION

THOMAS E. RANGE II and

SEAN PATRICK SMITH

THE PENNSYLVANIA STATE UNIVERSITY PRESS
UNIVERSITY PARK, PENNSYLVANIA

Library of Congress Cataloging-in-Publication Data

Range, Thomas E., 1967–
     The Penn State Blue Band : a century of pride and
precision / Thomas E. Range II, Sean Patrick Smith.
          p.   cm.
     Includes index.
     ISBN 0-271-01960-3 (alk. paper)
     1. Penn State Blue Band—History.   I. Smith, Sean
Patrick, 1968– .   II. Title.
ML28.U65P4647   1999
784.8'3'06074853—dc21   99-24468
                                                        CIP

Published by The Pennsylvania State University Press,
University Park, PA 16802-1003

It is the policy of The Pennsylvania State University Press
to use acid-free paper for the first printing of all clothbound
books. Publications on uncoated stock satisfy the minimum
requirements of American National Standard for Information
Sciences—Permanence of Paper for Printed Library Materials,
ANSI Z39.48–1992.

ENDPAPER PHOTOGRAPHS BY TOM MAIRS

To Maureen, Shelli, Megan, Sherilyn, and Ray

Contents

Foreword
by Graham B. Spanier,
President, Penn
State University
page ix

Foreword
by Joe Paterno,
Head Football Coach,
Penn State University
page xi

Preface
page xiii

Acknowl-
edgments
page xv

1 A Brief History
of Marching Bands,
by Thomas E.
Range Sr.
page 1

2 Laying the
Foundation,
Pre-1899
page 5

3 Carnegie's Gift,
1899–1909
page 9

4 Receiving
Professional
Direction,
1910–1919
page 23

5 Gaining
National
Recognition,
1920–1929
page 43

6 Passing the
Baton,
1930–1939
page 59

7 Surviving
the War Years,
1940–1949
page 69

8 Setting New
Standards,
1950–1959
page 87

9 Creating New
Traditions,
1960–1969
page 103

10 Growing and
Changing,
1970–1979
page 127

11 Continuing
the Excellence,
1980–1989
page 143

12 Joining
the Elite,
1990–1999
page 159

13 For the Future
That We Wait:
1999 and Beyond
page 175

Afterword
by O. Richard Bundy,
Director, Penn State
Blue Band
page 179

Appendixes
1. At a Glance: The
Blue Band Compared
with Other College
Marching Bands
2. How the Band
Has Grown
page 181

Index
page 187

Foreword
by Graham B. Spanier

PRESIDENT, THE PENNSYLVANIA STATE UNIVERSITY

EVERY TIME I HEAR *the Penn State Blue Band, I think*
about how each note resonates with so much tradition and
pride that it is impossible not to be caught up in the spirit
of this great University. Whether it is performing the Alma
Mater, a Penn State fight song, or a half-time show,
whether it is the full marching band, a smaller ensemble,
a symphonic group, or the ever loyal alumni band, the Blue
Band has a magical ability to capture the attention and
rouse the emotions of those in its presence. Few other
groups can quiet a crowd of nearly 100,000 people to a
hush, bring them to their feet for a deafening cheer, or lead
them to raise their voices in song.

A marching band plays a unique role in university life.
The musicians, baton twirlers, flag bearers, drum major,

and others associated with the band are highly visible ambassadors representing their school not only at home but to audiences far and wide. Band members create a public image of the quality and enthusiasm that characterize an institution. They generate important goodwill. They also support our athletic teams magnificently, involving fans deeply in the excitement throughout a game. And to the delight of so many, the band also entertains.

Yet our marching band does even more. In preserving cherished school songs and adding to this repertoire, the band knits generations of students and alumni together. The medium of music builds a special bond that unites Penn Staters all over the world in the warm feelings of all that our University has meant to students over the years.

The Penn State Blue Band does all of these things with a level of excellence that is unsurpassed. The commitment and hard work of the members and staff shine through in every appearance. The sounds—and sights—of a Blue Band performance are a perfect Penn State experience.

I am grateful for the outstanding job done by the Penn State Blue Band and deeply appreciative of the century of tradition that stands behind it. To all who have been associated with this great University tradition, I offer my thanks and admiration for the very special contributions the Blue Band has made over the last hundred years.

I love to listen to the band, and I know that the next century of Penn Staters will feel the same way.

Foreword
by Joe Paterno

HEAD FOOTBALL COACH, THE PENNSYLVANIA STATE UNIVERSITY

IT IS AN HONOR FOR ME *to salute the Penn State Blue Band on its 100th anniversary.*

As someone who has witnessed a lot of band performances in five decades around Penn State football, I can say without equivocation that the Blue Band's musical and marching precision are unmatched anywhere.

When the Nittany Lions charge through the team aisle formation prior to each home game, the verve that comes from the Blue Band's animated rendition of "The Nittany Lion" never fails to energize me and, I am sure, every player who has ever had the experience of making that dramatic entrance into Beaver Stadium.

Because of my involvement in coaching, I recognize the many hours of hard work that go into each and every

Blue Band performance. The excellence the band has consistently displayed does not come without a price, which thousands of young men and women have willingly paid to splendidly represent Penn State here and elsewhere around the nation.

The Blue Band never gets credit for a touchdown or a goal, but the enthusiasm its members have generated at Beaver Stadium and other athletic venues, from Rec Hall and Jeffrey Field to the Bryce Jordan Center, has carried from the stands to the playing field, fortifying every athlete wearing Blue and White.

As the Blue Band marks its centennial season, those who love Penn State should stand up and cheer the people who helped establish, and those who have preserved, the spirit that makes our band unique. May the next 100 years be filled with the same achievement as the century just completed.

Strike up the band!

Preface

A HUSH FALLS OVER *the 95,000 people in attendance as drum taps measure the seconds in the middle of the field. A whistle blows once, then four times rapidly, and suddenly the drums thunder in a staccato fury. Up from the depths of Beaver Stadium storm the 275 members of The Pennsylvania State University Marching Blue Band as they triple-time onto the field. The only thing louder than the fight song they play is the roar of thousands of football fans cheering them on.*

The excitement, the pride, and the tradition of the Blue Band have been experienced by generations of Nittany Lion fans for 100 years. The dedication to excellence of its members past and present instills a sense of pride in all who have watched them perform their precision maneuvers on the field and heard the music they play. It is the roar of the Nittany Lion that they hear in the sound of Penn State's premier band, at the football stadium, at the basketball arena, along parade routes, and at the concert hall.

The history of the Blue Band is filled with struggle and triumph, perseverance and perfection. As the years pass, the history of this band passes from living memory too, growing more silent each year through the march of time. As the band finishes its first century, those memories, stories, and traditions must be preserved for future generations to enjoy. This book attempts to do just that.

It starts with a brief historical overview of marching bands in general, to serve as a background for the story that unfolds at a small provincial college in rural Pennsylvania just before the turn of the twentieth century. The story becomes a short history of music at that college, known then as the Penn State College, and then becomes the story of the struggle to start one particular musical group that would evolve into one of the greatest marching bands in collegiate history.

The story of that group, which came to be known in 1923 as the "Blue Band," after its new, blue uniforms, will march through 100 years in the illustrated pages that follow. A word from the current Director of the Blue Band, Dr. O. Richard Bundy, closes our tale of this exciting and dynamic organization. The book also includes two comprehensive appendixes: (1) "How the Band Has Grown," which shows changes over the years, and (2) a comparison, "At a Glance," of Penn State's Blue Band with some other American college and university marching bands, including an overview of the various "styles" of marching.

The authors have made every effort to see that the facts mentioned in this book, such as names, dates, and places, are accurate. However, historical records often contain variations and even contradictions that cannot be resolved. In those cases, we have chosen the most likely version.

As former members and student leaders of this great marching band, the authors are proud to present this broad history. We really can't say we alone wrote this history, though, because it has been the thousands of former band members who really wrote it. We merely chronicled that which was accomplished by those who went before us and who came after us.

We hope you enjoy reading The Penn State Blue Band's history as much as we have enjoyed putting it down on paper. Thank you for participating in the celebration of the Blue Band's Century of Pride.

Thomas E. Range II, Class of 1989, Sousaphone
PRESIDENT, ALUMNI BLUE BAND ASSOCIATION

Sean Patrick Smith, Class of 1990, Mellophone
CHAIRMAN, ALUMNI BLUE BAND ASSOCIATION
HISTORICAL COMMITTEE

Acknowledgments

Although there were only two authors of this book, many individuals have helped "write" the rich history recounted in these pages. Without the dedication to excellence of the past and present members of The Penn State Marching Blue Band, this book would never have been written. We thank them all for their 100 years of devoted service to The Pennsylvania State University.

The authors would especially like to thank the following former and current band members for agreeing to be interviewed: Llewelyn Fisher '28, Howard Widenor '33, William Dye '37, Edward Pollock '42, Dorothy Ann (Young) Pollock '43, Glenn Orndorf '46, Hubert H. Haugh '54, Dwight Tothero '54, Ronald Reinhard '61, Duane Alexander '62, Richard Ammon '64, Allen Garbrick '67, Lawrence Newmark '67, Timothy Vought '68, Ned Trautman '70, William Arnold Jr. '71, Jeffrey A. Robertson '75, Kenneth Fultz '78, Gerrie Delaney' 79, Mark Harrington '79, Jay Weitzne '79, Jeffrey Rohrbeck '81, David Hartman '83, Mark King '83, Cheryl Roth '88, Terri Ruch '88, Bryan Stevenson '88, Duane Bullock '89, Mark Sperry '90, Vince Range '91, David Arnoldi '92, Arthur Miley '92, Kathleen Reish '92, Donald Cramer '93, Barbara Garbrick '93, Michael Harrell '93, Shawn Reish '93, Amy Wilson '93, Drew Yingling '93, Erin (Eck) Arnoldi '94, Thomas Roberts '94, Jon Sanford '95, Jessica Schumacher '95, Jennifer Davis '96, Brian Legutko '96, John Palchak '96, Brandy Sheaffer '96, Kari Blase '97, Katy McDowell '99, and Matthew Kologi, Class of 2000.

The authors would also like to thank all the past Blue Band

historians who created the informative and interesting scrapbooks summarizing their years with the band. Without these yearbooks, collecting all the information found in this book would not have been possible. Additional research materials were made available by the staff of the Penn State Room at Pattee Library. Our appreciation for their hard work is great.

Thanks are also in order for the staff of Penn State Press, without whose efforts and support this history would have been merely a small book of little interest to any save the most ardent Blue Band fans. Of all the staff at Penn State Press, the authors especially thank Sanford G. Thatcher, who listened to the dreams of two Penn State graduates and helped those dreams become a reality, and Peggy Hoover and Sigrid Albert, who helped create that reality.

A special thank-you goes to Thomas E. Range Sr., who not only wrote the first chapter of the book, "A Brief History of Marching Bands," but also acted as our mentor and "voice of experience" as a published author himself. We also thank Edward Barry, Michael Bezilla, O. Richard Bundy, Ned C. Deihl, Louise Dye, Scott P. Gitchell, Greg Grieco, Liz Mills, Suzanne Musselman, Coach Joe Paterno, Daniel Simon, Graham B. Spanier, Mark Sperry, Lena Spinneweber, and Karen Walk for their contributions to and support of this project.

Last, but most important, we would like to thank our wives and daughters, Maureen Range, Shelli Smith, Megan Range, and Sherilyn Smith. Without your inspiration, love, patience, and sacrifice, we would never have realized this dream.

PHOTOGRAPH AND ILLUSTRATION ACKNOWLEDGMENTS
Unless otherwise noted, the photographs and illustrations in this book are provided courtesy of The Pennsylvania State University Archives / Penn State Room; University PhotoGraphics, Penn State University; the Penn State Sports Information Office; the Penn State Blue Band Office; and the following individuals: Dick Ammon, Erin Arnoldi, Jere Fridy, Greg Grieco, Hubie Haugh, Kris Kokosko, Tom Mairs, Steve Manuel, Ed Pollock, Michael Rancik, Thomas E. Range Sr., William Rubert, Mark Sperry, and Alan Wood. We are grateful to all for sharing so generously. Other sources of illustrations were the Big Ten Conference office in Park Ridge, Illinois; Blue Band Historian scrapbooks; and *La Vie* *1902, 1906, 1908, 1909, 1910, 1913, 1927, 1930, 1940, 1998.*

by THOMAS E. RANGE SR.

I A Brief History of Marching Bands

THE HISTORY OF MARCHING BANDS *is intertwined with that of organized warfare, just as the cadenced step of a marching unit has its roots in the tactical maneuvering of troops. As better-trained and better-disciplined armies were being formed from the unorganized hordes of armed warriors that typified clan and tribal warfare, a need developed for instant communication of battle commands from the leaders of the combating forces to their subordinates in the field. Drums, the earliest form of musical instrument, fulfilled this function at first. In the din of combat, the beat of the drum, signaling orders from the field generals, rose above the sounds of the clashing troops. Later in military history, horns fashioned from animal antlers and then of bronze and brass served as a more*

GUARDS' BAND RETURNING FROM BUCKINGHAM PALACE
AFTER CHANGING OF THE GUARD, LONDON.

L.P.465

ABOVE The Queen's Guard in London has always been a marching band spectators love to see.

RIGHT The Queen's Guard in Williamsburg, Virginia, is quite similar to the one in London.

sophisticated method of communication. Even cavalry horses in ancient Mediterranean civilizations were trained to obey the commands of the bugle. Drums, bugles, fifes, and bagpipes also served to hearten warriors as they faced their grim tasks on the battlefield. Stirring their emotions with the sounds of their musicians, the troops were able to fight with excessive fervor.

It is significant that one of the first units to be established at the United States Military Academy at West Point was its marching band. The Academy, the first permanent military school in the United States, was established in 1802 by President Thomas Jefferson. During the early years of the school, the field activities of the cadets were dictated by cadet fife and drum corps. In 1813 the 3rd Artillery band of Governor's Island in New York Harbor was transferred to West Point, becoming the first band to be stationed at the Academy. Sporting red coats trimmed in blue, the band wore uniforms opposite in color scheme to the artillery and engineer regiment uniforms, making it instantly distinguishable from the combat troops. The original twenty-member band, led by a drum major with the unlikely name of George Washington, became a popular fixture at the Academy and became renowned in military circles away from the school as well.

The popularity of concert marching bands with the general public in America began with bandmaster Patrick Sarsfield Gilmore, born in Dublin, Ireland, in 1829. Organizing his own concert marching band in 1859, Gilmore sponsored huge music festivals in Boston and New Orleans during and after the Civil War, sometimes with tens of thousands of musicians and choral singers performing. Playing hundreds of concerts around the United States and abroad in the 1860s, 1870s, and 1880s, the band became quite famous, and march music began to grow in popularity. Gilmore wrote one such popular march during the Civil War that is still well known today: "When Johnny Comes Marching Home."

But the man most responsible for the popular appeal of the marching band was known as the March King, John Philip Sousa. This monumental figure in American music was born in Washington, D.C., in 1854 to his Portuguese father and Bavarian mother. Sousa

and his nine siblings were exposed to band music at an early age; their father, Antonio, was a trombone player in the United States Marine Band. Studying vocal music and seven musical instruments, young John became so enamored of performing that at the age of thirteen he attempted to run away and join a circus band. To curtail future impulsiveness on the part of his adventurous son, Antonio Sousa enlisted him in the Marine Corps as a musical apprentice.

While in the Marine Corps, John Philip Sousa wrote his first published musical composition, "Moonlight on the Potomac Waltzes," at the age of eighteen in 1872. The next year, Sousa published his first march, "Review." When his military service was finished in 1875, Sousa performed professionally on the violin, touring with the Offenbach Orchestra. He eventually conducted theater orchestras on Broadway as well.

Sousa was enticed back to Washington in 1880 to assume leadership of the United States Marine Band. He conducted this most famous military band, nicknamed "The President's Own," for twelve years, serving during the administrations of Presidents Hayes, Garfield, Arthur, Cleveland, and Benjamin Harrison. During this twelve-year span, Sousa composed his well-known marches "Semper Fidelis" (the motto of the Marines, meaning "always faithful" in Latin) in 1888 and "The Washington Post" in 1889, commissioned by and titled in honor of Sousa's hometown newspaper.

During the last two years of his tour of duty Sousa took the Marine Band on tour throughout the nation. While on tour Sousa met David Blakely, a professional event promoter, who convinced him to resign from his position with the Marines and start his own civilian band, based in Willow Grove, Pennsylvania. The first performance of Sousa's new band was on September 26, 1892, at the Stillman Music Hall in Plainfield, New Jersey. From there Sousa's band toured with great success throughout the United States, Canada, and, in 1900, Europe. In 1910 the band toured the world for one year, adding to the fame and popularity of Sousa and his band. Sousa died on March 6, 1932, at a rehearsal of the Ringgold Band in Reading, Pennsylvania, ending a conducting career that stretched more than fifty-two years.

LEFT One of the first "college bands" was established at the U.S. Military Academy at West Point. Now the military bands at West Point consist of career musicians.

RIGHT The military has always relied on music for morale-boosting.

Sousa wrote more than 100 marches, including "Stars and Stripes Forever" (1897), which Congress eventually declared the nation's national march. He surpassed his musical predecessor Patrick Gilmore as America's premier bandmaster and did much to improve the quality of band music and instrumentation of marching bands. Sousa designed the sousaphone, a tuba that wraps around the musician and is supported on the shoulder while marching or standing. Another concert tuba used primarily in military bands, the helicon, was also developed by Sousa. Responsible for the tremendous popularity of marching bands, John Philip Sousa did much for the rise of marching bands prevalent at college sporting events around the nation today.

It was but a small journey for marching bands to travel from the battlefield to the football field and the Via Appia to the homecoming parade route. Football is often described in military terms, as when gridiron "warriors battle their foes." Essentially, a football game is something of a mock war, where two opposing forces invade each other's territories and defend by force against such encroachment. Natural parallels bring other aspects and terminology of warfare to the gridiron, such as armor, tactics and strategy, a chain of command, and marching bands.

TOP Many colleges provide marching bands for halftime entertainment during football games.

BOTTOM An offshoot of the marching band is the drum corps, where percussion and brass players perform nonstop drills. The Concord Blue Devils drum corps has been World Champion numerous times.

Colleges and universities, with their emphasis on excellence and achievement in many different fields, have turned football and sports in general into one of the more visible and identifiable aspects of their scholastic spirit. Part of the pageantry, tradition, and excitement of college sports today is provided by college marching bands. Bands at some universities have even become as popular and as famous as the sports teams they perform for, such as Ohio State, Michigan, Texas, and the University of Southern California.

Above all, each college marching band represents the united spirit of fellow college students, alumni, and sports fans in supporting its college's athletic teams. Marching bands are an integral part of the nation's top autumnal pastime, and no Division I football college or university is without one. Without them, much of the emotion and sense of identification with a particular school would be lost. Indeed, Saturday afternoons would be gray.

THE ORIGIN OF *The Pennsylvania State University Marching Blue Band is clearly defined as beginning in the year 1899. But to begin our story at that date would be to ignore much of the detail behind the band's foundation, and that would be an injustice to the broader picture and indeed to the band itself. To understand and appreciate the history of the Blue Band, we must also understand the background against which the members of the Blue Band perform. To do this, we must look to a time almost fifty years earlier, to the founding of The Pennsylvania State University itself.*

When Penn State was established it was intended to be an agricultural institution. In the early 1850s, agricultural societies dedicated to using science and technology to improve farming methods advocated the creation of agricultural schools around the United States, with some success. The Pennsylvania State Agricultural Society, at its second annual meeting in Harrisburg in January 1853, proposed to hold a special convention in March of that year to plan an agricultural college in Pennsylvania. The March convention endorsed founding the Farmers' High School, so named in order to allay suspicions of farmers who may have been distrustful of traditional colleges. Nevertheless, the school would award baccalaureate degrees and include instruction in classical as well as agricultural subjects. The Pennsylvania State Senate passed the bill incorporating the school, and Governor William Bigler signed it into law on April 13, 1854.

Later that year the Pennsylvania General Assembly (the state's lower legislative house) revised the charter, reducing the number of Board of Trustees members of the Farmers' High School from sixty to thirteen when the required quorum repeatedly could not be reached to discuss where the school should be built. Governor James Pollock signed the new charter on February 22, 1855 (the recognized founding date of Penn State) and in so doing ensured the establishment of the college. Built on 200 acres of rolling farmland near the geographic center of Pennsylvania, the mission of the Farmers' High School was to instruct its students in the application of science to improve agricultural methods.

The original "Old Main" as it looked in 1859.

Although the school was primarily an agricultural institution of study, a healthy interest in music was always present among the student body. As early as 1859, the first year the college enrolled students, the Farmers' High School Board of Trustees entertained a communication from a number of the sixty-nine students enrolled who wanted to form a musical band. While the Board approved of the idea of a band, it felt it "did not require any other action on their part than the expression of their individual hopes that [the students] be successful in their efforts." Woefully lacking in resources at the time, the school was unable to make any facilities or funding available for such an endeavor.

The admission of women to the college in 1871 further stimulated the study of music, which became an academic subject at Penn State in 1874. Later, with the establishment of student fraternal organizations and the removal of the ban on dancing on campus, musical organizations began to proliferate. Student singing and instrumental trios, quartets, and other musical ensembles often performed at dances, student social occasions, and not a few faculty functions.

Eventually, before the turn of the century, the school made avail-

able facilities for piano and organ lessons, but such activities were charged separately from tuition, and students were tutored on an individual basis. The college also had a small volunteer chapel orchestra with fewer than ten members who performed for the compulsory church services held every weekday morning in the Main building.

Unable to formally support a band for the students in its early years, the college did, however, support marching. From very early in the history of Penn State, the college has had a strong military training organization. In 1863 Penn State, then known as The Agricultural College of Pennsylvania, solidified its financial future when it was guaranteed revenues from the sale of federal land, in accordance with the Morrill or "Land Grant" Act. The act, proposed as a federal bill by Vermont Congressman Justin S. Morrill, supported the endowment of at least one college in each state where the leading objective was to teach agricultural science and mechanical arts. Each state was to receive 30,000 acres of federal land to sell for each U.S. senator and representative it had in Congress. Pennsylvania, having little federal land, received land scrip to sell instead, which entitled the purchaser to buy federal land anywhere in the United States. Signed into law by President Abraham Lincoln on July 2, 1862, the act eventually allowed The Agricultural College of Pennsylvania, the only college in Pennsylvania at the time that could adhere to the act's guidelines, to be the sole recipient of Pennsylvania's interest in monies generated by the sale of federal land scrip.

In exchange for designation as Pennsylvania's only land-grant college, the Agricultural College required its male students to take four years of military tactical training and to be treated as cadets. Under certain conditions these students were entitled to appointment as brevet second lieutenants in the Pennsylvania National Guard before the turn of the century. Freshman and sophomore participation in what eventually became the Reserve Officers Training Corps (ROTC) was mandatory at Penn State until 1964.

Mention of fife and drum musicians in the college's military organization goes back to 1874 and three musicians: fifer William T. Read, tenor drummer B. Frank Knoche, and bass drummer George L. Potter Jr. The fife and drums were used primarily to set cadence for battalion marching drills and parades but not for much else. Later, in 1877, the Board

LEFT Women were admitted almost from the beginning of Penn State's history. Of course, there were no coed dorms at the time, so the ladies stayed at the "Ladies' Cottage."

RIGHT The Armory was one of the first buildings erected at the college. It was right next to the Obelisk.

One of the first pictures of musicians at Penn State. This fife and drum corps dates back to the mid-1870s.

of Trustees hired Read and Knoche at the rate of $13 per annum to instruct the drum corps, but lack of musicians caused the corps to fall apart in the early 1880s. In 1889 the fife and drum corps was restarted under the direction of another cadet, Lieutenant Silas Wolfe. Consisting of four fifers, four tenor drummers, and one bass drummer, it was considered by the students to be a much desired acquisition for the college battalion. In spite of the energies of these early musicians, however, they were without college sanction or organization, and no musical corps received official recognition as an integral part of Penn State until 1899, when the true precursor of the Blue Band, the Cadet Bugle Corps, was founded.

3 Carnegie's Gift, 1899–1909

ON SUNDAY MORNING *September 17, 1899, Penn State's commandant of cadets and mathematics instructor, Captain Thomas H. Taliaferro, was making his first weekly semester inspection of the cadet barracks, which were on the upper floors of Old Main building at the time. While inspecting the dormitory room of two students, freshman George Herbert Deike and his roommate Harry E. Leety, he noticed a bugle festooned with a haversack and a canteen hanging on the wall over an American flag. When asked about the bugle, Cadet Deike told Taliaferro that it was his: he was the regimental bugler for Company F of the Fourteenth Pennsylvania Volunteer Infantry during the Spanish-American War. Intrigued by the young man's tale, the commandant instructed him to report to his office with his bugle on Monday afternoon.*

That next day Deike arrived at Taliaferro's office and was instructed by him to demonstrate the sounding of service calls. Impressed, the commandant appointed Deike chief musician and added him to the noncommissioned battalion staff. Taliaferro also authorized organization of a Cadet Bugle Corps if Deike could find qualified members.

By October 1 of that year three other freshman buglers, Edwin Ray Norris, Percy Marvin Snoeberger, and Spanish-American War veteran Edgar Earle "Paddy" Godard, along with senior bass drummer Oliver Christmas "Irish" Edwards and junior snare drummer George Washington Dodge joined Deike to become the first members of the Cadet Bugle Corps. The Corps was in full operation from that point on, performing for the battalion drills and on other college occasions. At the end of the school year it led the final dress parade from Old Main to the Armory (where Willard Building now stands) during June Commencement in 1900. Edwards, graduating that year, retired from the Bugle Corps before Commencement. Junior John Monroe Craig took his place.

During those two semesters the six members of the Bugle Corps met frequently and discussed organizing a full Cadet Band along the lines of Cornell University's. First they had to find enough musicians on campus and the funding for instruments. The six canvassed the student body at the beginning of the fall semester of 1900 to find more musicians. There was much interest among the student body and the faculty in organizing a Cadet Band. *The Free Lance*, the college's student publication at the time, advocated organizing a full band: "The advantages to be derived from a military band are plainly to be seen. It would add much to the ordinary drills, and at Commencement and other occasions when State wishes to appear at her best, the appearance would be improved. Such a band, after being well started, could also be used as a concert band. It is to be hoped that the trustees will favor the idea and aid in carrying it out."

The cadet musicians eventually found twenty-five musicians with some band experience. Fortunately about half owned their own instruments. With Captain Taliaferro's help, the musicians drew up a petition to start the Cadet Band and presented it to the college's Board of Trustees. The petition asked the Board for funds to purchase twelve more instruments and included bids from musical instrument manufacturers and dealers ranging from $215 to $415 for brass instruments and from $260 to $523 for silver-plated instruments. Regretfully the Executive Committee of the Board, in its October 1900 meeting, responded that "there were no College funds now available for such a purpose," but that they recognized the importance of the object in view and earnestly hoped that it might be successfully accomplished.

General James Addams Beaver, president of Penn State's Board of Trustees at the time and a former governor of Pennsylvania, was also in favor of a Cadet Band. He had been impressed by the performance of the Cadet Bugle Corps at the Commencement ceremonies that June. While having to deny the Corps' petition for budgetary reasons, General Beaver and College President George W. Atherton each donated $50 to help pay for the instruments. Another trustee, H. V. White, made a $100 donation to the fund.

Professor A. Howry Espenshade, an instructor in the English Department, was also

sympathetic to the cause of the band and approached President Atherton with an idea. "You know that Andrew Carnegie has a great fondness for donating organs," suggested Espenshade, "and I believe that he might perhaps be prevailed upon to buy the necessary instruments for a cadet band for our student battalion." President Atherton replied, "Well, there would be certainly no harm in asking him." He asked Espenshade to draft a letter to the steel magnate and Board of Trustees member over the signature of General Beaver, a friend of Carnegie's, asking for a $100 donation to the Cadet Band fund. A week later, in reply, Beaver received from Carnegie the following cablegram, which Dr. Atherton read to the assembled student body at chapel services that late autumn.

The 1900 Cadet Band. Sitting from left to right are George Herbert Deike and Percy Marvin Snoeberger. Standing are John Monroe Craig, George Washington Dodge, Edgar Earle "Paddy" Godard, and Edwin Ray Norris.

My Dear Governor:
Please let me furnish the music for the College boys. I have directed my cashier to send you a check for eight hundred dollars.

With that reply the State College Cadet Band was ensured a place at Penn State that

George Herbert Deike

George Deike, one of the founders of the Penn State Blue Band, is arguably the most distinguished Penn State band alumnus. His life has left its mark indelibly on the university, on Pennsylvania, and on the mining industry. After his graduation from Penn State in 1903 as a mining engineer, George began working for different mines in the towns of Altoona, Charleroi, and Creighton, Pennsylvania. In 1910 he joined the U.S. Bureau of Mines, which had been created in response to a series of disastrous mine explosions and other mining accidents, as an engineer. When he reported for his first day of work at the bureau's Pittsburgh office, he found it deserted: all the other engineers had rushed to Briceville, Tennessee, where they began to recover the bodies of eighty-four miners killed in still another explosion. For the next four years George helped recover the bodies

of many other unfortunate miners killed in dozens of accidents. The horror of those experiences so affected George that he vowed to change the safety standards and equipment employed by coal miners. In 1914 he and fellow engineers John Ryan and Harrison Denning "Joe" Mason (a classmate of Deike's and the originator of the Nittany Lion as Penn State's Mascot) formed the Mine Safety Appliances Company, which provided miners with safety equipment. In 1915 Deike asked the famous inventor Thomas Edison to devise a battery-powered lamp for coal miners, to replace the dangerous open-flame lamps then in use. Edison later described his new invention as his greatest humanitarian achievement.

Deike's mark on Penn State is equally notable. Starting in 1922 Deike served as president of the Penn State Alumni Association until 1925, when he was elected to the Board of Trustees of the college. He served as vice-president of the Board from 1947 to 1956 and then as president from 1956 until 1958. In 1955 University President Eric A. Walker appointed Deike regional director of the Association of Governing Boards of State Universities.

Perhaps recalling the generosity of an earlier industrialist, Andrew Carnegie, Deike donated more than just his time to Penn State. Among his many philanthropic endeavors is a scholarship he started in 1951 in memory of his late son, Kenneth, who was a Penn State graduate in 1930 and died suddenly in 1939. The scholarship, consisting of 100 shares of common stock of Phillips Petroleum and valued at the time at $7,700, would be granted to applicants who demonstrated leadership

and athletic ability, as Kenneth did as a freshman football player and student manager of the Penn State varsity baseball team. Participating in the fiftieth anniversary of the Blue Band in 1949, Deike donated to the band six silver-plated sousaphones valued at the time at $4,000.

Mine Safety Appliances became a multimillion-dollar corporation with many offices around the United States, making George Deike a wealthy man. When he died in 1963 he left a personal fortune of almost $2 million to his wife and son, George Jr.

In 1965 a new earth sciences building, bearing Deike's name, was erected at a cost of more than $3 million. The building added more than 115,000 square feet of research and instructional space for the College of Mineral Industries and honored a man whose interest and involvement in Penn State continued for a lifetime. George Deike will always be remembered not only as an enterprising and successful Nittany Lion but also as a philanthropist and a humanitarian.

December, when the Executive Committee graciously accepted the gift and had the instruments purchased. According to the minutes for December 27, 1900, the Executive Committee expressed to Carnegie: "No single act in many years has awakened so warm an enthusiasm among the entire body of students, and the friends of the College regard this gift as one of the most stimulating and healthful towards the growth of a vigorous and manly College spirit." So appreciative of Carnegie's generosity were the students of Penn State that they dedicated their 1901 yearbook, *La Vie*, to him. The letter to Dr. Atherton from Carnegie that accompanied the cashier's check added: "I take particular pleasure in making this gift, because I have long held that there is no better way for a boy to get the devilment out of his system than to blow it out through a brass horn."

George Deike was named president of the new Cadet Band; George Dodge was named drum major; George Gilbert Pond, Professor of Chemistry and dean of the School of Natural Sciences representing the college administration, was treasurer; and "Paddy" Godard was secretary and bandmaster. According to Deike, Godard was a "real musician" and, because of his ability as such, "much credit is due him for the fine start [the Cadet Band] made."

Godard, a former member of the Fifth Pennsylvania Regimental Band during the Spanish-American War, was integral in deciding which of the original band instruments should be purchased. The instruments, which were the finest quality made by the Distin Company of Williamsport, Pennsylvania, consisted of drums and twenty other instruments, including cornets, trombones, alto horns, baritones, basses, clarinets, and saxophones.

President Atherton officially authorized the permanent organization of the Cadet Band in a letter dated October 23, 1901: "The Cadet Band of the Pennsylvania State College will hereby be regarded as an integral part of the Military Organization and will be subject to the orders of the Commandant of Cadets accordingly."

The Free Lance suggested in November 1900 that the band would be prepared to attend the inauguration of President William McKinley on March 4, 1901. Although other Pennsylvania colleges were well represented by their cadet battalions at the inaugural parade, there is no mention of Penn State's Cadet Band traveling to Washington, D.C., that spring in any publication. Perhaps for one reason or another the band was unable to participate or was not invited.

By March 1901 the twenty-four-member Cadet Band practiced regularly and performed several times in public, and not only for military functions but for social occasions as well. The Cadet Band often held "stag dances" at the Armory on campus, which had a large dance floor. The dances often were used to raise money for the band to buy music and miscellaneous equipment for football game performances, such as bells and whistles. They were well attended, sometimes with more than 100 couples dancing.

Even in 1901 the Cadet Band performed at Penn State football games. The first mention of a performance at a football game was by *The Times*, State College's local newspaper at the time, for the November 16, 1901, game against Lehigh College. Penn State's football team, with the band and 200 other students and fans, arrived by train in Williamsport, Pennsylvania, to compete against a strong Lehigh team. State won the game handily, 38 to 0,

ABOVE Once funds for instruments were acquired, membership in the Cadet Band grew quickly.

RIGHT Within only a few years the Cadet Band grew to almost thirty members.

backed by a solid showing of spectator spirit and a powerful performance by the Cadet Band.

The band also played at military functions off campus in the local area. Memorial Day in Central Pennsylvania was then and still is today a big event. The first community to celebrate this holiday, according to some scholars, was the town of Boalsburg, Pennsylvania, some three miles southeast of Penn State, in 1865. The town was placing flowers on the graves of veterans every Fourth of July three years before the formal order was called by General John A. Logan for a day to commemorate fallen veterans. Being a military organization, and especially one that contained war veterans, the Cadet Band was often at memorial services in various locations in the region. On Memorial Day, May 30, 1902, the band appeared at the memorial program held by the Grand Army of the Republic post in Pine Grove Mills, a few miles south of State College. Also appearing there that day was the State College Band, a community band affiliated not with the college but with the town of State College, Pennsylvania.

By the start of the fall semester of 1902 the band had grown to twenty-eight members. It continued to hold stag dances on Saturday nights, playing popular dance music, including some new selections, to large audiences. The Cadet Band also continued to support the football team. A notable performance by the band during the 1902 football season, when the football team traveled to Dickinson College in Carlisle, Pennsylvania, was recounted in *The Times*. This was the biggest game of the year for the football team, according to *The Times*, and well over half the student body arrived in Carlisle by train with the Cadet Band. Gathering after dinner at the Hotel Washington, the Penn State fans lined up behind the Cadet Band and marched to the football field, meeting the Dickinson fans and its own group of musicians, the Dickinson Indian Band. The team, supported by the enthusiastic crowd, won the game 23 to 0, surprising Dickinson on her own field.

In December 1902 Pennsylvania Governor William A. Stone visited the college, inspecting the different departments, the buildings, and the battalion. The Cadet Band, as well as the rest of the battalion, escorted the governor as he visited different points of interest on campus.

With the graduation of the remaining original members of the Bugle Corps in June 1903, the Cadet Band leadership passed to a new group of students. But the legacy of the founding members was not lost. Baritone player Earle B. Norris, younger brother of Edwin Norris, became bandmaster after Edgar Godard graduated. Earle Norris became the first relative of a band member to join the band. First cornet R. W.

Bowers became president, J. D. P. Kennedy was first sergeant and drum major, and trombone player P. G. Elder became secretary of the band.

Those who heard the band's performance considered it much improved that year over the last. Many more members with three years of Cadet Band experience returned, and the new members who joined were considered talented musicians.

As the band became more of a special-occasion organization in 1903, Captain Lawton, the new commandant of cadets, felt the need to organize once again a separate bugle corps to call the battalions to action. The bugle corps was to consist of six buglers (one for each student battalion) and fall under the direction of the chief bugler and Cadet Band president, R. W. Bowers. Thirteen buglers tried out for the five remaining spots. Even early in the band's history, competition for spots was difficult.

Later in 1903 Penn State football's "game of the decade," as advertised by *The Times*, was played on Thanksgiving against William and Jefferson College near Pittsburgh. W&J, as it was known, was matched favorably against Penn State. W&J had more fans rooting for them on their home field, but Penn State had heftier players, was looking for revenge after coming off a disappointing loss to Dickinson the week before, and had the Cadet Band with them. Penn State won the game, 22 to 9.

The Pennsylvania State College in the fall semester of 1904 enrolled more than 730 students, compared with 602 the year before and 461 in 1902. Clearly the college's recognition and popularity were growing considerably. The prestige of the Cadet Battalion also grew, after its annual inspection earlier that June. M. F. Harmon, captain of artillery at Fort Hamilton, New York Harbor, after inspecting the Cadet Band and the Cadets' skill in military movements and at arms, said that State College's battalion was in far better train-

Blue Band Families

Keith Alexander '92 and
Barbara Garbrick '93.

Although Edwin and Earle Norris were the first brothers to be band members, they did not remain the only relatives to have been in the Blue Band. Over the years there have been dozens of brothers, sisters, cousins, nephews, nieces, and grandchildren who followed relatives in the band. Since women were admitted into the once all-male Blue Band there have also been a number of marriages. In 1987 the first third-generation Blue Band member (who had a parent and a grandparent in the band) joined the rank and file: Sousaphone Keith Alexander '92, son of sousaphone player Dr. Duane Alexander '62 and nephew of baritone player Arnold Alexander '67, and grandson of sousaphone Fred Alexander '34. Duane Alexander recalls auditioning for the Blue Band using the same instrument his father played in the band. "Our family still owns that horn, though Keith chose to audition on his own instrument." Duane still brings the same sousaphone to every homecoming performance of the Alumni Blue Band.

Mellophone Barbara Garbrick '93, daughter of percussionist Allen Garbrick '67 and granddaughter of clarinetist J. Henry Garbrick '26, also proudly continued the musical legacies of her father and grandfather. Who will be the first fourth-generation Blue Band member?

ing than any other organization he had ever had the privilege of inspecting.

As the enrollment increased in 1904, other musical organizations also increased in membership. The first mention of the College Orchestra occurred that year as it performed for the Baccalaureate services on Sunday evening, June 11, at Schwab Auditorium on campus. The concert also featured the college president's wife, Helen Atherton, an accomplished pianist. The orchestra was composed of some members of the Cadet Band, the Mandolin Club, and other students not in other school musical groups. The orchestra also performed for the second YMCA open house reception of the year and at a number of stag dances of its own, which became at least as popular as the Cadet Band's dances.

The Cadet Band gained a valuable alumnus back in October 1904 when Edgar "Paddy" Godard returned to Penn State as an instructor. Godard, an electrical engineer, was hired by President Atherton as an assistant in the college's electrical laboratories and as instructor of the band; his salary was charged from the general expense account of the band, from the Department of Electrical Engineering, and from Electric Light & Water Supply.

Godard and the band led the parade of almost 800 State fans to Seminary Field at the Dickinson game in Williamsport in mid-November. With both Dickinson's band and the Cadet Band playing its fight songs in the stands, it was clear that the football teams were not the only ones competing. Penn State proved to be the victor, in the stands and on the field, defeating Dickinson 11 to 0.

Godard also led the band in a performance in late November on Pennsylvania Day, an annual event started in 1903 by the trustees of the college honoring the state of Pennsylvania and corresponding roughly to Founders' Day at other colleges. Many distinguished guests, including Governor of Pennsylvania Samuel Pennypacker and his wife, Mr. and Mrs. Andrew Carnegie, and Mr. and Mrs. Charles Schwab of Bethlehem Steel, were in attendance. They were serenaded by the Cadet Band at President Atherton's residence on campus the evening before. During the dedication of the $150,000 Carnegie Library on campus on Pennsylvania Day, Board of Trustees President James Beaver referred to an earlier act of philanthropy by Andrew Carnegie toward the Cadet Band. "You have heard, Sir," addressing Carnegie and the gathered audience, "on the platform in the Auditorium today what impetus was given to the music of this College by that donation for a band. I believe it was the foundation of what I regard as one of the great elements in a complete education—the knowledge of music and the ability to express that knowledge in song."

The State College Cadet Band members began to see themselves as more than merely the Penn State band. While they performed at the major functions on campus for the college, such as for Pennsylvania Day, they also performed for functions not directly related to Penn State. It was in some instances a band-for-hire, but at all times when away from campus the Cadet Band represented the college. An example was a parade performance for the conclave of the Knights Templar in Williamsport on May 22, 1905. Secured by the Bellefonte Commandary of the Knights Templar, the band spent the night before the parade in Bellefonte and had the opportunity to serenade Governor Beaver at his home there. During the day of the parade the Cadet Band combined with the other bands that had also

TO THE CADET BAND.

TO THE CADET BAND.

There was a time when quiet reigned within these college halls,
When no heartrending din of noise re-echoed from these walls,
When our tympannums ne'er were pained by any brazen blast,
But now, I tremble to relate, those peaceful days are past.

There came a day, a plan was formed, we thought the scheme was grand,
When 'twas proposed in chapel here to organize a band.
We cheered to help the thing along, but then we did not know,
That we were bringing on ourselves unutterable woe.

At last they came, those instruments, all silver plated o'er—

How strange it seems, such pretty things make such a deafening roar.
And then in gasping wonderment we question, How can they
Help dissipate our devilment in an effective way?

For we were told once on a time, and at a certain place,
That a brass band could often be a saving means of grace.
Perhaps it is, but it must be a persecution plan,
For thoughts inspired by the din don't make a better man.

In silent resignation then we'll stop our ears and pray
That at some not far distant time the band may learn to play.
So we may place it carefully among our college joys,
And let Old Time obliterate all memory of its noise.
A. R. D.

A humorous poem describing the change in student life that the band provided was published in the 1902 *La Vie*.

performed there and played "Onward Christian Soldiers," an appropriate piece for the occasion.

Although more than just the college's band, the Cadet Band did not forget it was one of Penn State's major sources of instilling school spirit. Being a military organization, the Cadet Band performed every Memorial Day. Memorial Day 1905 was rather quiet in Happy Valley, where Penn State is located. Rain dampened most cemetery services, and turnout by veterans and families was low. The band planned to hold a concert that evening in McAllister Hall, expecting attendance to be disappointing. However, word arrived that evening that State's baseball team defeated arch-rival Princeton 8 to 3 that afternoon on the Tigers' home field. The Cadet Band, filled with pride for the team, turned the concert into a dance and livened up the usually somber holiday for a larger-than-expected audience.

As well as supporting the baseball team, the band did its part to support the Penn State football team in 1905, encouraging it to victory and supplying dignity in defeat. The game in Harrisburg against the Carlisle Indian School was notable as both the Cadet Band and the Carlisle Indian band fought for musical supremacy in the stands for more than half an hour before the start of the game. Upward of 8,000 students and fans cheered for each band as they traded school songs across the football field. Penn State was defeated by Carlisle and its legendary coach Glenn "Pop" Warner 11 to 0 in what was described in the *Collegian* as a "valiant gridiron battle."

The band's enthusiastic spirit spurred not only valiant effort by the sports teams but also a loyalty for the band's role at the college. The Blue Band in its long history has had many ardent supporters. Many students and fans have spoken out in defense of the band in the past when they felt the band was treated with disrespect or even apathy. One such case occurred in late March 1906. After Instructor Godard went through some difficulty arranging it with the Board of Trustees, the Cadet Band was able to hold a concert on March 23 of that year in Schwab Auditorium. Charging twenty-five cents for admission, the band hoped to defray expenses for a series of free spring concerts and to purchase new music to play at the upcoming baseball games and track meets on Beaver Field. Musically, the band had improved considerably over the short time it had existed. It also had many new selections, including the overture to Orpheus and the waltz "Tales from Vienna Woods." Although it performed superbly at the concert, its audience was only 300, a disappointing number for an auditorium that could hold almost 1,000 people.

In response to such a poor turnout, one person, calling himself "The Spectator," wrote a castigating letter to the editor of the *Collegian*, criticizing the school spirit shown by the students:

> The Cadet Band is a college organization. It works just as hard, in its own way, as does any organization in the College. It is just as much entitled to your support. You go to the football games, the baseball games, the basketball games with regularity, and claim that you show your spirit in so doing. You DO NOT go to the Band Concert and can give no good reason for not going. The Spectator is forced to this conclusion: that your college spirit is a matter of dollars and cents. You pay an athletic fee which entitles you to go to the games with no extra charge, and so you go to get your money's worth. When a college organization which deserves your support equally with the football team asks you to pay twenty-five cents to hear the results of its hard work—that is a different story, and your much vaunted State spirit goes up in smoke.

Even with zealous support from such people, there were those who were not afraid to be critical of the band. In mid-May another letter to the editor of the *Collegian*, after its author had witnessed the band performing at a Penn State baseball game, stated: "The playing of the Band at athletic games is appreciated between innings, but during the actual playing it is a source of annoyance to both teams and visitors."

The fall of 1906 brought an interesting trip for the Cadet Band and rest of the battalion. On October 10, Harrisburg dedicated its new Capitol building, after the old one had

The Cadet Band in 1906, wearing new uniforms.

TOP TO BOTTOM

The Cadet Band also performed concerts. Note the upright bass in this photo of the 1907 band.

The Cadet Band provided parade music, especially before football games, as here before the 1908 Bucknell game.

In the early 1900s, the band practiced at Old Main, which had changed considerably since 1859.

been destroyed in a fire in 1897. Traveling by train, the battalion arrived in Harrisburg that rain-soaked morning and marched in a parade to the Board of Trade building. Afterward the 400 cadets of Penn State had a free afternoon and evening to see the sights of the state capital before the midnight train for State College left again. One of the dignitaries present at the dedication was President Theodore Roosevelt, who was said to have been impressed by the cadet battalion and band as a whole.

In spite of these noncollege events the primary focus of the marching band at Penn State in 1907, and still today, was sporting events. In these early years, the band performed for baseball games, track and field events, and of course the football games. To this point, however, there had been no mention of the band playing at any of the basketball games at the Armory or away. The band in 1907 did not need to travel with the teams in order to stir State spirit with the students. On May 1, State's varsity baseball team defeated Cornell 3 to 1 in a seventeen-inning marathon in Ithaca, New York. Back at State College, the students, overjoyed at the victory, gathered on campus to give the college yells and fire the Cadet's cannon. The Cadet Band, always ready to lend its support, also gathered and started an impromptu parade around the town. Holding a bonfire on the site where the old University Inn had been years before, the students celebrated until the early morning.

An appearance by the Cadet Band when it did travel did not always spell victory for the Blue and White, however. On October 5 the football team once again competed with the Carlisle Indian School in Williamsport and lost 18 to 5, in spite of the more than 800 State fans and the Cadet Band cheering the team on from the north bleachers. Even in defeat, Penn State fans kept their dignity with the help of the Cadet Band, as they marched from the field after the game and held a parade through the main streets of Williamsport. The residents of Williamsport

The Cadet Band
continued to grow
during the 1900s.

were also appreciative of the event and gave high praise to the visiting Cadet Band.

The band also performed for on-campus events away from the football field the same year. On Sunday, June 9, the band performed an outdoor concert of sacred music in front of Old Main after the Baccalaureate sermon, and on the following Tuesday, June 11, performed its annual Commencement Week Concert at the same place. The next semester, on Pennsylvania Day, November 22, the Cadet Band escorted Pennsylvania Governor Edwin Stuart from the train station to Schwab Auditorium, where he addressed the college and later dedicated the new $300,000 Agricultural Building, one of the finest structures of its kind in 1907.

The spring of 1908 marked the beginning of the administration of Dr. Edwin Sparks, the eighth president of the Pennsylvania State College. Dr. Sparks was well liked by the students, being more personable than the late Dr. Atherton had been. Sparks was an 1884 graduate of Ohio State University and a former member and student leader of Ohio State's now famous marching band. The students planned a welcoming parade for the new college president at the State College train station, but Dr. Sparks arrived two days early. Not to be denied their celebration in his honor, however, the students rescheduled the parade for the following Wednesday, May 13, 1908.

That morning the 500-student cadet regiment assembled on the parade grounds west of the Armory and marched to the east campus parade grounds. With the annual U.S. Army inspection taking place the next Monday, Commandant Hay took advantage of the opportunity and inspected the cadets. Afterward, leading the parade of cadets, the varsity baseball team, and the academic departments and their floats, the Cadet Band marched up what was a continuation of modern-day Allen Street (what is now the elm tree-lined mall from College Avenue to Pattee Library), and passed in front of the grandstands erected at Schwab Auditorium. The band peeled away from the rest of the parading students to stand between Old Main and the auditorium to play as the parade passed by. The band and the cadets, clothed in their parade-dress blue jackets, white trousers, and gloves, received thunderous applause from the gathered spectators. President Sparks stated that he was well pleased with the parade and saluted the band and cadets as they passed in review.

The Cadet Band continued to live up to its popular appeal. Remarkably, the band's high level of performance at this time was achieved with a shoestring budget. Because Penn State had no School of Music or School of Arts and Architecture, and the athletic budget was much slimmer, the Cadet Band was funded mostly by the interclass college budget, which came from the funds of the student body through class treasuries.

Compared with today, entertainment choices were much more limited during the first decade of the twentieth century, so attending musical concerts was much more common back then among the general populace. With the popularity of John Philip Sousa, marching bands were much in demand. Most of the concerts the Cadet Band held were well attended, and the admission was usually not free. The money from each twenty-five-cent ticket benefited the band directly and went a long way to defray shortfalls in the collegiate budget.

The Cadet Band also held many other fund-raising activities. One of the most innovative was on Saturday night, October 21, 1909, when the Cadet Band held a "moving picture" show in the auditorium. Movies were rare in 1909, and State College did not have a movie theater, so the event was of high interest to the students and general public. The Cadet Band hired the Lubin Company, a movie-projector manufacturer and movie producer that ran a number of "moving picture palaces" in the Philadelphia area. The band showed Lubin's films as well as films from other movie producers, such as Vitagraph and Edison, that evening. During the silent movies, the band performed the incidental music, as well as a number of selections during each intermission while the films were changed in the projector.

The show was a rousing success for the Cadet Band. The attendance was high, and the movies and music were quite entertaining, according to the *Collegian*. In return for holding the motion-picture show on campus, sixteen members of the band performed in Bellefonte the night before, at Lubin's request, for another picture show presented by the movie company.

The year 1909 also saw the start of a second orchestra. Because of the popularity of instrumental music on campus, many who auditioned for the main orchestra did not make the cut. Those musicians usually played in the new orchestra, improving their musical skills and filling in for vacancies in the first orchestra that occurred during the school year.

In spite of the popularity of instrumental and vocal music on campus, by the end of the decade the band remained about the same size as during its first few years of existence. It continued to be student-led and student-organized, and remained so until 1914. But from its beginnings the Cadet Band matured from a small bugle corps to a full-fledged college marching and concert band, receiving many accolades from the students, faculty, and townspeople in and around Penn State. Its reputation, as well as the college's, was already becoming one of pride, competence, and spirit.

As the Cadet Band changed, so did the college. This view, looking northeast from the tower of Old Main, shows how much it had grown by 1909.

THE NEW DECADE *brought new promise to the Cadet Band.*
The band went from being a small but popular student
club to a large, professionally conducted and instructed
organization. The quality of the band's musicians, music,
field performances, and concerts increased tremendously
owing to the skill of its members and its first professional
bandmaster, Wilfred Otto Thompson.

The early years of this decade started rather ordinarily.
For the Cadet Band, "ordinarily" in most cases meant "with
distinction." In 1910 the first concert of the Cadet Band's
spring season was on Sunday afternoon, April 17. A B-flat
bass (tuba) player and student director, L. R. Meissner,
conducted the thirty-five-member band in performing
The Barber of Seville *by Rossini and the Bridal Chorus*

Penn State had a very respectable football team even at this early stage of development. Coach William "Big Bill" Hollenback had undefeated teams in 1909, 1911, and 1912.

Coach Hollenback.
Mauthe
McGleary Hirshman   Capt. Vorhis   Smith
Very   Arnold   Grey   Watson   Johnson   Brown
McNary & Swope.
Photo.

from *Lohengrin* by Wagner, among other pieces. The next concert by the band was also on a Sunday, May 8, on the steps of Old Main, where the band played Chopin's "Funeral March," "The Drummer of the Guard," and "Hungarian Dance Number 5." Because the Sunday afternoon concerts were so popular, the band began performing regularly every Sunday until Commencement. This tradition of Sunday afternoon concerts in the spring lasted many years, until well after World War II.

The autumn semester of 1910 saw the band perform to capacity crowds at Schwab Auditorium. On October 9 the band again played a Sunday afternoon concert, this time with P. M. Snavely, the first trombone and assistant student leader, conducting in Meissner's absence. Snavely, according to the *Collegian*, "proved himself to be a capable leader." Another standing-room-only concert at Schwab was performed on Pennsylvania Day in mid-November; it featured a solo by H. P. Armstrong on cornet, and a duet by Mrs. Atherton on piano and Miss Katherine Foster on baritone horn.

The Cadet Band cheered the football team that autumn as well. As usual, the band was the catalyst for student spirit at the games, whatever the fortunes of the football team. In October, after one particular game Penn State happened to lose, one *Collegian* editorial read:

> In spite of the fact that last Saturday's game did not mark any particular epoch in our
> football history, the display of spirit by the undergraduates was by far the best that
> has been seen on Beaver Field this year. To be just and give credit where credit is due,
> the band was the distinct factor which was instrumental in bringing about this much
> hoped for show of enthusiasm. Undoubtedly music has its effects everywhere in one
> form or another; not only does it stir up crowds in the bleachers, but its influence
> invades the playing field and rouses the players to their utmost efforts there.

The Cadet Band added a "cord" to its uniform in 1911.

Another tradition, the Thanksgiving Day game with the University of Pittsburgh, also continued that November. The band traveled to Forbes Field in Pittsburgh the day before and performed at the alumni smoker at its hotel as well as at the game the next day.

By winter the football season was over and the Sunday concerts soon ensued. In February 1911 Snavely conducted the band once more, this time as its director. The band played such marches as "Chicago Tribune" and "Stars and Stripes Forever," as well as classical selections. Alexander Gray III, a baritone with the Glee Club, was on hand to sing "Life's Lullaby" by Gerald Lane with the band. His performance was only the first in a number of band concerts over the next few years in which Gray was a guest soloist. The concert was well received and continued to provide Penn State with a source of good entertainment that few other colleges could boast. The band performed four more Sunday concerts that semester in Schwab Auditorium and, as the weather grew warmer, on the steps of Old Main.

As a well-known and well-respected student activity, the Cadet Band was often asked to represent the college, either tacitly or explicitly. Such appearances were almost always at college functions for which a musical setting would be appropriate—for example, sporting events, commencements, and parades. Alumni Day, a homecoming celebration during Commencement week in June 1911, was just such an occasion. The alumni festivities included a celebration of the fiftieth anniversary of the first graduating class of the college in 1861, and a parade downtown. Originally the Cadet Band was asked to lead the parade, but because the college could not pay for the expenses of its service the band did not participate. The organizers of the events that week felt the members of the Cadet Band would gladly volunteer their services, so they were naturally disappointed. In spite of the band's lack of participation on this occasion, Alumni Day was successful and enjoyable; many other events besides the parade took place, such as a baseball game pitting the alumni against the 1911 varsity baseball team, and an alumni dance in McAllister Hall.

During the fall of 1911 the band, sporting new shoulder cords that dressed the uniforms nicely, once again traveled to Pittsburgh for the annual Thanksgiving Day football game. Joining the band were the Glee Club, the Mandolin Club, and Pitt's musical clubs, all of which held a combined concert at Soldiers' Memorial Hall the day before. This was the first year of many that musical organizations of Penn State and Pitt performed together

In 1912 the Cadet Band's director was Captain W. A. Moyer. Moyer was one of the last student directors before Wilfred Otto "Tommy" Thompson was hired in 1914.

during the events preceding the annual football game. With an audience of more than 1,200, the concert was quite successful, and so was the dance that followed in the ballroom of the Hotel Schenley, where most of the Penn State fans and the band were staying.

In spite of the band's numerous accolades and successes, its membership had been decreasing in recent years. By the fall semester of 1912 it had twenty-nine musicians, the lowest number since 1904 and more than a dozen fewer than in 1906. This, however, marked the nadir of membership for the rest of the band's history.

Although smaller, the Cadet Band was becoming better organized, with more officers and special positions. The band director, Captain W. A. Moyer, had graduated, but he stayed one more semester to conduct the band and take additional courses. O. B. Gippel was listed as drum major, the first since 1908. The band's treasurer, Dr. George Gilbert Pond, was on sabbatical in Europe for the fall, so Professor John S. Crandell controlled the purse strings for the band that semester. A new band position was created that year: property master. The duty of the property master, J. E. Graham, was similar to that of today's student band managers: to take care of the physical equipment the band owned.

As in past years, the band started the fall semester at the Young Men's Christian Association freshman reception and orientation meeting and ended the spring semester at Commencement, performing at football games, concerts, and special occasions between. The YMCA was an important social and religious organization at Penn State, and more than three-quarters of the student body belonged to it. After Yale's it was the second largest college YMCA in the nation in 1912. The fall reception in late September promised to be larger than ever, with the number of incoming freshmen and the popularity of the YMCA with upperclassmen. To accommodate all the guests the reception was held on the grounds of the Ladies' Cottage. Lit by electric lights and Japanese lanterns in the trees, the occasion was further illuminated by the talent of the Glee Club and the Cadet Band, which played "The American Medley" and "A Spring Maid Pot-Pourri."

The Glee Club and the Cadet Band joined together again later in the fall at two Sunday evening concerts. With the Orchestra and the Mandolin Club, the Glee Club and band played to packed houses at Schwab Auditorium. Many of those who attended hoped that the musical clubs and band would make its combined concerts a tradition.

The Glee Club's accomplishments overshadowed those of the band in 1913. Winning many intercollegiate competitions, the Penn State Glee Club was considered by many college singing groups to be the best on the East Coast. In March of that year, the club began a coast-to-coast tour, promoting the name and welfare of its alma mater at many concerts. Such locations as Pittsburgh, Chicago, Amarillo, Dodge City, Albuquerque, San Francisco, and Los Angeles were all whistle-stops for the Glee Club on its long tour.

The Glee Club was not the only musical organization that was becoming more prominent. The Cadet Band continued to provide quality Sunday concerts and football performances as it had in the past. The Thespian Orchestra, in performing for the production of *Yankee Brigands*, was the largest ever, with nineteen musicians. The Symphonic Orchestra was also held in high regard and showed much promise for the future during its

ABOVE AND LEFT
One of the more popular events at the college during this time was the sophomore-freshman pushball scrap.

WILFRED OTTO THOMPSON

Wilfred Otto "Tommy" Thompson was born on May 10, 1868, in Boston, Massachusetts. At an early age he showed a great talent for music and a drive for perfection. When his parents, Theodore and Augusta Spangler Thompson, grew weary of listening to him play his trumpet in the house, they sent young Wilfred outside, where he practiced for hours in the chicken coop. By the time he reached high school, he was already filling in on trombone for the Boston Symphony Orchestra and was regarded as one of the finest young musicians in the nation. When Thompson was offered a chair with the Orchestra after graduating from high school, he turned it down in order to enlist in the Army and attend the U.S. Military Academy's famous Bandmasters' School at West Point, New York. By this time he had married his hometown sweetheart, Clarabel MacEntire, with whom they had a son, Harold, in 1895.

From May until October 1893, just after he completed his coursework at West Point, Thompson conducted daily band concerts at the World's Columbian Exposition in Chicago, performing before literally millions of people in those six months. By 1894 he was directing Army bands all over the United States, and later in Cuba during the Spanish-American War, in China during the Boxer Rebellion, and in the Philippines on three separate tours of duty. While in the Philippines in 1901, when the civil government was established, Thompson was in charge of the music

for the inauguration of Governor-General William Howard Taft, later President of the United States. About ten years afterward, President Taft put him in charge of the music for Taft's conference with Mexican President Porfirio Díaz in El Paso, Texas.

In the course of his military career, Thompson became a well-known and highly respected bandmaster. He was a personal friend of John Philip Sousa, and on a few occasions Thompson's army bands performed with Sousa's band.

Retiring in 1913 from active service, Thompson worked as an office manager with the Brockway Smith Corporation in Boston and continued to conduct local bands. In 1914 Pennsylvania State College President Edwin Sparks, a former student president of the Ohio State University Marching Band as an undergraduate, appointed Thompson as Penn State's Bandmaster. Thompson was also appointed property custodian of the college's Department of Military Science and Tactics,

handling all the cadet uniforms, weapons, and supplies. In September 1917, when Commandant of Cadets Captain A. E. Ahrends was called to active service during World War I, Thompson became Acting Commandant until the War Department appointed Retired Army Major James Baylies later that month. Thompson remained on emergency active duty until July 1925, when he was retired by the War Department again. In October 1925 his request to be recalled to active duty was granted and he was appointed Assistant to the Commandant. When the Department of Music was reorganized in 1929, Thompson became Assistant Professor of Music. He directed the Blue Band until 1938, when he retired from all his duties at Penn State. In recognition of his service to the college, the graduating class of 1939 dedicated its yearbook, *La Vie,* to him and to two other retiring professors, Ralph Watts, dean of the School of Agricultural Sciences, and Elton Walker, who headed the Department of Civil Engineering.

Thompson, with his Bismarck mustache, rough tongue, and confident manner, was a colorful figure. The *Collegian* once quoted him as saying: "Two great men came to Penn State in 1914. Bob Higgins [Football All-American and Penn State Head Coach] was the other one." Although Thompson had a high opinion of himself, it was not undeserved. His success as a musician and a bandleader stemmed from being a perfectionist and a taskmaster. Former Blue Band percussionist Bill

Dye '37 remembered his years under Thompson as a great deal of hard work. "If Tommy heard someone play something wrong, he would stop the whole band and make that boy play his part. If he messed it up more than once, he sometimes would throw his baton at him!" Thompson often used rough "army" language when his men did not follow directions. "Tommy would grab one of the boys' trumpets and tell us, 'This is the way it's supposed to be played!' Then he would play it himself, and then continue to yell and swear at us."

But Thompson was not always cross. "He may have had his rough edges," recalled Dye, "but you couldn't meet a more caring or loyal individual once you got to know him." When a rehearsal or a performance was over, Thompson usually did not restrict band members' free time, especially on trips. In later years he often received letters from former students recalling how much they appreciated his instruction in music and the discipline on the field. Thompson often invited those former band members to his home when they came back to Penn State, to reminisce about "the good old days." Thompson remained active in retirement and almost never missed a Penn State football game, a Blue Band concert, or a Symphonic Orchestra concert until his death in April 1950 at the age of eighty-one.

The legacy Thompson left for the Blue Band and for Penn State is significant. During his tenure he turned the Cadet Band, which was little more than a small student activity and not well known outside State College, into a large, well-run unit of crack marching musicians that was considered one of the top college bands in the nation. The band started with just over twenty-five musicians and during his twenty-five-year career grew to more than 150 musicians in three bands at Penn State. Thompson also organized the Symphonic Orchestra and many other instrumental music ensembles, and in so doing played a major role in the impetus to create the Department of Music in 1915. Under Thompson's direction the fame of Penn State's band program was spread around the United States, especially in Pennsylvania and New York, and even in Europe. Above all, Penn State's Tommy Thompson will be remembered best as one of the world's top bandmasters. ≋

well-attended concerts. In December 1913 the College Quartet, a foursome of quite talented student singers, was invited to the nation of Panama to perform. The quartet traveled to Panama numerous times in the next few years, entertaining the Panamanians, the canal builders, and American dignitaries during the completion of the Panama Canal.

Over these years more than 100 students belonged to some instrumental music organization at Penn State, and many more belonged to the Glee Club or other college singing groups. Even with a second orchestra in place it was clear that before long there would not be enough positions in the musical groups to accommodate all the students who were interested. At this point many students were in favor of starting a school of music in order to organize the musical groups and develop musical talent among the students. Such a school, some argued, would benefit from the leadership of a professional musician, who would give some permanency and direction for these bands, orchestras, and other musical clubs. Talk grew in 1913 of at least hiring a bandmaster to lead the instrumental music organizations much the way vocal instructor Clarence Robinson did for the singing clubs. Such talk was not meant to diminish the current student leadership of the Cadet Band, whom most of the student body believed were quite capable—especially G. L. Sumner, the student director in 1913.

The start of Penn State's Music Department was greatly facilitated when a professional musician was hired by the Board of Trustees in September 1914 to lead the Cadet Band and the Orchestra: Wilfred Otto "Tommy" Thompson. Right away Thompson began to fundamentally change the Cadet Band. He increased the size of the band to sixty members, almost doubling its size. And his very presence did away with the band's structure as a student-run club, eliminating the offices of president and vice-president, and even the need for a faculty treasurer. The musicians would still have student leaders, but Thompson was in charge. Another notable yet subtle change in the structure is evident in the listing of band musicians in *La Vie* during his tenure. The students were not grouped by instrument, but rather by class rank in *La Vie*, as student seniority became more important for discipline. This seniority system even was more pronounced later in the band's history, when Thompson split the band into three organizations according to ability and, largely, class status.

Thompson was also in charge of the Regimental Drum and Bugle Corps, which consisted only of freshmen and sophomores. Male students at Penn State were required to take two years of military training, so all first-year and second-year students were cadets. The Drum and Bugle Corps participated in the regular compulsory drilling and performed for military exercises and demonstrations. As no member of the Cadet Band was a member of the Drum and Bugle Corps, and Thompson expanded the Corps to approximately two-thirds the size of the band, with thirty-eight members, both organizations had almost 100 members all told, a far cry from the original six band members just sixteen years earlier.

The first official appearance of the new Cadet Band was on Pennsylvania Day, November 13, 1914, where the Nittany Lion gridders battled the Michigan Agricultural College Aggies (later to become the Michigan State University Spartans) at New Beaver Field. Michigan Agricultural, a land-grant school itself, brought its own cadet band and about 100 other fans from East Lansing. The game was witnessed by Governor John K. Tener, Governor-Elect Martin G. Brumbaugh, and some of the newest members of the Pennsylvania House and Senate, as it was usual for the state leadership to attend Pennsylvania Day. The Aggies won the contest that day "in a clean, hard fought game," according to the *Collegian*, posting only the second loss on New Beaver Field for the Lions since it was dedicated in 1909. The newspaper went on to describe the visiting band as "a wonderfully well-trained organization," among other accolades. Penn State's Cadet Band received no such mention in the paper, but the Aggies' band was well established as one of the best in the nation at the time and definitely deserved the praise.

This was not to say that the Penn State band did not deserve or receive distinction by the press or the student body that year. Thompson made a remarkable start in improving the quality of the band, which was evident at the Lehigh College game in Easton, Pennsylvania, later in the season. At the time, Lehigh's marching band was known to the local region as the "best band in the East." One Penn State fan wrote to the *Collegian*: "Wait 'till they [at Lehigh] hear our stirring organization of sixty pieces at State!" Although Penn State lost 20 to 7, the *Collegian* stated: "State rooters made a fine impression on the entire crowd by their spirited cheering when victory seemed hopeless. The band was pronounced by many critics to be the best that has ever played at a Lehigh game."

The positive exposure the band received that year was highlighted in a concert at Fort Pitt just before the annual Pittsburgh game on November 26. Featured in this concert was an original march arranged by Thompson, "Penn State." No longer a club, the band did not participate in the music-club combined concert at Carnegie Hall the day before, although the Glee Clubs and Mandolin Clubs of both schools did perform.

At the beginning of the spring semester the Cadet Band participated in the inauguration ceremonies for Governor Brumbaugh on January 15, 1915. Accompanied by Company F of the cadet regiment and by officers and dignitaries from the college, the band marched in the inaugural parade in Harrisburg. The students, worried about the inclement weather of mid-January, began a movement to purchase overcoats for the cadet regiment, although for budgetary reasons it was not successful that year.

Members of the Pennsylvania Senate Appropriations Committee once again received an opportunity to listen to the Cadet Band in late March. Making a whirlwind tour of Penn State, the state senators were greeted in the auditorium by the entire student body. During the assembly, President Sparks addressed the senators, pointing out the needs of the college and expressing his confidence in their collective judgment. The Cadet Band, as well as the Varsity Quartet, then performed for the visitors in a lively fashion and was quite favorably received.

Proof of the need for increased funding at the college was evident at the start of the 1915 fall semester with the long-overdue organization of the Department of Music. With the number of talented musicians and faculty already participating in musical clubs and courses, the department had been in existence in all but name well before 1915. Technically, all it needed was formal recognition by Penn State's administration and funding. Dr. Clarence Robinson was appointed head of the new department, which was placed in the School of Liberal Arts. With college credit now offered for almost all music courses, the status of Penn State's fine arts program was raised significantly. The Cadet Band was not included in the new department, however, because it was technically still part of the Department of Military Science.

At the beginning of that semester, the band met in Schwab Auditorium on September 30 for the first mass meeting, or pep rally, of the season just before the football game against Lebanon Valley State. Most students arrived early, excited about the prospects of the football team, so when the Cadet Band came out on the stage the auditorium erupted into loud cheering. Along with other stirring pieces, the band played a new arrangement of a popular college song, "Victory," written in 1913 by James Leyden, a Penn State student and Glee Club member. At the mass meeting the assembled students, consisting of almost the entire student body, voted to raise fees in order to send the Cadet Band to the University of Pennsylvania game in Philadelphia. Convincing many of the students to attend the game on October 9 themselves was the appearance of the band at Franklin Field.

At another football game show, this time at Beaver Field against Lehigh, the Cadet Band formed the letter "L" and played Lehigh's Alma Mater, then formed an "S" and played "Victory." During the playing of "Victory," the students held blue and white streamers and lifted them up in the air, alternating colors with the beats of the song. The effect was considered "novel" and delighted all who had attended the game. The new cheering style

OVERLEAF The 1912 Cadet Band at the New Beaver Field.

The Fight Songs: "Victory," "Nittany Lion," "Fight On, State"

James Leyden

Many prominent band-music arrangers and songwriters, such as Paul Yoder, Jerry Bilik, Tom Wallace, Rich Miller, and John Tatgenhorst, have written stirring music for the Blue Band. The songwriter who has written the most memorable music for the band, however, was Jimmy Leyden, a 1914 graduate of Penn State and a member of the Glee Club. The reason his music is so memorable, at least for Penn State fans, is that two of the three school fight songs, "Victory" and "Nittany Lion," were written by him.

Leyden went on to become a prolific and popular songwriter. He worked mainly for another former Penn State student, Fred Waring, the famous bandleader of "The Pennsylvanians" and star of his own radio and television music variety shows. Leyden was also the father of James A. Leyden Jr., Blue Band drum major from 1939 through 1941.

VICTORY

Come now Classmen, let us
  sing, loyally support the team,
We're here today with our colors
  gay, ready to win the fray.
Whether it be Pitt or Penn,
  Harvard or Cornell,
Play the game, every man, and
  we will win again.
Chorus:
Fight, Fight, Fight, for the Blue
  and White,
Victory will our slogan be;
Dear Alma Mater, fairest of all,
Thy loyal sons will obey thy call
To fight, fight, fight, with all
  their might,
Ever the goal to gain,
Into the game for Penn State's fame
Fight on to Victory!

The legend of "Victory" begins in 1913 when Leyden, a very musical student with a penchant for composing songs at a moment's notice, began singing a song he "just made up" at the old trackhouse, where he and his roommate, Albert A. Hansen, lived. After hearing the song his roommate was singing, Hansen made a bargain with him. "Write it down and I'll publish it and give you two cents royalty for every copy sold," Hansen told him.

Hansen did have the song published, although Leyden never made a fortune from it. It was introduced to the student body that year at the freshman orientation at the beginning of the fall semester and was a huge success. The Blue Band today still plays "Victory," usually when exiting the field after halftime performances, in the stands to pep the football team, and during parades.

NITTANY LION

Every college has a legend, passed
  on from year to year,
To which they pledge allegiance
  and always cherish dear.
But of all the honored idols, there's
  but one that stands the test,
It's the stately Nittany Lion, the
  symbol of our best.
Chorus:
Hail to the Lion, loyal and true,
Hail Alma Mater, with your
  White and Blue.
Penn State forever, molder of men,
Fight for her honor, Fight! and
  victory again!
There's Pittsburgh with its Panther,
  and Penn her Red and Blue,
Dartmouth with its Indian, and
  Yale her Bulldog, too.
There's Princeton with its Tiger,
  and Cornell with its Bear,
But speaking now of victory, we'll
  get the Lion's share.
Repeat Chorus

Leyden composed "Nittany Lion" between 1922 and 1924. He brought it to Penn State just before Alumni Day one year. Professor Hummel Fishburn and Bandmaster Tommy Thompson, with Leyden, polished the lyrics and music in a private "jam session" and introduced it to the students at the pep rally the night before the game. It was instantly popular, and the band and campus choral groups have been performing it ever since. The Blue Band today not only plays this song, especially during the pregame fanfare and downfield block, but also sings it as the band marches over to Beaver Stadium just before each football game. The upperclassmen make sure the freshmen learn the words to the song before the first game. In 1995 the second verse was changed to reflect the Big Ten Conference teams Penn State was now playing:

Indiana has its Hoosiers, Purdue
  its Gold and Black,
The Wildcats from Northwestern,
  and Spartans on attack.
Ohio State has its Buckeyes,
  up North, the Wolverines,
But the mighty Nittany Lions,
  the best they've ever seen.

FIGHT ON, STATE
Fight on, State; Fight on, State,
  strike your gait and win,
Victory we predict for thee,

We're ever true to you, dear old
  White and Blue.
Onward, State; Onward, State,
Roar, Lions, roar,
We'll hit that line, roll up the score,
Fight on to victory evermore,
Fight on, on
On, on, on.
Fight on, on,
Penn State!

"Fight On, State," which the Blue Band performs with instruments flashing side-to-side every time the football team scores, was written by Joseph Sanders '15, who sent it to the head of the Music Department, Dr. Richard Grant, in 1933. Grant, along with Hummel Fishburn and

J. E. "Sock" Kennedy, the Thespian coach, introduced this song to the freshman mass meeting soon afterward. Although the song was sung by the freshmen at every football game thereafter, it did not become popular until the next few classes learned it. The Blue Band today performs this song after the team scores and, along with the other two fight songs, during parades and in the stands. It also is one of the fight songs played during the Blue Band's famous trademark, the Floating Lions. ⌐⊞⊣

was devised by Dr. Sparks, who, with most of the rest of the student body, had become dissatisfied with the old cheers. Penn State exacted revenge for last year's loss by beating Lehigh 7 to 0.

The band traveled to Pitt once again in late November. A statement overheard at the game by a *Collegian* reporter and reprinted in the December 2 issue was: "The Penn State Band made the Pitt organization look like a German band." Given that America's position on the events in Europe was officially neutral but shifting toward enmity toward Germany because of its aggressive behavior at sea toward American merchant vessels, it was probably a good thing that a *Collegian* reporter overheard this statement and not a Pitt Panther fan.

As the United States moved closer and closer to becoming involved in the European war, the Department of Military Science at Penn State began to prepare for that eventuality, increasing the length of the weekly cadet drills. The students participating in the drills began to take them a bit more seriously as well. Another preparation by the Military Science Department was the replacement of the cadet regiment's uniforms that November, including the uniforms of the Cadet Band. Instead of a dark-blue "Civil War" style uniform, the dress was now standard army issue olive drab. The new uniforms were five dollars cheaper per uniform and were made of cotton instead of wool, making them much more comfortable to wear.

The newly attired Cadet Band ended 1915 with a Sunday afternoon concert on December 5. The concert was held before another capacity crowd at Schwab Auditorium, with Thompson on the podium. Many traditional pieces, such as the march "Second Regiment Connecticut National Guard" and "Catharina Cormare," were on the program, as well as popular songs. Thompson, notorious for hating popular music, apologized to the audience for feeling compelled to mix styles in order to please more listeners, some of whom had begun demanding of late that the band play more modern "ragtime" pieces. One *Collegian* reader, annoyed by the students' insistence on selecting popular music, wrote to the editor:

> Bandmaster Thompson's apology … should set every man in the college to thinking. It stands as a confession of weakness on the part of the student body which is little short of disgraceful when one considers that in a very short time these same students will go out into the world as representatives of the character and culture of their Alma Mater. Whatever else music may be, it is a measure of culture. … What, then, is to be the status of the student who incessantly demands that "popular" airs be played, who steadily refuses the opportunities for advancement and education in musical lines and demands something noisy, spectacular, something that appeals to his feet rather than his head.

Requests for "popular" music were not the only ones that Thompson tried to accommodate. One frequent concert attendee was President Sparks, who was himself a musician and former marching band member at Ohio State as an undergraduate. At the last concert of the spring semester of 1916 Sparks requested that the Fife and Drum Corps, accompanied by the band, perform a patriotic march played earlier as its last number. Thompson gladly obliged, much to the satisfaction of the president and the rest of the appreciative audience.

Enticed by a full-fledged Department of Music at Penn State, the incoming members of the 1916 freshman class that fall proved to have many talented musicians and singers. The 1916–17 season proved to be one of the best ever for all the musical organizations. At the intercollegiate vocal trials in New York City, the Glee Club received second place in a quite competitive field of colleges. It traveled again that upcoming spring, at Easter, across the country via

Uniforms

The Blue Band's uniform has evolved in its 100-year history from a military uniform to the current jacket and overlay style that today's band members wear. The first band uniform worn by the Cadet Bugle Corps and the Cadet Band was similar to the blue Civil War–era Union Army uniforms worn by all Penn State cadets at the time. The Cadet Band kept this uniform until 1915, when it received new khaki outfits from the War Department, which were less expensive and relatively comfortable. The most historically significant band uniform change occurred in 1923, when Penn State bought fifty new-style blue uniforms—all it could afford at the time. Because there were more than 125 musicians vying for the new uniforms, Bandmaster Wilfred O. Thompson issued them to his most

talented musicians, and that became the group that traveled to away games and other events when the full band could not. From that point forward, this elite group of fifty were known as the "Blue Band," and its name would be synonymous with the best of the best musicians.

In 1934 the uniform was revamped again, this time to a "West Point Cadet" style uniform, even though most band members were not part of the military program at college. The uniforms were a brighter blue, had double-breasted jackets, and had a white cross-belt across the chest. In 1947 the uniforms changed again but remained military in styling, patterned after U.S. Navy officers' uniforms. Another change to the uniform style appeared in 1956, when the color of the jacket and the trousers became a lighter blue that almost looked light gray from a distance and that featured more white trim around the sleeves and shoulder straps.

One of the most dramatic updates

to the Blue Band uniform occurred in 1963, with new outfits that were similar to what the band wears on the field today. Consisting of a navy-blue single-breasted suit jacket and blue trousers, the uniform's most obvious difference from years past was a white tunic vest, called an overlay, worn over the blue jacket. This "overlay," which prominently featured an image of the Nittany Lion Shrine on the back and a huge "s" on the front, could be removed for the spring Concert Band season. Far removed from its previous military style, the uniforms were distinctly for a marching band, with white spats, a white cap with plume, and white gloves easily seen by the highest seats in Beaver Stadium. In 1971 the current-style band overlay was purchased, adding a letter "P" to the "s" on the front and the words "Nittany Lions" in block letters on the back, replacing the Shrine. Other than minor changes, this uniform has not been modified in almost thirty years. Replaced every eight to ten

years, the uniforms were last renewed in 1994 after a Blue Band fund-raiser raised the money for this purpose.

Today, as it has always been since 1923, those who wear the Blue Band uniform are proud to represent some of the best marching musicians in the nation.

The Cadet Band traveled to many away games during the 1910s.

rail, providing concerts for many western and southern cities. The Mandolin Club traveled to Pittsburgh with the Glee Club for the annual combined concert at Carnegie Hall with the Pitt clubs.

The Cadet Band also improved its musical talent. Most of the older members had returned, and competition for the open spots in the band was especially keen: there were several men auditioning for each seat. The improvement in the reed section, which had been slightly weak the previous year, was substantial, and this balanced the entire band much better.

Among the football game shows and normal Sunday concerts, the most notable performance by the Cadet Band in 1916 was during Pennsylvania Day in mid-November. With funds in the band's treasury low, the concert receipts went toward offsetting the expenses of purchasing gold and silver medals given to seniors and juniors, respectively, for their service to the Cadet Band. Featured in the concert was the college president's wife, Mrs. Sparks, who performed a scarf dance to the musical number by the band, "Pas des Echarpes." A humorous reading was also well rendered by a sophomore coed known as Miss Baker. Another humorous number was performed by the band. Playing a song known as "Banddidntstrike," the musicians left the stage as the music continued, leaving only the percussion section. The piece was sustained by the drummers, and one by one the rest of the band returned to finish the song for the delighted audience. Closing the concert was "The Star Spangled Banner," which Thompson always had as the last piece. By all accounts the concert was a huge success and definitely put the Cadet Band's financial resources back on solid footing.

In January 1917 the band participated in another financial campaign, this time for the entire college. "Fight for Penn State's Rights," as the mass meeting of students was called, was organized to inform the students about the various funding appropriations requested from the state legislature and to start a student letter-writing campaign to impress on the legislators the importance of passing the appropriations bill. Performing at the meeting was the Cadet Band, providing the necessary Penn State spirit to persuade the students to participate. Although Governor Brumbaugh cut some of the appropriations as presented by the Board of Trustees, the state funding received that year was far greater than the funding for the previous two-year period.

By April the budget battle was all but forgotten. On March 12, owing to attacks by German U-boats in the Atlantic on unarmed merchant ships of neutral nations, American merchant vessels began to arm themselves, and the U.S. Navy instructed them to fire on the submarines. One week later, word was received that three American vessels had been torpedoed and sunk by the Germans, which prompted Congress on April 6 to declare war on Germany and enter World War I.

Through the National Defense Act of 1916, Congress authorized the formation of the Reserve Officers' Training Corps (ROTC) to instruct future military officers. Penn State did not participate at first, already having a military organization, but by the autumn of 1917 President Sparks formed the college's ROTC through the U.S. War Department. Unlike the previous Department of Military Science on campus, the ROTC offered army commissions, and many more upperclassmen were involved.

In September the commandant of cadets, Captain A. E. Ahrends, was called to active duty and assigned by the War Department to lead a regiment from Gettysburg. Until the government appointed a new commandant, President Sparks appointed Bandmaster Thompson as acting commandant, and the War Department reinstated Thompson to emergency active duty as a staff sergeant. The cadets progressed remarkably well under Thompson's authority, but his appointment was short-lived: Retired Army Major James Baylies succeeded him as commandant the next month. Coincidentally, Baylies and Thompson had served together in the Ninth Infantry Regiment in the Philippines and knew each other from their time spent there.

The Cadet Band did its part to serve those going off to war. At a farewell reception in September in Bellefonte, the band led the parade of student majors in the cadet regiment, deans of various schools, and members of the Centre County Red Cross to help send off fifty-three draftees headed for boot camp and then to Europe. Later, in November, the band at the Pittsburgh game performed "America" while unfurling a huge United States flag with a white number "1,043" emblazoned on the blue field instead of stars. This number represented the approximate number of Penn State students and alumni in the armed services to that date.

To take the students' minds off the war temporarily that following spring, the Student Council decided to hold a student "get-together" in February. A circus held in the Armory on February 16 was the idea that met with approval by the student body. It was known as "Zarney's Big Circus," named for S. J. Czarnecki, a champion Penn State wrestler who offered to take on all challengers at the circus. A Penn State boxer, R. F. Henney, issued a similar challenge. Another feature of the circus was a "stag" dance, wherein upperclassmen, borrowing dresses from their "weaker sex acquaintanceships," forced freshmen to don the dresses and dance. The Cadet Band performed pieces appropriate for the occasion, ending the event with the playing of "The Star Spangled Banner" and the Alma Mater.

During the fall semester of 1918 the Cadet Drum and Bugle Corps, unable to fill its ranks because so many were going to war, was disbanded. All the band musicians were put into the Cadet Band, which changed its name that year to The Penn State College Military Band. However, the band performed no concerts, and the football schedule was severely restricted. The reason for the lack of performances was the Student Army Training Corps (SATC). The SATC was originally designed to provide additional noncommissioned military training to volunteering college students over the age of twenty-one. However, when Congress lowered the draft age to eighteen and decided to make the SATC compulsory, student social life during that semester became virtually nonexistent. The whole campus became a quasi-army base, with the male undergraduates wearing uniforms at all times, following military regulations, and observing a strict curfew.

Fortunately, on November 11, 1918, the armistice ending World War I was signed, and Penn State demobilized rapidly. By mid-December the SATC had been completely disbanded. As campus life returned to normal, many more musicians tried out for the band. The band grew to 107 in number that semester, making it one of the largest college marching bands in the United States at the time and one of the first to reach 100 members. The first appearance by the new band since the spring of 1918 was on Sunday afternoon, January 19, 1919, at a concert in Schwab Auditorium, where the band played Thompson's march "Penn State" and classical pieces by Verdi, Brahms, and Dvořák.

The second public appearance by the Military Band was just two days later, at the inauguration of Governor William C. Sproul in Harrisburg. Joining the band was an entire battalion of 300 men from Penn State's ROTC. As well as marching in the parade in downtown Harrisburg, the band later performed a concert in the rotunda of the State Capitol. Although the listeners attending that event enjoyed the concert, the band members believed that the echoes from the rotunda had diminished the quality of their performance.

In the fall of 1919 the band began to perform at football games again. Traveling to Philadelphia and Pittsburgh for the Penn and Pitt games, respectively, the Military Band helped propel Penn State to victory on both Franklin Field and Forbes Field, the first time ever that Penn State won both of these away games. Penn lost its run for a national championship the day it played Penn State, demonstrating that the Nittany Lions had one of the strongest teams in the nation.

Tommy Thompson kept the tradition of the Cadet Band spring concerts and sometimes used string instruments to enhance the performance.

By the end of the decade, Penn State's marching band was in excellent shape. Having tripled in size from 1910 to 1919, the band was also clearly positioned as a major college band. With the hiring of a professional bandmaster with the pedigree of Thompson, the quality and discipline of the musicians increased dramatically and enhanced the band's reputation as one of the top marching and concert bands in the country. As the next decade began, the fortunes and fame of the College Military Band promised to be like no other.

5 | Gaining National Recognition, 1920–1929

THE GOAL OF ATTAINING *further eminence among other bands in the collegiate world was realized during the 1920s. "Tommy" Thompson spread the fame of his young charges beyond Central Pennsylvania and into much of the rest of the United States. Those who knew anything about concert and marching bands were familiar with Thompson's renown, and those involved in college band circles began to see that Penn State's marching band was worth watching closely.*

The beginning of the 1920s saw the campus return to a focus on academics, leaving World War I behind. Completely military-oriented in 1918, the pendulum of Penn State's collective military mind-set by 1920 was swinging back toward a much more pacifist orientation. Across the nation during these early years of the postwar era, compulsory

THE BAND AT PENN

After its creation in 1923 the Blue Band became the premier marching band at Penn State and was usually the band that played at away football games. This is a picture of the Blue Band at the University of Pennsylvania game in 1924.

military training by land-grant colleges and the continuance of the Selective Service Act of 1917 were being debated by the general population. With World War I over, most Americans were ready to put the war behind them, some even suggesting that the United States spend less money and energy on military preparedness.

The *Collegian* published numerous editorials in the 1920s arguing for abolishing compulsory ROTC enrollment for Penn State undergraduates. The paper took the position that the Morrill Land Grant Act never intended that land-grant colleges make military training mandatory, but only merely available as a course of study. Furthermore, the University of Wisconsin, another land-grant college, abolished compulsory drill in 1922 without losing federal appropriations. Secretary of War John W. Weeks affirmed in 1924 that the National Defense Act of 1920 makes optional the instruction of military tactics at land-grant colleges and subject to the approval of each college's administration. Nevertheless, Penn State's Board of Trustees and the college presidents during the 1920s were convinced of its importance and did not vote to make the ROTC optional. Compulsory military training for freshmen and sophomores lasted at Penn State until 1964.

In spite of generally pacifist sentiments on campus, most Penn Staters were proud of the Department of Military Science, with good reason. As representatives of the college at many military functions, the ROTC students of Penn State always made an impressive showing. During Field Day in May 1920, visitors to the college watched the ROTC perform admirably when the military regiment held a review. At 10:30 that morning a bugle sounded to assemble the regiment on the drill field. After the roll call and the issuing of orders, the regiment, led by the College Military Band, marched to Beaver Field. The regiment passed in review before President Sparks and hundreds of spectators, to the sounds of Sousa marches supplied by the band. The audience was then treated to demonstrations by the machine-gun company, the 37 mm or "one-pounder" gun squad, and a select bayonet squad. The review provided many of the visitors who witnessed it an impressive example of the importance of military training at Penn State.

Another boost to Penn State's ROTC occurred later that year when U.S. Secretary of War Newton D. Baker visited Penn State at Opening Exercises on September 15. Met at the city limits by the band and a company of the cadet regiment, the secretary was escorted to Schwab Auditorium, where he gave his address, titled "Physical Value of Military Training." Because his message was broadcast via radio nationwide, Secretary Baker also took the opportunity to outline the new military policies that all ROTC units around the nation should follow.

Another successful organization during this period was the Nittany Lion football team. All Penn State students attending the football games and other collegiate events in the first half of the century sang the Alma Mater and school fight songs: "Victory," "Nittany Lion," and "Fight On, State." To help provide more spirit for the team, Professor Clarence C. Robinson, head of the Music Department, wanted to have a corps of "song leaders" who would start the mass singing at these events. A course on song-leading was started by Robinson at the beginning of the fall semester, where the students learned the rudiments of music and how to direct. Sixteen men who expressed an interest in becoming song leaders took the course and led songs for the mass meetings, football games, and pep rallies.

Another notable event in 1920 was the passing of a beloved faculty member, Dr. George Gilbert Pond, in May. "Swampy" Pond had been dean of Penn State's School of Natural Sciences and was acting president of the college after Edwin Sparks took what became a permanent leave of absence for health reasons. Funeral services for Pond were held on Sunday, May 23, and out of respect for the professor and former faculty treasurer of the band, Bandmaster Thompson canceled the Sunday concert scheduled that day for the front lawn of Old Main.

During May of the next year, the band participated once again in the Memorial Day observances in State College. That year's holiday was like no other in Central Pennsylvania. The main feature was a huge parade that rivaled in size the parades of many much larger communities. The marching units consisted of many local veterans' groups from three wars, plus the Daughters of the American Revolution, the Red Cross, the YMCA, the entire college regiment, and various other patriotic groups in the Centre County region. Led by the College Military Band, the parade wended its way through the streets of State College to Schwab Auditorium, where the band halted and let the rest of the parade file past in review. At the auditorium, the memorial service began with a bugler playing taps and a rifleman firing a volley over the grave of President Atherton beside the building.

By the fall semester of 1921 Sergeant Thompson had split the Military Band into two organizations because it was becoming too large to hold an effective practice together. The first band, consisting mostly of upperclassmen, had seventy-five members, while the second band, mostly freshmen, had forty members. The second band was also the band of

The Rookie Run

Today, singing the school fight songs is rare at Penn State athletic events. Many Penn Staters, even some of the older alumni, do not know the words to the fight songs or even the Alma Mater. During pregame at football and basketball games, the words to the Alma Mater are displayed on the scoreboards to help those who do not know them. The words to the fight songs are rarely taught in any student activity outside the vocal music organizations. One group of students, however, is expected to know the words to at least one fight song: The Penn State Blue Band.

During the days when first-year men wore "dinks" (small caps) and the women wore green ribbons to advertise their class rank, the senior class set many rules for the first-year students to follow to demonstrate their respect for their "elders." These rules included not being allowed to walk in the grass on campus, not being allowed to be seen talking to members of the opposite sex, and at all times having matches available to light cigarettes for seniors. Such rules were enforced by the sophomore class and the student tribunal. Punishment for violations was usually an experience of public humiliation, like being forced to wear a sandwich board with the infraction written on it, or being made to publicly confess numerous times how foolish they were to break the rules and defy the upperclassmen. Since the mid-1940s such activities have faded, however, and no freshman is required to wear special attire signifying class standing.

But the tradition of freshmen rules has not died out, though it is carried on now in a harmless and even fun experience. First-year members of the Blue Band, or "rookies," have a special requirement: Learn the words to "Nittany Lion" before the first home football game. Because the Blue Band sings this fight song while marching just before it enters Beaver Stadium, it is important for all members to know it. After the first full practice of the season, the band gathers in what they call a "huddle" for last-minute remarks and announcements. The president of the Blue Band addresses the band and congratulates the new members. Finally, the president asks the first-year members to start singing "Nittany Lion." Since it is the first practice and the new members had not been told to learn the song beforehand, this command is usually a surprise to the rookies, so none of them knows the words. When they attempt to sing a song they didn't know they had to learn, the traditional "Rookie Run" commences right away.

Standing at the corners of the practice field, four upperclassmen mark the boundaries of the run holding 7.5 foot poles marked every 22.5 inches used to measure the "eight-steps-per-five-yards" marching interval. Then the upperclassmen order the rookies to run a lap around these poles. While the rookies run, the upperclassmen begin to sing "Nittany Lion." Some upperclassmen run with the rookies, singing along to help them learn the words. The last part of every practice from then until the first home football game is the "Rookie Run," unless the rookies can demonstrate that they have all mastered the song. If the upperclassmen are not impressed, they begin to yell "Run!" and the rookies take off for the poles to the sound of the upperclassmen singing. To date, no freshman class has ever learned the song to the upperclassmen's satisfaction before the first game.

Because of their interest in music and familiarity with the school songs, most Blue Band members know the words to "Fight On, State," "Victory," and the Alma Mater. By the first home football game, however, every single band member knows the words to "Nittany Lion," thanks to the Rookie Run.

choice for those who did not have a seat in the first band. Both units, still collectively known as the College Military Band, performed together for the football games, other athletic events, and parades, but for formal concerts only the first band was used. The second band, however, did perform its own formal concerts. As with the two-orchestra system that Thompson directed, open seats in the first band were filled by audition from the members of the second band. By 1927 Thompson split the second band into two military drill units: the Engineers' Band, consisting of freshmen, and the Infantry Band, consisting of sophomores.

Penn State's football team traveled to New York City's Polo Grounds for a gridiron battle against Georgia Tech on October 29, 1921. A month beforehand, Penn State's campus heard that the students of Georgia Tech had raised enough money to send their Golden Tornado Marching Band from Atlanta to the game too. Penn State, much closer than Atlanta to New York City, was not planning to send its College Military Band until the news came from the South and Penn Staters felt their school spirit was in question.

The annual trips planned to Philadelphia and Pittsburgh, and the trip to Annapolis to play Navy, depleted the yearly travel budget for the band. The Athletic Association paid for all the expenses of the Pittsburgh trip, and the interclass budget paid fully for the band's travel, lodging, and meals for the Penn and Navy games. Sending a thirty-five-piece band to New York would have cost an extra $400. With the students overwhelmingly in favor of sending the band to the game, they decided to raise the money for the trip themselves, just as Georgia Tech did.

To that end the students staged a Tag Day. During the Lehigh College football weekend at Penn State, the students sold tags to wear that stated that the purchaser had supported the college and its Marching Band. Within one hour, students and alumni had purchased

The Blue Band also played at Commencement, as shown here during the 1925 ceremony.

The Blue Band still accepts alternate band members. In an organization that has reached 275 members, it is not unrealistic to expect that, due to unforeseen circumstances or a previous engagement, some members would from time to time be unable to participate in the current weekend's football show. Because of the intricate designs and patterns that unfold during a pregame or halftime performance, it is necessary to fill in the "holes" when a band member is absent. This is a job for the alternate band member.

Alternates are full band members who participate in every way that the other Blue Band members do, including attending each rehearsal, parade, and football game. They are, however, not guaranteed to march in every pregame or halftime performance. These are band members who have the potential to gain a "ranked" spot but need a little extra experience or practice to reach that coveted goal. Some alternates are definitely qualified for a ranked position but, because of the balance of instrumentation and the limited number of sectional spots, there may not be a ranked position that needs to be filled. Alternate band members in subsequent years generally get full-time positions, and some have gone on to distinguish themselves as instrumental section leaders, band presidents, and drum majors.

Alternates have a difficult and respected job. Learning a different halftime drill in only one week is difficult enough for most band members, but learning a halftime drill in two hours the morning of a football game, as alternates must often do, is especially trying. And the Blue Band's famous pregame performance is the same all year round for the full-time band members, but it is different for the alternates, who must march a new "hole" every week. The Blue Band owes a generous debt to these unsung heroes who are among its most dedicated members.

all the tags, raising $460, enough to send forty-five musicians to New York City. The success of this sale was attributed to the generosity of the alumni and students, who donated anywhere from one cent to $10 for each tag, and to the coeds, who conducted the sale.

Staying at the McAlpin Hotel in New York City, Penn State's band played an informal concert in the lobby the morning of the game, consisting of marches, college fight songs, and popular numbers of the day. At noon, traveling by elevated rail, the band arrived at the Polo Grounds ahead of the Georgia Tech band. When Tech's band arrived, Penn State welcomed it with music as it entered. Before long, both bands were playing, each trying to outdo the other. During the game, both bands provided inspiration for their respective teams and for each other's team. When a Golden Tornado player ran the length of the football field for a touchdown, the Penn State band played "Dixie" in honor of the long-distance visitors, which the mayor of Atlanta, attending the game, remarked was a "fine bit of courtesy." The Nittany Lion football team was younger and less experienced compared with the previous year's team, and most of its difficult games were away games. Having the band at the Georgia Tech game contributed much to the young squad's victory that day, according to the spectators who attended.

Another football trip to New York City, on October 27, 1922, gave the College Military Band the opportunity to become the first college marching band to perform an on-air concert in the history of radio broadcasting. Arranged by Penn State alumni living in New

York City, the concert was held at the WEAF studios of the American Telephone & Telegraph Company, which was impressed with the performance of Penn State's band the year before.

Fifty-four of the band's top members, and the Varsity Quartet, joined by Bandmaster Thompson and Music Professor T. E. Grant, traveled by train to New York the day of the concert. At 8:30 that evening, the band and the quartet began the concert of college songs and popular pieces. The band started off with "Penn State," a march written for the band by James Leyden and arranged by Bandmaster Thompson. All the other radio stations in New York City were idle at this time of the evening, so the concert was the only music broadcast throughout the city. Indeed, it was the only music heard over the airwaves for much of the United States. The broadcast, which went to all radio stations east of the Mississippi, gave hundreds of thousands of listeners the opportunity to enjoy the music of the Penn State students. And Penn State alumni attending the banquet at the Hotel Pennsylvania could hear the concert too, with the help of amplifiers set up in the banquet room.

The concert, by all accounts, was a huge success and filled the Penn Staters who heard it with pride. The band proved to most of the nation's radio audience that it still upheld its reputation as the nation's leading college band. The Varsity Quartet, already quite well known around North and Central America, was also praised for its performance. Professor Grant, who directed the quartet, believed that the concert greatly benefited the college—both because of the quality of the music and because between musical selections the educational programs offered by Penn State, which had plans for enlarging its enrollment and improving its classes, were described.

In the fall of the next year, 1923, the band ceased to be known as the College Military Band and became known as the Blue Band. Today it is easy to see why it has that name when we see the more than 275 blue-clad musicians, silks, and majorettes perform on the field or in concert. But the Blue Band was not always uniformed in blue during its long history, and even in the fall of 1923 most of its members were dressed in tan.

The cadet uniform during the first years of the band was a dark blue, much in the Civil War style. Just before World War I, the standard army-issue khaki became the ROTC and marching band uniform. Because upperclassmen were not required to be in the ROTC, most in the band were not military. The fact that the band as a whole was no longer part of the military organization of the college was a subject for some debate among the student body about whether it was proper to have the band continue to use the army-style uniforms for every occasion. This argument was especially convincing because the ROTC already had two other marching bands it used for drill and parades: the Engineers' Band and the Infantry Band. This debate was ended during the first Student Council meeting of the new year in January 1923, when it was decided to buy new uniforms for the band. W. R. Auman, the Student Council member appointed to investigate the purchase of uniforms, stated that it would cost at least $2,500 to uniform only 100 men. The funds were expected to come from the Athletic Association and the interclass budget, but because the budgets were already drawn up and approved for the school year, purchasing uniforms would have to wait until the beginning of the fall semester.

When the 1923 fall semester began, the Student Council had at its disposal the $2,500, gathered from the college's Finance Committee and the Alumni Association. Bandmaster Thompson, an expert in uniforms as property master of the ROTC, told the Student Council that, with the bitter winters that often occurred during late-season football games, overcoats for the band would be needed as part of the uniform. Overcoats had not been considered by the council until then, and this almost doubled the price of the uniforms. However, the council agreed with Thompson and decided to purchase only fifty uniforms with overcoats that year, based on the bids from various uniform manufacturers.

The uniforms selected by the band were from the William Rowland Company of Philadelphia and cost $55 each. The cut of the uniforms was similar to that of the old dress khaki uniforms. The most noticeable difference was that they were dark blue. Because there were only fifty new uniforms for a 125-piece band, the fifty top musicians received the coveted new uniforms. Soon thereafter, this group became known as the "Blue Band," and these were the band members who traveled when it was too expensive to send the full band. Almost without exception the new uniforms went to the upperclassmen, although a few freshmen so impressed Thompson that they got to wear the blue also.

This Blue Band first appeared on the field on October 26, 1923, at Yankee Stadium in New York City, where the Nittany Lions played the Mountaineers of West Virginia. Thompson was more than satisfied with the appearance the band made at this game. "There is no doubt in my mind," he stated when asked his opinion on the game, "that the organization made a very favorable showing, both in appearance and musical ability." Thompson also stated that he had earlier felt at a disadvantage because the band did not have a distinctive uniform, but that he was happy to see that situation was being rectified, if only in part at first.

The first appearance of the new uniforms on campus occurred during one of the last Pennsylvania Days, November 9. The full band performed at the mass meeting that night, and at New Beaver Field the next day for the Georgia Tech game. The Blue Band, under the direction of student leader K. R. "Danny" Dever, sat in the west stands while the rest of the band, under Thompson's baton, was located in the east bleachers. During the game, both bands played college songs separately and one piece simultaneously. At halftime, the two bands then met in the middle of the field and performed their routines as one.

One highlight of the decade for the band occurred that semester when it hosted John Philip Sousa and his famous concert band on October 12. Sousa was invited to Penn State by the band and by Bandmaster Thompson, who had known the March King for years. Based in Willow Grove, Pennsylvania, Sousa and his band were only a few hours by train from Penn State and accepted the invitation. After touring the campus with representatives of the Penn State band, Sousa and his musicians attended a luncheon in their honor hosted by the honorary music fraternity Kappa Kappa Psi, of which Sousa and Bandmaster Thompson were members.

Sousa and Thompson knew each other quite well. Thompson, a 1894 graduate of the United States Military Academy at West Point and distinguished as an Army band leader before coming to Penn State, met with Lieutenant Commander Sousa, who was the former leader of the U.S. Marine Corps Band before starting his own band, a number of times. On a few occasions their respective bands performed together during Thompson's tour of duty. They had a great respect for each other's talents both as band leaders and as musicians.

After the luncheon, Sousa went to Schwab Auditorium and listened to the rest of the Blue Band play an afternoon concert. When the concert was over the band escorted Sousa's band to the banquet hall of the Methodist Church playing "Saber and Spurs" and "Washington Post," both written by the March King. A few words by Thompson and Band President A. F. Texter followed, and then Sousa praised the Penn State band members and band leader for their performance and expressed appreciation for their invitation.

After such a heady year in 1923, the Blue Band in 1924 had its share of challenges. Once again the band struggled with finances. Every year approximately fifty members of the band went to Philadelphia and Pittsburgh for the University of Pennsylvania and the University of Pittsburgh football games. At these away games the band played not only in the stands but also at an alumni smoker and a concert at the band's hotel. The band often went on a third football trip, if the money could be raised. That year it was expected that the band would again travel to Annapolis, Maryland, for the Penn State game against Navy.

The full College Band (or the College Military Band, as it was known during World War I) consisted of three bands—the Blue Band, the ROTC Infantry Band, and the ROTC Engineers' Band— shown here on Alumni Home- coming Day, 1926.

There were also rumors that the band would go to Atlanta in mid-October to perform at the Georgia Tech game, which at the time would have been the longest trip the band had ever taken. Friends of the band hung posters all over campus—"Who'll Play the Alma Mater in Georgia?" "Will the Band March Through Georgia?"—to gain popular support for the idea.

Unfortunately the band was unable to secure sufficient funds to go to the Georgia Tech game, and just after that game some students began to speculate about whether the band could even afford to make the third trip to Annapolis. The Blue Band was still mostly "tan": fifty more blue uniforms had been planned to be purchased for the next season. There was no way the athletic, interclass, or even college budget could both afford to purchase these uniforms and send the band on an extra trip that season.

As it turned out, the band did not go to the Navy game, as most had anticipated, in order to have money to purchase the remaining new uniforms. It was rumored on campus that the band members were disgruntled and discouraged with the college because it could only go to two games that year. While certainly disappointed, the band members dispelled rumors of dissatisfaction at their business meeting in early November. In a unanimous decision, the band passed a motion that stated that the band had implicit confidence in the college authorities and would give them its wholehearted support regarding any athletic engagements. Whether it could travel with the athletic teams or not, the Blue Band supported the teams and their alma mater, as it continues to do today.

Although it could not go to any other away football games, the band did make its annual trips to Philadelphia and Pittsburgh. On the Pittsburgh trip it did a radio performance at the nation's first radio broadcasting station, KDKA in eastern Pittsburgh. A. B. Zerby, a 1911 Penn State graduate and a publicity manager at Westinghouse, the owner of KDKA, invited the band, the Varsity Quartet, College President John Martin Thomas, and Penn State football coach Hugo Bezdek all to appear on KDKA's famous midnight review program on November 26, the day before the big Pitt game on Thanksgiving Day. The singing quartet was under the baton of Music Professor Hummel Fishburn, the future Blue Band director and future head of the Music Department. Along with the normal band selections, Director Thompson organized jazz pieces for some of the band members who were also in dance orchestras on campus to play. Westinghouse, which normally restricted "popular" music, such as jazz, on its station, made an exception that night for the Blue Band. Between musical numbers by the band and the quartet, President Thomas and Coach Bezdek were interviewed and spoke about the college and the football team.

The program was heard by more than one million listeners around North America and Europe—by far the largest audience ever for the Blue Band, or indeed for any college marching band at the time. KFKX in Hastings, Nebraska, carried the program on a lower frequency, so the program was also heard in Canada. Transcontinental broadcast testing that night also made it possible for many people in England and continental Europe to hear the sounds of the Nittany Lions. The band received many postcards from Penn State

The Alma Mater

For the Glory of old State,
For her founders, strong and great,
For the future that we wait,
Raise the song, raise the song.

Sing our love and loyalty,
Sing our hopes that bright and free
Rest, O Mother dear, with thee,
All with thee, all with thee.

When we stood at childhood's gate,
Shapeless in the hands of Fate,
Thou didst mold us, dear old State,
Dear old State, dear old State.

May no act of ours bring shame,
To one heart that loves thy name,
May our lives but swell thy fame,
Dear old State, dear old State.

Penn State's Alma Mater was written by Fred Lewis Pattee, Professor of American Literature at the college and the first professor of this subject in the United States. A member of the Penn State faculty for thirty-four years, Dr. Pattee was dedicated to Penn State. In 1901 he decided that it was time for Penn State, which was rapidly growing into a large college, to have its own song. Instilled with school spirit, he wrote an article in the April edition of The Free Lance suggesting that a contest be held to compose an Alma Mater in order to foster pride in the college. At the end of the article he attached an example of lyrics, composed by himself, to give the students an idea of what the song should be like. His words were sung to the hymn "Lead Me On," which was well known by the students because it was sung at Commencement by the graduating seniors.

As it turned out, no contest was necessary. Pattee's song became popular on campus and was first sung at the alumni Commencement banquet in June the same year. After the singing ended, the president of the Board of Trustees, James A. Beaver, rose and formally announced to the alumni attending that the trustees had declared the composition to be the official Penn State Alma Mater.

Later, some of the original lyrics, such as standing "at boyhood's gate" and being "molded into men," began to bother Pattee. By then Penn State had been a coeducational institution for more than thirty years, and Pattee believed that the Alma Mater should represent the spirit of all its students, male and female. Aware that he was not the only one troubled by the masculine tone of the lyrics, Pattee, in his autobiography, suggested changing the word "boyhood" to "childhood" and changing the line "into men, into men" to "Dear old State, dear old State." With many students and faculty in agreement that such a change was long overdue, the Board of Trustees adopted the changes suggested by Pattee in 1975 and molded the Alma Mater into its modern form.

alumni in London, Paris, and other European cities who happened to tune in to the program. They expressed their pride and admiration for their band and for their beloved alma mater half a world away.

With the new uniforms paid for last year, the band in 1925 was able to make its three trips that year to Syracuse, Pittsburgh, and Morgantown, West Virginia. Fifty members of the Blue Band traveled to Syracuse, receiving a hearty welcome by the Syracuse University football fans and the blue-sweatered Orange Band. The following weekend, those fifty Blue Banders went to Morgantown for the game and helped dedicate the new West Virginia University Memorial Stadium. The final trip of the year saw seventy-five blue uniforms march on the University of Pittsburgh, celebrating the inaugural year of the new Pitt Stadium. Not only did the Blue Band play at the game, at the alumni smoker, and at the hotel concert, it also performed for the second annual KDKA Penn State Night. Joining the band for that evening broadcast were the Penn State Glee Club and the Thespians. Also appearing on Penn State Night were guest speakers, such as Penn State Board of Trustees President Judge H. Walton Mitchell, who discussed the Lions-Panthers game and other topics of interest to Penn State enthusiasts. Again the radio broadcast was widely listened to and considered a success both for the band and for Penn State.

The Blue Band's football game shows and spring concerts were not the only music offerings the college served up during the school year. Enrollment in music courses during the summer sessions was increasing rapidly by 1926. Many who took the courses were not full-time students at Penn State, but public school teachers who wanted to earn more credits. Because of this demand Penn State's School of Education launched a summer Institute of Music Education under the leadership of Professor Richard Grant. The institute was based on the success of the college's Institute of French Education, where students lived for six weeks in French-speaking-only dormitories. The Music Institute had the students live together in campus cottages and concentrate all their attention that summer on studying music.

The Institute of Music Education enrolled sixty students the summer of 1926. Students took music courses, but also had the opportunity to perform in the Summer Session Band, the orchestra, and other various musical groups. The success of the institute was helped when the Pennsylvania State Department of Public Education approved the courses and allowed public school teachers who attended to meet state certification requirements. Some who had sufficient advanced courses could receive a bachelor of arts degree in education as well.

Later in 1926 the Blue Band once again began its fall season. En route to an away football game, the Blue Band often made a concert stop somewhere in the opponents' town or at another town along the way. Train trips to the University of Pennsylvania were often preceded by a Blue Band demonstration in the state capital of Harrisburg, through which the trains passed on the way to Philadelphia. Such was the case that year in early November. Traveling to march at Franklin Field, the band stopped near the state capital and presented a semi-classical music concert at Lemoyne High School arranged by the

OPPOSITE TOP
The Blue Band was quite noticeable in its dark-blue uniforms.

OPPOSITE BOTTOM
The 1928 Blue Band played concerts all over the campus, even in front of the Obelisk.

Harrisburg Alumni Association. Seventy-five band members were present for the concert and the Penn game.

In February of the next year the Blue Band and the other two Penn State bands participated in Military Week, a week of celebration focused on the Department of Military Science. The Blue Band performed its first spring concert of the year to close Military Week in Schwab Auditorium. The band played, among other pieces, a fantasy called "The Battle for Democracy," described as a musical panorama depicting the strife in Siberia during World War I and the ultimate victory of the Allies.

Selected members of the Blue Band, thirty in all, played another concert later in the week on WPSC, Penn State's own radio station, for the first time. The station, often plagued by insufficient equipment, resumed broadcasting for the first time in two years that month, bringing to the air the Blue Band, the Penn State basketball game versus Ursinus, and a number of one-minute talks by Professor A. Howry Espenshade. Later that spring, in May, WPSC broadcast another Blue Band concert in celebration of National Music Week. From its new and enlarged studio, the station broadcast a performance by a larger group from the Blue Band after receiving many requests from all over the listening area to have the band back on the air.

The next spring, 1928, the band performed again for the Knights Templar in Reading, this time as the featured unit leading the parade. W. O. Thompson arranged original music for the event, combining traditional Knights pieces with Penn State school songs for an additional concert. One piece arranged by Thompson, "Grand Commander," was a tribute to Boyd Musser, an 1894 Penn State graduate and former Eminent Commander of the Knights Templar of Pennsylvania. Originally scheduled to perform in Lebanon, Allentown, Harrisburg, and Lewistown during their trip, those band appearances were cut from the schedule by Thompson because of approaching final exams.

That fall saw the Blue Band travel again to Philadelphia's Franklin Field for the gridiron battle against the Penn Quakers. The band performed at the huge alumni pep rally and dance at the Bellevue-Stratford Hotel. Also featured at the rally were the famous Adelphia Quartet, five vaudeville acts, and three movies featuring the Penn State campus and Penn State alumni. Earlier in the evening the band performed a short concert on WIP radio, which also featured College President Ralph Dorn Hetzel and some of the Nittany Lion football coaching staff speaking about Penn State and college football. Along with the praise received as a result of the radio and pep rally performance, the next day at the game proved to be praiseworthy as well; the Philadelphia newspapers likened the band to a symphony orchestra on the field.

The Blue Band broadcast another concert in 1929 over the radio when it performed in New York at the NBC studios of WJZ in mid-October. Earlier in the day the band performed at Yankee Stadium for the football game between Penn State and New York University. Only a week before the game the band was not even scheduled to travel to New York. The *Collegian* was mainly responsible for stirring up the movement to send the band when it printed an editorial saying:

There is scarcely a more fitting ceremony for between the halves of a football game than a parade over the gridiron by a band, suitably uniformed and well trained. As a prelude to the game such a band marching upon the field is still more appropriate. When the whistle blows for the opening of what will presumably be one of the biggest games in the East that afternoon, Penn State will be ably represented on the gridiron, but unorganized in the stands [without the Blue Band]. The Collegian feels, therefore, that the importance of the event to Penn State warrants the presence of our premier musical organization.

Meeting with the finance committees of the Athletic Association and class funds, the Music Department demonstrated that sending the band by bus rather than train would make up for the more than $3,000 needed to send the band to New York. With the finances worked out, the committees agreed to fund the third trip. It was up to the band, however, to decide whether it would go to New York or to the Syracuse game later in the year. The band chose New York, mainly for the golden opportunity to promote itself and the college to a wider audience.

In late 1929 the music programs at the college had grown to the point where the Department of Music could reorganize and offer more courses. Dr. Richard Grant was appointed by President Hetzel to be the first Department of Music department head after the reorganization. Because of the new band- and orchestra-directing courses offered, the

Some members of the 1929 Blue Band with Director Wilfred Thompson.

Recreation Hall

Ⓞne of the big events of 1929 at Penn State was the dedication of Recreation Hall. The impetus for the idea of a recreation building began ten years before its dedication, when the college decided that the Armory was not well equipped for all athletic uses. Raising money to build the hall did not begin in earnest until 1922, when the college emergency building fund listed it as a major objective. Construction of the 6,000-seat sports hall began in February 1928 and was completed a year later. A major event on campus associated with athletics, the dedication was attended by the Blue Band, where it performed fight songs and the Alma Mater for the large crowd who came out to the event.

From that point on until 1996 "Rec Hall" was the home of the major indoor sports teams, such as wrestling, men's and women's basketball, and gymnastics. It was also the main arena for Penn State's Basketball Pep Band, another athletic band on campus.

In 1996 most of the activities held at Rec Hall were moved to the newly created Bryce Jordan Center, where the Basketball Pep Band (now called the Pride of the Lions) performs. One activity that remains at Rec Hall is women's volleyball, which has recently experienced a significant increase in attendance. The Pride of the Lions sometimes performs for the many fans present at the games. ⌁

Blue Band and the orchestra were removed from the Department of Military Science and moved to the Department of Music. In October the college appointed Wilfred O. ("Tommy") Thompson Assistant Professor of Music. He was in charge of the band and orchestra and was responsible for teaching the conducting classes for future directors. He was able to keep his position as Property Manager of the Department of Military Science.

The development of the music programs at Penn State increased dramatically by the end of the decade. Improvements in the curriculum, such as the start of the summer music institute and new conducting courses, all stimulated growth in the Music Department. And as part of the Music Department the Blue Band was contributing to its growth, in a major way, as the band continued to increase in membership and improve performance quality in the years to come.

6 Passing the Baton, 1930–1939

DURING THE 1930S *the Blue Band seemed to be in stasis. Throughout the Great Depression, although Penn State increased its enrollment as students waited out the tough economic times at college, the Blue Band did not increase its membership dramatically. It continued to earn the respect and admiration of alumni, students, and fans, but during this decade few new features were introduced. When Hummel Fishburn succeeded the retiring Wilfred O. Thompson as Band Director in the late 1930s, however, the band began to expand and change.*

In the 1930 football season the Blue Band accompanied the football team to three away games: Lafayette, Bucknell, and Pittsburgh. Before the Pittsburgh game the band once again broadcast a concert from the studios of KDKA.

Practice Fields

The Blue Band does not really have a practice field to call its own, and it never did. Over the years, the Blue Band has practiced at many different places around Penn State's campus. In the earliest years the Cadet Band held indoor practices in Old Main and practice field maneuvers on old Beaver Field. During the 1930s and 1940s, the Blue Band rehearsed on a field behind Recreation Hall. Then, in the 1950s, the band was moved to the golf courses on the west side of Atherton Road at the edge of campus. Night rehearsals were conducted at the site where Fisher Plaza and Kern Building are now located, because that area was well lit.

During the mid-1960s to the early 1970s the Blue Band had to hold marching practice in the parking lot adjacent to Beaver Stadium. Later in the 1970s the band moved again to its current home on the Intramural Sports Fields near the parking lot by the Flower Gardens. That is where it practices now on Monday, Wednesday, and Friday afternoons. On Tuesday evenings and Saturday mornings during the 1970s it practiced at the Astroturf field next to the ice rink. Because of the intramural football schedule, the Blue Band must often remove itself from the football field and practice its music in sectional rehearsals instead. In addition, the intramural fields overlap the Blue Band field, and often a goalpost is in the way of the practicing band. Tall sousaphone players beware!

Tuesday night practices were moved in the early 1980s back to the golf courses, a mile away from the band-instrument storage trailers. That made the logistics of moving the instruments quite difficult for the band's equipment managers. Saturday morning practices are now held at the IM field early in the morning, because the field doubles as a parking lot on game day.

Of the eleven college marching bands in the Big Ten Athletic Conference, only two do not have a practice field of their own: Penn State and the University of Wisconsin. Most of the Big Ten schools have indoor practice facilities for their bands as well. The Blue Band prides itself in practicing outside no matter what the weather conditions, but the truth is that they have nowhere else to go.

In 1934 the college decided to acquire new uniforms for the Blue Band. The new uniforms were in a military style and patterned after those worn at West Point. The new uniforms and the company that manufactured them, Hirsh Weintraub Company of Philadelphia, had been selected by a committee consisting of Bandmaster Thompson; Claude Shappelle, the previous Blue Band president; John Ryan Jr., president of the Class of 1934; Neil Flemming, graduate manager of athletics; Richard Grant, director of the Department of Music; and Jacob Stark, chairman of the Interclass Finance Committee. The cost of each uniform was approximately $60.

To ensure that the new, form-fitting uniforms would fit the 1934–35 Blue Band, special auditions were held at the *end* of the 1933–34 season, the first time this had ever been done. Of special interest were the new caps worn by the band. These caps were blue with a white band across the top with the words "Penn State" written in silver letters on the white band. The new uniforms also had a white keystone enclosing a blue "s" on the left shoulder and a detachable cape.

In 1936 Thompson received some help in creating formations for the Blue Band to perform. Hum Fishburn, who was to become the band's director in 1939, began designing field formations for Thompson. One of the first field shows Fishburn wrote was for Dad's

ABOVE The size of the Blue Band continued to grow under the leadership of Wilfred O. Thompson.

LEFT The Blue Band's pregame usually consisted of a march around the track before performing on Beaver Field.

Day, the annual event where the college officially welcomes students' fathers to campus. One particular formation showed a little of Fishburn's humor. "The band formed a huge dollar sign," Hum recalled in an interview in 1951, "but nobody seemed to catch the significance of it. I still think it was appropriate."

In May 1937 the students' satirical college newspaper, *The Froth*, printed a small article about "Major" Thompson that was criticized by some Blue Band members, some students, and a few faculty members. The article included a photograph of a "claycature" of Tommy Thompson holding a baton in his right hand and leaning against a music stand with his left. The claycature was made by Richard Ellenberger, a trombone player who joined the Blue Band in 1938. The article stated:

> Standing before a map showing part of his musical travels, Major W. O. Thompson raises his baton, silences the patient boys, and tells us for three hours of his astonishing career. Through the colorful occident and the mysterious East, the Major inspired downtrodden composers to bring forth works of genius which he always had the honor of playing first. Indeed, the Major has not been unrewarded as the thicket of tinwear he carries on his breast mutely testifies. Sultans fell at his feet and Maharajas inevitably gave him cigaret cases. "Here's the cigaret case to prove it," says the Major. Meanwhile the annual spring concert of the Blue Band is waiting. At last, the Major runs down, the Blue Band fills its lungs and the patient listeners will have a brief interlude of music as an overture to the major's address before the second number.

The Blue Band also led the Commencement procession during the 1930s.

Officers

The role of student officers has been quite important to the Blue Band. Even though the original Cadet Band had only three student officers—president, secretary, and bandmaster—and one office held by a faculty member (treasurer, held by Dr. George Pond), as the band grew in number the officer positions did too. The current Blue Band has approximately eleven positions to which students from the band are elected. Each has its own responsibilities.

The president of the band is responsible for the morale of the general membership and for organizing and providing leadership to the other officers. One of the chief responsibilities of the president is to be the liaison between the members of the band and the Blue Band staff.

The vice-president's responsibility is to assist the president and all other officers with their duties. The vice-president also fills in for the president when necessary and accompanies him or her when greeting bands from visiting universities.

The secretary is responsible for recording the notes at meetings and helping to organize social events.

The treasurer is responsible for tracking the student monies of the Blue Band. He or she must collect money for social events, as well as instrument rental fees and the like.

The librarians are responsible for collecting, storing, and distributing music to the Blue Band membership. The Blue Band might have up to forty different pieces of music per season. Multiply that by a total membership of 275 and you get more than 1,000 sheets of music that must be accounted for—and that is only if the piece is written on one page. Three people usually hold this position, with one being known as the "head librarian."

The managers are responsible for the upkeep of the school-owned instruments, for distributing the uniforms at the beginning of the season, for collecting the uniforms at the end of the season, for transporting the instruments to practice fields and bowl trips, and for setting up and breaking down of the yard-line markers, the sound system, and marching equipment used during practices and performances. Usually three band members share these responsibilities, one of which holds the distinction of being "head manager."

The historian is responsible for keeping a record of the events that have transpired during the season. Usually at the Blue Band Banquet the membership is presented with a photo album containing pictures of important events during the season. Some historians have created videotapes of the season as well as a printed yearbook.

Although there is a standard hierarchy among the positions, all are equally important for the smooth running of an organization that is approaching 300 members.

Blue Band managers making "turning dots" for the pregame performance at an away game at the University of Maryland in 1987.

The Blue Band always enjoyed performing at Beaver Field for Dad's Day.

The article was humorous and in jest, and it is believed that Thompson found it funny as well.

Hummel Fishburn changed the pregame show, which consisted of playing the march "National Emblem" and marching down the field as a block, slightly in 1938: he added a fanfare to the beginning of the piece. According to Ed Pollock, a member of the Blue Band from 1939 to 1942, each week a trumpet or trombone player would create a new fanfare and implement it for the next game.

The year 1938 marked the end of an era in Blue Band history. On November 5, 1938, Tommy Thompson, after announcing his retirement, directed the Blue Band for the last time. It was the last home game of the year, and the one in which Penn State was defeated by Lafayette. Even in defeat the Blue Band played "There Will Be a Hot Time in the Old Town Tonight" as a retirement song for Thompson. With a gleam in his eye, Thompson had these parting words for the Blue Band on Beaver Field: "I'm 103 years old, but I can still make more noise on a trumpet than the whole damn bunch of you!"

Thompson had many stories to share about his experiences with the Blue Band. His favorite experience, according to the *Collegian*, had taken place at a game between Penn

State and Navy in the early years of the band's existence. When an official had made a controversial decision, fans of both teams began to pour out of the stands to settle the argument about the decision physically. Thompson quickly got the attention of the Blue Band and led the band in a rendition of the National Anthem. The music immediately halted the progress of the Midshipmen and the Lions, averting a riot.

In the spring of 1939 Thompson was on campus receiving gifts and accolades. The 1939 *La Vie* wrote:

> With the departure of the Class of '39, there will terminate the active professional duties of three outstandingly popular men, three men who have their periods of service bridge the gap between the Old Penn State and the New Penn State, three men whose contributions will never be forgotten and whose memory will enter the sanctity accorded to past Penn State greats.
>
> These men, Dean Ralph L. Watts, Professor Elton D. Walker, and Major W. O. ("Tommy") Thompson, have compiled between them 95 years of service. During these years they have established enviable reputations that have bound them close to the hearts of the faculty and the student body.
>
> As due credit to their splendid records, the staff of the Penn State *La Vie* dedicates this, the 1939 edition, to Dean Ralph Watts, Professor Elton Walker, and Major "Tommy" Thompson.

Two days before the largest Penn State Commencement exercises to date took place on June 12, an alumni luncheon was held. At the luncheon, Thompson was presented with a gold watch in recognition of his service as bandmaster for the past twenty-five years. The letters W O THOMPSON replaced the numbers on the watch, and the second hand ticked over the Penn State seal. On the face of the watch was engraved "TO TOMMY, FROM THE PENN STATE CLASSES FROM 1914 TO 1939." The Blue Band was there to perform for

After Thompson's retirement, Hummel Fishburn became Director of the Blue Band in 1939.

HUMMEL FISHBURN

Hummel Fishburn was born on March 18, 1901, in Washington, D.C., to the Reverend Ross Fishburn and his wife, Emma. "Hum," as he came to be known on Penn State's campus, was introduced to music as a young child by his mother's sister, Sue Hummel. Aunt Sue, a talented pianist, often took Hummel to symphony concerts in the Washington area, sometimes to as many as twenty-five a year. As a teenager, Hummel studied at the Washington Music Conservatory, where he learned to sight-read piano music and play it in any key. But because his thumb knuckles had been fused since birth, he could never be a concert pianist. That did not keep him from choosing music as a profession, however. His older sister, Margaret, also helped Hummel pursue a music career indirectly by applying to Penn State for him without his knowledge. After graduating from high school in 1918, Hummel found a job working at the Newport News shipyards for $300 a month with three other boys. "While I was there, I got a letter from Penn State saying I'd been accepted, but I hadn't even applied," Fishburn recalled. "I was making a lot of money. I didn't want to go to college!" His sister, a senior at Penn State and one of the first coed Thespians at the time, knew what was best for her brother, so Hummel became a Penn Stater that fall.

Hummel also joined the Penn State Thespians, where he excelled as a playwright. His first show, the comedy "King Pomp Pompous I," was a smash hit at Schwab Auditorium in 1921,

and Fishburn followed that with at least three more plays. As an undergraduate student, Fishburn also played piano with a local dance band known as "'Schlop' Schlosser's Orchestra," and he also played incidental piano music for silent films at the Pastime Theatre, which "Hum" fondly recalled: "Films weren't scored in those days, so the pianist 'jammed' as he saw fit." Fishburn was also the chapel organist at the college, and he learned to play bassoon for Tommy Thompson in the college orchestra when no one else could be found for the instrument. With Thompson, Fishburn was a founding member of Penn State's chapter (Alpha Zeta) of the professional music fraternity Phi Mu Alpha.

After graduating with a bachelor's degree in finance, Fishburn was offered the position of assistant to the dean of men, Arthur R. Warnock, and held that job for four years. His main duty was to supervise organized

student activities, such as music and dramatics, a job for which he was eminently qualified. During his years in this position, he earned a master's degree in psychology in 1925 and met his future wife, Becky Clingerman of Tyrone, Pennsylvania.

After Becky graduated from the Grier School and left Tyrone to attend Wells College in New York, Hummel left Penn State for Chester, Pennsylvania, to direct the high school music program there. During those high school teaching years he earned a doctoral degree in music from the University of Montreal. In 1929 Becky graduated from Wells College and returned with Hummel to Penn State, where he had been hired as a professor and as head of the instrumental music program at the newly reorganized Department of Music. The following year Becky and Hummel were married, and eventually they became the parents of three sons, David, Ross, and Peter, all of whom became excellent musicians in their own right, and Penn State Blue Band members.

Fishburn was responsible for directing the Symphony Orchestra, the Women's Chorus, and the Men's Glee Club, all of which continued to improve and blossom during his tenure. He founded the Women's Symphonic Orchestra in 1929 when the male students objected to including coeds in the orchestra. Then in 1930, Fishburn developed a course in music appreciation, which included everything from classical music to jazz. And because there was no textbook at the time for this type of course, Fishburn wrote one: *Fundamentals of Music Appreciation*, which eventually became the standard textbook for music appreciation courses for most colleges in the United States offering such a course. He also penned many scholarly papers as well as nonacademic articles and editorials for various publications both on and off campus. In 1943 he was elevated to head the Department of Music, and a few years later to head the Music Education Department too, which positions he held simultaneously until 1965. As head of the music schools, he restarted and expanded the high school band, chorus, and orchestra summer school program at Penn State, which was recognized as one of the best in the nation.

In addition to being a professor and an administrator, Fishburn was closely involved in various organizations at Penn State. His roles on campus included returning as chapel organist, serving on the Thespians' board of directors, serving on the Athletic Advisory Board from 1948 through 1959, adjudicating most track meets and a few wrestling and swimming meets for thirty-plus years, and serving as a member of the University Faculty Senate for more than thirty-five years, longer than any other faculty member at that time. Fishburn also served as Marshal at Commencement and at college inaugurations.

Off campus, Fishburn was equally active. He was a volunteer fireman for the Alpha Fire Company, served on the board of directors of the Mount Nittany Savings & Loan Association, was a member and past president of the Pennsylvania Music Educators' Association, and was active nationally in many honorary

fraternities. He was also appointed Centre County jury commissioner in 1968 by Judge Campbell.

Fishburn also remained active creatively during his tenure. He composed many published Glee Club songs and orchestral works during his years directing the Blue Band, and for a few years after he stepped down from that position, he wrote all the drill maneuvers for the Blue Band until 1962. His sing-alongs with Music Professor Frank Gullo were legendary in Happy Valley. The duo traveled all over Pennsylvania performing with Fishburn at the piano. The 1953 graduating class recognized his many years of dedication to university life when it dedicated its yearbook to him.

In 1938 Fishburn took on the directorship of the Blue Band when longtime bandmaster Wilfred Otto Thompson retired that fall. In this position Hum wrote all the drills, conducted all band rehearsals, and administered the off-field functions of the Blue Band. When he retired from the university as Professor Emeritus in 1965, he continued to help out as the official home game announcer for the Blue Band until his death in April 1976.

Fishburn's mark on the Blue Band as an innovator and as a catalyst for moving the band from a military-style drill band to a more modern college marching band is significant. Among his innovations as head of the Blue Band were integrating women into the ranks, playing student-composed music at Penn State football games, and increasing the performance marching speed of the band from an army-regulation 120 steps per minute to a speedy 180 steps, making the Blue Band one of the fastest marching units in the

nation. His creation of intricate field maneuvers and inclusion of popular music with the march repertoire became a hallmark of the Blue Band's style. He also eliminated the upperclassman-status requirement for being a member of the Blue Band, making everyone audition for his or her block position each year, a tradition that continues today. It was not unheard of for a freshman to unseat a fourth-year band member if performance warranted it under Fishburn's direction. Described as a modern "Renaissance man," Fishburn was an active participant with the Blue Band for well over half its existence, and his innovative touches are still felt by the current band today. ≽

During the 1930s the Blue Band formations usually consisted of letters and numbers.

its retiring leader and to learn who the next director would be.

The new director of the Blue Band was Hummel Fishburn, a Penn State graduate of the Class of 1922 and a graduate school graduate in 1925. Fishburn was a former Blue Band member, playing bassoon. One of the first things he did as director was expand the band, increasing its membership in 1939 by twenty members. Another change was that freshmen were permitted to be in the band. Ed Pollock was one of the freshmen from 1939 that earned a spot in the now expanded Blue Band. When asked about the benefits of being a freshman Blue Bander, he replied that he was assumed to be an upperclassman and did not always have to wear a "dink" cap signifying class rank.

With the retirement of Thompson as director of the Blue Band, an era had truly ended. The military marching band in the Sousa tradition prevalent for so many years at Penn State was ending, although its military character remained. With the elevation of Hummel Fishburn in 1939, the Blue Band began to reinvent itself. New traditions were in store for the band in the decade that followed, as Fishburn began putting his mark on the Blue Band, the Music and Music Education Departments, and the university at large.

THE DECADE OF THE 1940S *was one of change for the Blue Band. With a new director, the band began to move in new creative directions both on the field and off. World War II, which left dramatic and lasting changes on every institution across the world, did not leave the Blue Band untouched. In some respects, the band became a reflection of the changes occurring in the Music Department, the college, and the nation as the decade brought dramatic upheaval, struggle, triumph, and eventual prosperity for each.*

A positive change for the Music Department took place early in the decade as Professors of Music George S. Howard and Hummel Fishburn reorganized the Band, Orchestra, and Chorus School during the summer session of 1940. Wanting to improve its recruitment of musicians, the Music

Department shifted the emphasis in the revamped summer music institute to high school students. While at the institute, high school boys and girls attended band and orchestra rehearsals, sectional rehearsals, marching classes, dance band performances, and took classes in voice, drum-majoring, flag-swinging, and conducting as well as private instrumental instruction. High school teachers too participated in the summer institute, earning undergraduate and graduate credits by using the student band and orchestra as a clinical laboratory.

The students made public appearances performing at concerts, recitals, and radio broadcasts all summer. Every morning just before 8:00, a group of about 70 of the 100 summer music institute students participated in the formal flag-raising ceremony in front of Old Main. The band marched to the flagpole and played "To the Colors" and "The Star Spangled Banner." Between 100 and 200 people gathered to attend the ceremony each day.

The summer music institute was rated one of the best of its kind in the United States. After spending three weeks lecturing and instructing the students, Pierre Henrotte, conductor and concertmeister of the Metropolitan Opera House at the time, said that it was the finest musical training center for high school students and instructors in the nation.

The Blue Band also made a change for the better, albeit a cosmetic change, early in the decade. The All-College Cabinet recommended a $1.20 increase in March 1941 to purchase new band uniforms for the fall semester. Estimated to cost $6,500, the new uniforms were to replace the old-style uniforms purchased just six years earlier. In September the ninety-member band donned the new suits: navy-blue coats with lighter blue lapels and trim, light-blue trousers with navy-blue braid and a gold stripe down the seams, and a white keystone on the front. The band debuted in the new outfits at the pep rally for the first home football game of the season later that week.

In early October the band took an interesting away-game trip to Buffalo, New York, for the football game at Colgate University. The band had not been originally scheduled to go to Colgate. The band's budget allowed for travel to only two away games that year: to the Temple University game in Philadelphia and to the University of Pittsburgh later in the season. It was through the generous efforts of the students, the Athletic Department, and the Buffalo Junior Chamber of Commerce that the band went to this third game.

Buffalo residents started to become "Penn State minded" through the efforts of the Penn State alumni living there, who believed that the Nittany Lions would need extra motivation, knowing that Colgate's Red Raider Band was already planning to attend. Buffalo residents who were Colgate fans already knew this was going to be a big game. Five thousand advance tickets had been sold the weekend before the game, and newspapers from all over the Buffalo region reprinted road maps leading to Buffalo's Civic Stadium. The Buffalo Junior Chamber of Commerce, quite interested in bringing the famous Penn State Blue Band to town, raised $750 toward that endeavor. The additional $750 needed to send the ninety-member band would have to come from Penn State.

The Athletic Association began to feel the pressure from the students, alumni, and local newspapers to finance part of the trip. The popularity of sending "musical ambassa-

ABOVE The Blue Band created morale-boosting formations during World War II. In this photo (part of a montage) an air-plane formation marches over and destroys a swastika. The drum major was the plane's propeller.

LEFT Women were performing in the Blue Band on the football field for the first time in 1943. They are the band members wearing skirts.

dors" to the game was enormous: Colgate was relatively new on Penn State's football schedule, and Penn State fans wanted to introduce themselves to Buffalo as something more than just a college that "exists somewhere between Pittsburgh and Philadelphia." The Athletic Association reluctantly pitched in $375 raised from money set aside for sudden unforeseen expenses after the Inter-class Finance Board raised the other $375. Athletics was hesitant to give the money because it did not want to start a precedent of having to raise money for the band every time fans petitioned to send it to events not budgeted for. Unfortunately for the department, it was already on that slippery slope. The zealous Penn State alumni in New York, heartened by the actions of the Athletic Association, suggested that the Athletic Association also help pay to send the band to the New York University game at Yankee Stadium two weeks later. The Athletic Association flatly refused to help fund a fourth trip by the band. To its credit, sending the band on another nonbudgeted trip that year was also not popular among the student body, the local newspapers, the college administration, or even the band, which had already traveled more that year than its members themselves had anticipated.

In Buffalo the band participated in the huge alumni smoker at Buffalo's Memorial Auditorium. The band was led by Assistant Professor Frank Gullo, who took Dr. Fishburn's place while he was convalescing from minor surgery. Although the team lost to the Red

SPOTLIGHT

Marching

The Blue Band and most other college marching bands today march differently from military drill units. The pregame show cadence is approximately 180 beats a minute, while the regulation army cadence is 120 steps. The fast, "high-stepping" style of the Blue Band was started by the band's former director Hummel Fishburn in the late 1930s to the early 1940s. The Blue Band was the first college band in the Northeast to march that way, but it was not the first to employ a quickened pace. It is generally accepted that the practice began with colleges in the South and West years earlier. At that time it was believed that the Penn State football team was made up of young men who were not fast enough to make the Blue Band (though that was surely not stated within earshot of the football practice field).

Proper pregame marching style for the Blue Band is sometimes also known as a "chair step," for how the legs look when marching this way. To take a "high step" (or "chair step") is to lift each leg fully so that the thigh is parallel to the ground and the calf is at a 90-degree angle to the ground while the toes point straight downward. While stepping down, the feet should roll toe to heel so that the upper body remains motionless and erect. Each step should be exactly eight steps per 5 yards, or 22.5 inches per step. This ensures that the ball of the right foot always strikes the yard line when marching down the football field. Band members must be able to do this without looking at the ground because they also have to march across the field (sideline to sideline), which has no yard lines to guide them.

To appreciate the level of athleticism that the Blue Band members must possess, try marching in place this way yourself: 180 beats per second is three steps per second—and remember to pick your feet up high and point your toes. Don't bounce! At the same time, you must keep your upper body still in order to blow through your instrument while you are stepping. Now do this for at least five minutes straight, which is the approximate time of the fast-tempo pregame opening. (The total length of pregame is approximately 12 minutes.) Keep in mind that the Blue Band does this numerous times at every practice and once during each football game—while wearing a heavy wool suit and carrying heavy musical instruments. (The sousaphones weigh about twenty-five pounds each!)

If you have succeeded, congratulations! Now memorize the pregame music and marching maneuvers, memorize the new halftime formations (you may have more than fifty different precision moves to remember each week), and practice this week's challenging halftime music. Is it raining cats and dogs? Snowing? Below zero degrees? The show must go on, so hit the practice field anyway. The Blue Band always does, no matter what the weather. If you can do all that, you have met the minimum *marching* requirements to be a Blue Band member. Have fun at the Penn State football games and remember: pick 'em up!

Raiders 7 to 0, the Penn State fans attending the game were satisfied that the Blue Band was there to cheer for their Nittany Lions. After the Temple and Pittsburgh trips, the band in that year covered more than 1,400 miles to and from away games, making 1941 the most widely traveled season for the band to that time.

The end of 1941 witnessed events that called for great personal sacrifice from every American. As in all other communities around the nation, Penn State and the Blue Band were not unaffected by America's participation in World War II. Indeed, the war was the cause of significant and even historic changes that occurred in both the band and the college.

The war years actually started on a positive note for the band and the Music Department. In 1942 the Blue Band again benefited from the philanthropy of Andrew Carnegie, although not in as direct a way as it had forty-three years earlier. The Blue Band and the rest of the Department of Music moved from the fourth floor of Old Main to nearby Carnegie Hall across from the Armory in late January. Carnegie Hall, built in 1904 with a gift from Andrew Carnegie and used previously as Penn State's library, became the music building after Pattee Library was built. "Dean" Richard Grant, director of the Music Department, had been planning the move ever since it was decided that Carnegie Hall was to be the department's new home a year before. Acoustical engineers from Rockefeller Center in New York City were consulted in refurbishing the old library, in order to incorporate soundproofing equipment that was said to rival even Radio City Music Hall's. The best room, according to Professor Grant, was the band room, which had been the library's skylighted main reading room. The entire room was specially redesigned for soundproofing and was near perfect in studio quality. It also had built-in storage compartments designed by Hum Fishburn himself, to stow the school's musical instruments.

Professor Grant was pleased with the redesigned building, personally showing off the new rooms to friends and colleagues that January. "Music on the campus is definitely on the upswing now that we have adequate facilities," Grant told the *Collegian*. "Now we have one of the finest music buildings in the whole country."

Also during that year, Hummel Fishburn really began to put his signature on the Blue Band. Gregarious and not nearly as gruff as Wilfred Thompson, Fishburn encouraged creativity in the marching and concert bands by allowing them to perform arrangements written by their own members. Former Band President Victor Dimeo, a junior entering the armed services in 1942, wrote "Vic Lick #1," a short jazz piece with a cheer, performed by the band at the first home game, against Bucknell, of that year. This was followed later in the season by "Vic Lick #2" and "Vic Lick #3," which, like the first piece by Dimeo, were played during time-outs. In the previous year, Band President Walter James also wrote a short jazz lick that the band played often. In 1943 the Blue Band performed jazz pieces by fellow band members Jim Burden and Don Smith.

Fishburn began to make the halftime performances a little less traditional and a little more fun by including novel formations and numerous stunts. The field maneuvers in previous years consisted of spelling simple words and numbers. One notable example of

Fishburn's more sophisticated movements was the "Day in the Life of a Soldier" show, which was seen between halves of the homecoming game against Colgate in mid-October. The most memorable part of the show had the band march onto the field and split in two. On the upper side of the field, half the band formed an airplane imitating the sound of propellers with drums and trumpets. Thunderous applause erupted from the spectators when, sweeping down the field playing the popular "Praise the Lord and Pass the Ammunition," the "airplane" dive-bombed and dispersed the other half of the band, which had formed a Nazi swastika.

Usually it took Fishburn somewhere between twenty minutes and eight hours to write halftime routines, but because of the intricacy of this show he left town and cloistered himself in a hotel room for two days to work out the maneuvers and arranging the halftime show's six musical pieces alone. The show was so popular that Fishburn had the band perform it again when Pittsburgh came to Beaver Field and when the band traveled to its only away game of the year, at Penn.

Penn State and its students made a number of sacrifices during the war years. In the foreword of the 1944–46 class annual, *La Vie*, a passage captures the mood on campus at the time: "These were grim years, and this book, though recounting a vital period in the life of the College, has a grim theme—war. Carefree college days, the frills of higher education, were missing from the undergraduate life of these students."

Penn State was declared an "essential industry" by the federal government, ensuring that the college would receive scarce supplies during the war. However, the individual student, faculty member, and town resident still had to cope with shortages and make do with ration stamps. In September 1940 the U.S. Congress enacted the first peacetime military draft in American history. The draft age was twenty-one, and students could receive a deferment in order to finish the academic year. But because of the draft, many potential freshmen decided not to go to college, opting instead to enlist or get jobs in the rapidly growing defense industries. This trend caused a decline in enrollment at the college in 1941, for the first time in almost ten years. By 1943 the need for soldiers prompted Congress to lower the draft age to eighteen and abolish educational deferments. With so many male students heading to war, for the first time in Penn State's history the women students outnumbered the men, making up more than 60 percent of the student body in 1943.

The personnel strain on the college was felt strongly by the Blue Band, an all-male organization. Women were allowed to be members of the Symphonic Orchestra, however. Hum Fishburn made the orchestra coed in 1930 after an unsuccessful and unpopular (with the male students) attempt to do so the year before. The men in the orchestra were opposed to allowing women into their organization in 1929, and as a result Fishburn established an all-female orchestra that year. When the men's orchestra was short a french horn, an oboe, and a cello in 1930 because of graduating seniors, the gender barrier was removed out of necessity and the two organizations were combined.

That was not the situation for the Marching Blue Band. With its military roots and masculine tradition, women did not even attempt to try out for the Marching Band any

more than they did for the football team. In 1943, however, nineteen of its eighty members were called up for military service, and, with more sure to go, the Blue Band was in desperate need of musicians. Faced with the inevitable, Fishburn once again turned to the coeds and allowed them to be in the Marching Band, starting with percussionist Lois Turner '47. Although these were not the first female students to perform in any college band, they were the first at Penn State, and the only women in the Marching Band until almost thirty years later.

To augment the band, Hum Fishburn used nonstudents as well. Along with forty-one undergraduate men, the band that year was comprised of six coeds, ten Navy and Marine V-12 students (who were at Penn State taking technical training requested by the federal government), one Curtiss-Wright cadette (who was taking courses through the Curtiss-Wright Corporation's contract with the college to instruct female engineers), five boys and seven girls from State College High School, five graduate students, one State College High School faculty member, one Penn State faculty member, and one town resident. Even some Blue Band alumni who lived locally returned to perform on those football weekends.

For the first time in Blue Band history, women were actually wearing Blue Band uniforms and performing on the field during the 1943 season at Beaver Field. Although travel by the band was severely restricted because of the gasoline shortages, the band did go to

After the war, the Blue Band returned to its word or letter formations.

The uniform of the 1947 drum major, P. Grove, was quite different from the current-day drum major uniform.

the University of Pittsburgh that year as its only away appearance and the only game during the war when the band was in uniform. The Pittsburgh Panther Band, owing to the adverse circumstances of the day, disbanded after the first two games of the season, and for that reason Hum Fishburn included several Pitt songs in the Blue Band's repertoire. It was the first time in the history of Penn State that female students had the opportunity to go on an interscholastic Blue Band trip. Mrs. Louise Dye, secretary to Dr. Fishburn, went along as a chaperone. "I remember that Dr. Fishburn was short a cymbal player on that trip, so he had me in a uniform playing the cymbals," Mrs. Dye recalls. "Not knowing where the crashes were supposed to be, Dr. Fishburn told me to watch him and he would point to me when I was supposed to crash them. So I did."

Fishburn took a while getting used to having women in his band. Mrs. Dye remembers the bandmaster saying to her with bemused resignation just after the Pitt performance, "I just can't get over seeing those girls in those uniforms!" After that game, Fishburn saw no point in uniforming the band and had them put away for the remainder of the war. The "Blue" Band dressed in jackets, ties, dresses, and military uniforms, as appropriate for each musician, from that point forward.

Participation in the war effort on campus was universal, and this included the Blue Band. The Blue Band was featured in February 1943 at the basketball game between Pitt and Penn State in Rec Hall during one of many Victory Raffles. The raffle was sponsored by five of the "hat" societies (which were and are honorary student organizations): Skull and Bones, Druids, Friars, Parmi Nous, and Blue Key. War stamps were sold by the hat societies before the game, and with the stamps came a raffle ticket that would give the ticket holder a chance to win numerous prizes at halftime. Between each drawing, the Blue Band played for the spectators. This was the first time the Blue Band participated at a Penn State basketball game, playing the National Anthem and other pieces before the game, at the half, and during time-outs.

For the Blue Band, 1944 was quite similar to 1943. More students were called up for the war that year. By April thirty-three members of the band had either graduated or been called to active service since the beginning of the semester, bringing its size down to fifty-five. Female students, high school students, and many nonstudent musicians again participated in the band that year. Tryouts in November eventually added twenty-six new members after the football season ended.

A lack of materials made it impossible for the Music Department to present the normal five or six Sunday concerts in the spring of 1945.

Only two concerts were held: one by the Blue Band and one by the Symphonic Orchestra. The band performed a program of overtures, marches, and other standard band music. Although the concert was considered interesting and well played, Professor Fishburn believed the band lacked slightly for "polish" compared with prewar bands, because of the shortage of students and resources. It was his policy not to make excuses for band performances, however, and for the most part the dedication of the band members caused the Blue Band to perform above its level of talent.

On Tuesday, August 14, 1945, when news of Japan's surrender reached State College, students, faculty, and the entire town suddenly stopped what they were doing and started heading downtown. Shops were closed, classes were canceled, and meetings adjourned abruptly as everyone celebrated the Allied victory in the Pacific. Later that evening a parade featuring members of the Blue Band and the ROTC band was hastily organized. It wound its way through the streets of State College to the cheers of the jubilant crowd.

Preparations for the transition back to peacetime operations at Penn State began as early as March 1944, although the postwar policies drawn up by President Hetzel and the college postwar committee members were implemented gradually until the end of the war in the Pacific. The college was still operating on the wartime schedule of sixteen-week terms in a twelve-month period, so the Blue Band was in session during the summer. With thousands of men returning from war and going to college on the G.I. Bill, Penn State was deluged with applications from former soldiers. In the fall of 1946 more than 2,800 freshmen were admitted to the branch campuses and state teachers' colleges that agreed to instruct the Penn Staters. No freshmen were admitted to the main campus in State College.

Because of the number of male musicians returning to college, Dr. Fishburn decided in June to split the Blue Band into two organizations. The first, the so-called football band, was to operate as an all-male organization once again, marching at Beaver Field and performing at a few away games. After a long hiatus from marching at the games, seeing the Blue Band back in uniform entertaining on the field again was a welcome sight for most Penn State fans and helped everyone return to a peacetime mind-set.

The second band, the Concert Blue Band, continued to give coeds the opportunity to play band music in concert settings, though they were excluded from the marching band. Both bands held separate tryouts, and participation in one band did not necessarily mean automatic admission to the other. This band would perform in the traditional spring concerts, making Blue Band participation no longer year-round (unless, of course, a musician belonged to both bands).

(AUTHORS' NOTE: In this history, from this point forward the Marching Blue Band is referred to also as simply "the Blue Band"; the Concert Blue Band is always referred to as "the Concert Blue Band" or simply "the Concert Band.")

In October of that year, thoughts of football began to consume the students once again. Those thoughts also turned to the Blue Band, which returned to marching after three years of performing in the stands. On Friday night, October 4, the pep rally for the opening-day game against Bucknell University featured the new Blue Band. Originally scheduled

Concert Blue Band

U ntil the spring of 1947 the Concert Blue Band was made up of the same members as the Marching Blue Band. After World War II, however, these bands became so popular that it was necessary to split them into two organizations. The Concert Band performed traditional band pieces in concert at Schwab Auditorium, Recreation Hall, Pattee Library, and other locations around the Commonwealth during the spring. The uniforms for the two groups were similar, with the men in navy jackets and trousers and the women of the Concert Band in navy-blue dresses and white blouses.

Dr. James M. Dunlop, Assistant Professor of Music Education, was hired in 1947 and became Concert Band Director as well as Assistant Director of the Marching Blue Band. As the Concert Blue Band programs grew in popularity, they began making concert tours around the state, including performances in Philadelphia, Pittsburgh, Williamsport, Erie, and Harrisburg, among many others.

The Concert Blue Band performed spring concerts and was one of the best college concert bands in the nation. Because of its popularity, other Penn State symphonic bands were formed by Dr. Ned C. Deihl in the 1970s: the Concert White Band and the Nittany Lion Band. In 1996, when the School of Music reorganized, the Concert Blue Band was retired, leaving the Symphonic Band, under the direction of Dennis Glocke, as the only Concert Band left at the University. In 1998 Glocke started another band, called the Campus Band, to provide another option for students interested in performing.

to take place in Schwab Auditorium, the rally was moved outside to the steps of Old Main because of the enormous turnout of enthusiastic football and band supporters.

The band performed well at the game the next day, according to those who attended, especially in view of the difficulties it faced in preparing for the 1946 debut. Hummel Fishburn had only three days to instruct the band on that week's drill, and in addition only twenty-six of the eighty members marching had marched with the band before.

The next game the band marched at was again at Beaver Field, versus Michigan State, which had brought its eighty-member Spartan Band on its first trip out of state since 1942. The Spartans too had a promising band that year, and the musical performances by both schools were outstanding and quite competitive. Michigan State and Penn State were both land-grant colleges with similarly ranked football teams and marching bands of equal size, which led to fierce competition on the field by both athletes and musicians. Excited about marching for the first time in years, the two musical groups tried to outdo the other, much to the delight of the spectators.

Another milestone performance occurred in mid-November, when the football team and the Blue Band traveled to Annapolis to meet Navy on the gridiron. In attendance at the game was President Harry Truman as a guest of the Midshipmen. Navy had lost six games in a row and was not expected to beat the Lions that day, in spite of the President's pep talk to the naval gridders before the game. The Navy students were quite enthusiastic during the game. Some Midshipmen hung a large sign stating "Grind Over Penn" directly across from the President's box. Unfortunately, the only letters that could be seen where Truman was sitting were the initials "GOP." Chagrined Navy officials tore the sign down at the end of the first half before Democrat Truman noticed it.

The Lions did not disappoint the Penn State fans that day by winning the game 12 to 7. At the half, the Blue Band, in one of the "finest performances [by a marching band] ever seen at Annapolis," according to naval officials, serenaded the commander-in-chief with the "Missouri Waltz," as it formed a grand piano. Forming an "N" for "Navy," and later "USN," the Blue Band sang "Navy Blue and Gold," led by Assistant Director Frank Gullo, and played "Anchors Away" and Penn State's own Alma Mater. President Truman was impressed with the Blue Band, saying its performance was "superb" and thanking the band members and the football team for the enjoyable day at the stadium.

The last game of the 1946 season was, according to tradition, against Pittsburgh. The Blue Band traveled west to Pitt, this time to perform with the re-formed Panther Marching Band. Pitt's bandmaster, Dr. Robert Arthur, a Penn State graduate, wrote a halftime show that would combine the two bands, with 200 musicians on the field at once. The show was a great success, and Pitt was grateful to the Blue Band for participating that day and for playing at Pitt games during the war, while the Pitt Band was disbanded.

As the football season wound down and the spring concert season of 1947 began, Dr. Fishburn began to consider replacing some of the old uniforms. Many of the uniforms had been damaged by moths over the years of disuse. At the time, the only mechanism for raising funds to replace the damaged uniforms was a student referendum on an all-college election ballot. William Keefauver, the Blue Band president, addressed the Student Council to convince them to have a referendum on whether to add 50 cents to the student fees over the next two semesters in order to raise the more than $7,500 needed to purchase the uniforms. The council agreed, and the referendum passed at the student elections that April. The new uniforms finally arrived in late October, because of labor difficulties experienced by the uniform manufacturer. The outfits were on the order of a naval officer's uniform, rather conservative. The uniforms also had white trim on the trousers, gold buttons on the coat, and a patch on the shoulder with the words "Penn State Blue Band."

Earlier in the football season, fifty-six experienced members of the band made their own arrangements and traveled to Hershey, Pennsylvania, to participate in the opening game against Washington State. Having practiced just two days before the game, the band members cheered the Nittany Lions to a 27 to 6 victory over the Cougars.

Another interesting occasion in 1947 provided the band members with an unforgettable experience. Fred Waring, the famous band leader, invited the Blue Band, as well as the College Choir, the College Symphony, the Glee Club, members of Phi Mu Alpha musical fraternity, and the Penn State Thespians to be his guests at two live broadcasts of the "Fred Waring NBC Show." The show, performed in Schwab Auditorium by Waring and his band, delighted the students and the rest of the audience. Waring, a Penn State student from 1918 through 1920, was quite familiar with the band and its former bandmaster Wilfred Thompson and was a classmate of Hummel Fishburn's. James Leyden, a songwriter and Waring's partner, had also been a Penn Stater and had two sons who had been in the Blue Band, Donald Leyden and James Leyden Jr., the drum major from 1939 to 1941.

The Nittany Lion football team shone all year. It was ranked fourth in the nation by the Associated Press without one scholarship athlete. With an exciting football season behind, Penn State was invited to play Southern Methodist University in the Cotton Bowl on New Year's Day. Enrollment had been dropping from the previous postwar years, however, and the college was sponsoring and paying for more varsity sports than any other institution of its size, so athletics was strapped for money. As a result, the alumni-controlled Athletic Association believed it could not afford to send the Blue Band to the game. Hum Fishburn estimated that $12,000 would be needed to take the band to Dallas, and that was too large an expense. The All-College Cabinet, always eager to help student spirit organizations, voted to recommend to the Athletic Association to send the band, the cheerleaders, and the student who performed as the Lion Mascot with a portion of the estimated $75,000 Penn State would receive as its gate share. However, because athletics had been a financial drain on the college's general fund for many years, the college felt that the proceeds from the bowl game were to make up for much of it. When the bowl game was played, the Blue Band stayed home and the White Oak High School Band of Dallas, Texas, volunteered to take the Blue Band's place. According to some bowl game attendees, who may well have been staunch Penn Staters, the high school band far out-shone SMU's band. In spite of the accolades that White Oak received, most Penn Staters were disappointed that the college did not send the Blue Band and was represented by a high school band instead, as the letters to the editor of the *Collegian* after the game showed. "If the football squad receives a bowl bid next year," one contributor wrote, "I hope the College feels it can spend a little of the money earned this year on the men who give their time and spirit to play for the scheduled football games, and send the Band as well as the squad." The editor of the *Collegian* too was skeptical about the decision not to send the Blue Band: "Evidently the College officials believed that the estimated $18,000 needed to send the Blue Band to Dallas could be put to better use in the athletic program. Whether the money is put to good use remains to be seen."

Although not part of the athletic program, Blue Band members were often treated by the "Beaver Field Pictorial" (the official Penn State football program at the time) as if they were a sports team. From 1948 through the late 1960s the name of each band member was listed, plus age, "position" (instrument), home town, height, and weight. In comparing the football players in size with the Blue Band personnel in the 1948 Temple game program, the football team was sometimes found wanting. Other than outnumbering the squad eighty-one to fifty-one, the band had three more men than the football team who were over six feet tall. Tom McDermott, the heaviest member of the football team at 220 pounds, was outweighed by 40 pounds by cornet player Eugene Golla, the band's largest member. Given these facts, and taking into account the stamina of the Blue Band members while performing the pregame show, the Penn State Thespians predicted that in a few years Football Coach Bob Higgins would be "hollering to the Blue Band to give him back his wingback."

The Blue Band in its new uniforms in 1948.

Changes in the faculty and administrators at Penn State were at its twentieth-century peak in the late 1940s; as many as five long-term deans and many more department heads retired or passed away. Ralph Dorn Hetzel, president of the college since 1926, died in October 1947. Many other prominent figures at the college had also retired around this time, such as Dr. Joseph Ritenour, head of the campus health center since 1917, and Willard Lewis, head librarian for eighteen years. As a result, many members of the remaining faculty were elevated to new positions, and new professors were hired to fill the vacuum.

This was the case in the college's music program too. Hummel Fishburn, elevated to head the Music Department in 1943, was appointed also to head the new Department of Music Education during this time of change. Fishburn, who was active in many other college and community activities as well, began to see the need for a full-time director of the Blue Bands, both concert and marching. Frank Gullo, Fishburn's longtime friend, sing-along partner, and assistant band instructor, was more of a vocal music professor as head of the Glee Club and College Chorus and so was not really in the running for the position. To lead his band programs, Fishburn needed a true instrumental music instructor.

BIOGRAPHY

JAMES W. DUNLOP

James W. Dunlop was born on October 12, 1913, in Morris Run, Tioga County, Pennsylvania, to Hugh and Isabel Woodhouse Dunlop. His music career before coming to Penn State was as a music director at a public school. Graduating from Mansfield State College in 1935 with a bachelor's degree in public school music, Dunlop was hired as supervisor of music for the Mount Jewett High School and remained there for two years. He held a similar position in Emporium, Pennsylvania, from then until 1941, when he became director of music at the Farrell School District. In 1940 Dunlop married Fay Kahley, and they eventually had two children: Joan and H. James. During his summers while teaching at Emporium, Dunlop received a master's

degree in music from the University of Michigan in 1939, studying violin and conducting under Michigan's legendary music director William Revelli. In 1944 Dunlop joined the U.S. Navy for a two-year tour of duty.

Dunlop's career at Penn State began in 1947 when Dr. Hummel Fishburn, head of both the Department of Music and the Department of Music Education, hired him as Associate Professor of Music. His responsibilities included directing the Concert Blue Band and assisting Fishburn with the Marching Blue Band, with the expectation that Dunlop would take over directing the marching band the next year to free Fishburn of that task. In 1948 Dunlop did indeed become Director of the Blue Band, giving Dr. Fishburn the opportunity to concentrate on creating more elaborate field formations and on his other duties. In 1964 Dunlop received an honorary doctorate of music from Salem College in West Virginia.

Dunlop was involved in many musical events outside of Penn State, and he often guest-conducted other bands. He conducted top high school musicians at many All-State Band Festivals, including Delaware, Florida, Maryland, Utah, West Virginia, and Pennsylvania. Starting in 1949 he was director of the Pennsylvania Future Farmers of America Band for more than twenty-five years. In 1956 he guest-conducted the University of New Mexico's concert band at the American Bandmasters' Association annual convention, and at the following year's convention he conducted the U.S. Air Force Band. He adjudicated many county, district, and state high school and intercollegiate band festivals across Pennsylvania. In 1963 he was elected president of the Eastern Division of the National Association of College Band Directors, the same position Hummel Fishburn once held. In 1971 he was elected president of the prestigious American Bandmasters' Association at its annual convention in Toronto, Canada. Also in 1971 he was cited by Penn State for excellence in teaching, and the next year he was voted one of the top-ten outstanding educational music directors in North America by *School Musician Director and Teacher* magazine. In 1973 Dunlop was guest conductor for a performance by the U.S. Navy Band at the John F. Kennedy Center in Washington, D.C. Jim Dunlop passed away suddenly from a heart attack on August 7, 1975, while he was at the University of Utah Snowbird Summer Arts Institute near Salt Lake City as a guest conductor.

A robust figure at six-foot-four, Dunlop was a commanding presence on the podium. His strict and authoritarian style often instilled fear and anxiety among those in his charge. Dr. Ned C. Deihl, his assistant and a former Blue Band director, remembers Dunlop's personality while directing: "He set high standards and was an iron-handed disciplinarian. … If a student got out of line, he'd come down hard on him." Dunlop was also strict about starting on time. "He was fanatical about punctuality, much the way Dr. Revelli was, whom Jim idolized," Deihl recalls. According to Alan Wood '71, a trombone player in the Blue Band under Jim Dunlop, punctuality for band members was a must. "If Dr. Dunlop said the buses would leave at 8:00 A.M., they were moving at 7:59 A.M. I remember that two guys missed the bus to the North Carolina State game and had to catch a commuter airplane to catch up!" It was Dunlop's policy to punish tardiness severely by scolding a late band member publicly, or in extreme cases expelling him from the band. With the number of musicians that auditioned for the Blue Band but did not make the cut, being replaced was no idle threat. According to another former band member, Dunlop believed that time waited for no one, not even himself. "During one trip, Dr. Dunlop was running late himself. When he saw that the bus was waiting for him, he bawled out the bus driver for not leaving him!"

Jim Dunlop was not all ogre though. "Off the field, Jim was very warm and was a dear friend," said Deihl. Carmen Cugini '61, a former Blue Band member and high school band director, also experienced Jim's warm side. "No matter how much he chewed you out on the field, he might walk arm-in-arm off the field with you." All business during rehearsals and performances, Dunlop was kind and caring with his students afterward. "I just love kids," he said in an interview in 1971. "I even do a little private teaching because I enjoy working with younger children and bringing them along on the horn."

Jim Dunlop molded the Blue Band in a number of ways during his twenty-seven years at Penn State. The band became a more disciplined, polished group on the field under his no-nonsense conducting style. Quality musicianship was Jim's emphasis, and it showed with the Blue Band. On occasions when Jim could have increased the size of the band much more, he limited growth so that the instrumentation would remain balanced and the band would retain a "concert band" quality. The musical standards that apply today to Penn State's Marching Blue Band were fostered under Dunlop's tutelage.

With his background at Michigan, Dunlop, with the help of fellow Michigan graduate Ned C. Deihl, began forming the Blue Band's Big Ten style and modernizing the band program as a whole. One of his major innovations with the university music program was the creation of Band Day, which brought thousands of high school musicians to Penn State every year to perform with the Blue Band and interest them in applying for Penn State and its Marching Blue Band after graduating. Dunlop will be remembered best by his students as the "Toscanini" of the Blue Band: a strict disciplinarian with a big heart. 🕮

As a result, in summer 1947 Fishburn hired James W. Dunlop, a well-respected music teacher from northern Central Pennsylvania with a master's degree from the renowned University of Michigan Music School, to assist with the Marching Blue Band and fully direct the Concert Blue Band. At the beginning of the fall semester of 1948, Hummel Fishburn relinquished the directorship of the Marching Blue Band to Assistant Director Dunlop. Dunlop proved to be a capable leader. Although Fishburn was no longer the marching band's director, he kept his hand in by continuing to chart all the field maneuvers for Dunlop until 1962.

Dunlop was much in the tradition of Wilfred O. Thompson in that he was more narrowly focused as a conductor than the jack-of-all-trades Hummel Fishburn was. As a result, the quality of the musical performances by both the Concert Band and Blue Band improved early under Dunlop's direction. With Fishburn's help on the field, Dunlop was able to concentrate on his forté as a podium master and continue to improve the Blue Band's "symphonic band sound" on the football field.

Off the gridiron, the band in 1949 participated in an interesting summit in October that brought dignitaries from around the world to the tiny town of Aaronsburg, Pennsylvania, some twenty-three miles east of State College in the geographic center of the state. Aaronsburg was founded by a Jewish immigrant from Holland, Aaron Levy, who by 1760 was a large landowner in Central Pennsylvania. He laid out the town hoping to make it the state capital, because it was the exact center of the Commonwealth. Aaronsburg in 1949 was the site of international sessions designed to further the cause of religious understanding during the celebration of Pennsylvania Week. Dignitaries who spoke at this event included Sir Mohammed Aly Zafrullah Khan, vice-president of the United Nations; Dr. Ralph Bunche, former mediator of the U.N. Palestine Commission; Pennsylvania Governor James H. Duff; Supreme Court Justice Felix Frankfurter; General William J. "Wild Bill" Donovan, former director of the Office of Strategic Services; and Dr. Abram Sachar, president of Brandeis University. During the weekend of the summit a pageant titled "The Aaronsburg Story" was performed for the dignitaries and 30,000 others gathered. The pageant, which dramatized the role that all nationalities and religious persuasions played in the formation of America, had more than 1,000 participants, including film star Cornel Wilde, who narrated. Providing the music for the pageant was none other than the Blue Band, under the direction of Director James Dunlop, in his third year with the college. Also helping prepare the celebration was Hummel Fishburn, who arranged much of the music, and many others in the Music Department.

The year 1949 also marked the fiftieth anniversary of the Blue Band. To celebrate this milestone, Hum Fishburn wrote a homecoming halftime show commemorating the founding of the Cadet Bugle Corps, the Blue Band's precursor, with six members of the band dressed as the original cadet musicians. Among those who witnessed the historical review at the Penn State–Nebraska game was George Deike, the founder of the Bugle Corps and a Trustee of the college. In honor of the band's golden anniversary, Deike donated six silver-plated sousaphones worth more than $4,000 at the alumni homecoming luncheon.

Each sousaphone commemorated the six original members of the Cadet Bugle Corps of 1899 and replaced the well-worn and unmatching sousaphones the band had been using previously.

At the halfway point of the current story of the Penn State Marching Blue Band, the band had seen its share of challenges and achievements. The changes experienced in the Blue Band in the 1940s would contribute both to its successes and to its shortcomings in the years to follow. In its next fifty years, the band faced other challenges from the Music Department, Athletics, the university as a whole, and other college bands around the nation for recognition. Above all, however, as it always had in its quest for perfection, the Blue Band would strive to challenge itself.

One of the most-loved formations the Blue Band displayed was that of the "P-S-C."

8 Setting New Standards, 1950–1959

THE LATE 1940S AND EARLY 1950S *marked a changing of the old guard for The Pennsylvania State College. Many of the most prominent names in the faculty and administration were gone, and the college itself began to look at itself anew. The attitude of the quaint "cow" college in pastoral Central Pennsylvania with inferior academic standards and accomplishments was incongruous with the true nature of Penn State. It was actually the largest college in the nation not designated a "university" and for many years had been a leading educator more of engineers in Pennsylvania than of agricultural students.*

Much of the change in Penn State's image was due in large part to the new president of the college, Milton Stover Eisenhower, who was hired in 1950. Brother of war hero

The 1950 Blue Band under the direction of James Dunlop (far right) and Hum Fishburn (far left), wearing topcoats and capes.

and future U.S. President Dwight D. Eisenhower, Milton was also a highly respected and able college administrator. He accepted the top position at Penn State after previously stepping down as president of Kansas State College, later University. In order to secure financial support for the college's future needs, Eisenhower successfully campaigned to change the name of the college to The Pennsylvania State University in late 1953. With the designation as a university, Penn State was able to finally cement in the minds of its students, faculty, legislators, and the public in general that the institution was indeed a major player in academia, at least in Pennsylvania in the mid-1950s.

The promise of the progress that starts this decade was not realized by either of the Blue Bands in the one area in which they were truly lacking: funding. Debate about the way the bands were funded was beginning to heat up in January 1950. Fourteen members of the Concert Blue Band were selected to participate in the third annual Intercollegiate Band Festival at Carnegie Tech in Pittsburgh scheduled in late February—one of the largest representations from any college in the state. It was estimated that the cost of sending these band members to the three-day festival would be $144, and the All-College Student Cabinet, which funded much of the band's activities, was asked for the money.

Because the $3,000 yearly appropriation to the Blue Band represented one-quarter of the cabinet's total budget, however, the cabinet felt it had to turn down the request. Although it was generous, it could not afford to spend such a large amount of money on a single student activity. But an unknown member of the cabinet made the unfortunate mistake of stating that the funding was refused because the Blue Band was not an all-college activity, but rather primarily a Music Department activity.

This comment elicited a strong rebuttal from many Blue Band fans and members. Hubert H. Haugh, a tuba player and the equipment manager of the band, wrote in response to the cabinet's decision in a letter to the *Collegian* editor:

[The] Cabinet maintained that [the] funds it administers are primarily for All-College activities. To keep the record (and the cabinet) straight, it would be timely to note that 71 of the 81 Blue Band members you saw, heard, and applauded at the football games last fall WERE NOT music or music education students. … I should like further to point out that 10 of the 14 musicians selected to go to the Intercollegiate Band Festival at Carnegie Tech next month ARE NOT music or music education students. In view of the facts stated above, I would like to know how any member of the All-College Cabinet or the Inter-class Finance Committee can justly claim that [the] Blue Band is not an All-College function.

Another Blue Bander, trumpeter Ralph J. Egolf Jr., argued along the same lines in another letter to the *Collegian*:

It is also interesting to note that the Cabinet granted $367 for Soccer team awards. There seems to be a great deal of false logic connected with the above actions. If the Blue Band, which draws its members from seven of the eight schools in this college, is to be considered as departmental, then the same logic would seem to indicate that the Soccer team is also a departmental activity. … I whole heartedly agree with the allocation of funds for Soccer team awards, but believe that the Blue Band is worthy of the same consideration. After all, both organizations represent Penn State on an inter-collegiate basis and both organizations embody members from many departments at the college.

The money was eventually raised, although whether it was through the All-College Cabinet is unclear, and the selected members of the Blue Band participated in the festival. The All-College Cabinet raised the student fees in May by 25 cents per semester to increase funding for the band, hoping to improve the financial situation. But the controversy sparked debate on campus and prompted a proposal that the bands' multiple financial sources be reorganized and placed in a single area: the college budget. Today a small portion of the Marching Band's funding is through the University's general budget, but it continues today to have multiple funding sources.

In late April of that year, the Blue Band and the College at large received sad news. Wilfred Otto Thompson, the retired Army bandmaster who had led Penn State's Blue Band for twenty-five years, had died at the age of eighty-one. A colorful figure and a fixture at the football games, music concerts, and military functions on campus, Thompson was sorely missed by his fellow band members, and his passing was another link to Penn State's past broken during the postwar years.

More unfortunate occurrences plagued the Blue Band that year. As usual, however, the band turned bad situations into positive ones. One notable example was the University of Pittsburgh game trip in late November. Scheduled to practice for the game on Friday afternoon, November 24, after performing at a "smoker" at the William Penn Hotel, the band was stuck in its own hotel, the Pittsburgher, after a terrible blizzard blanketed the city with almost thirty inches of snow. With the game canceled, the band decided to

Maintaining a marching band financially, in the broadest terms, involves paying for staff, instruments, uniforms, music, transportation, and accommodations in direct proportion to the number of students participating. This can be very expensive because marching bands tend to be quite large student organizations, often much larger than the athletic teams they support. Because band concerts usually do not draw audiences nearly as large as football games, the revenue generated by such concerts to offset these expenses almost always falls short. In order to raise funds to cover these expenses, marching bands at the public high school level often hold fund-raising events, which can be anything from selling hoagies to washing cars.

Today such fund-raisers are almost unheard of at the collegiate level. Most of the funding for today's college marching bands comes from the budgets of the colleges' schools of music, schools of arts, athletic departments, or a combination of these sources. Penn State's Blue Band, for example, today receives approximately 70 percent of its funding from the Athletic Department, 17 percent from the School of Arts and Architecture, and the rest from the general university budget, alumni donations, and sales of CDs and concert tickets.

leave the hotel and head back to State College on Saturday. Before leaving, however, it played an impromtu concert for the other snowbound guests. While at the hotel, clarinetist Ernest Skipper struck up a conversation with an older gentleman and told him how inefficient Pittsburgh's snow removal was. Unbeknownst to Skipper, the man was Pittsburgh's mayor, David Lawrence, who later vowed to improve the city's snow removal services.

The band walked six snowy blocks to the train station. When band members discovered that their train was delayed by at least three hours, they again took out their instruments and entertained the almost 2,000 people gathered at the station. Finally leaving for Tyrone at 6:00 in the evening, the band's train did not arrive until 3:30 Sunday morning, after blowtorches were used to unfreeze each switch along the way. Since the buses from Tyrone were still snowbound, the band was stranded at the Tyrone station. The National Guard and the American Red Cross, bringing high-axle trucks to the location, transported the Blue Band members to Tyrone High School, where they spent the rest of the night sleeping on wrestling mats. The game was rescheduled for the following week, but the Blue Band did not go.

Most of the band's fall season was not as disappointing. The band performed well in front of the home crowd all season. However, one particularly memorable event in mid-November made up for most of the unfortunate ones the rest of the year. That event was the first Band Day at Beaver Field.

Band Day was started by Jim Dunlop and Hum Fishburn as a way to get high school musicians from the Central Pennsylvania region to experience a Penn State football game, in hopes of attracting the better musicians to the college and the Blue Band when they graduated. Inviting nine Centre County high school bands to the Penn State game with West Virginia at Beaver Field on November 11, the Blue Band treated the 700 high school students to a collegiate-level marching band halftime show. Before the game the bands were allowed to march onto the field and perform a three-minute show each.

The day was a huge success. The high school students got to see a major college football game and marching band, the Blue Band received potential recruits for the years to come, and the spectators were treated to a fine performance by all the schools involved. Dunlop and Fishburn began making Band Day an annual event at little cost to music departments, because football tickets were relatively inexpensive in those days and the high school bands provided for their own transportation.

The fall of 1951 marked the first year that the Blue Band alone consisted of more than 100 musicians. The 98 full-time members and 3 alternates performed at the first game of the year, against Boston University. The halftime show consisted of school fight songs and the Alma Mater while the band formed the letters "BU" to honor the opponent, the word "STATE" for its own team, and the number "55" for the new freshman class.

The Blue Band hosted its second annual Band Day that October, inviting fifty-six high school bands directed by Penn State graduates. Twenty-four accepted the invitation

During the 1950s the Blue Band's pregame consisted of playing a fanfare that was a very fast version of the Alma Mater, then playing the march "National Emblem" downfield.

and arrived with 1,600 students. A pregame parade was organized and marched through the town of State College and the campus, ending with a mass formation and performance under the direction of Jim Dunlop. At the game the twenty-four bands joined the Blue Band in forming the letters "PSC" and playing marches under the direction of Carrol Chapman, Penn State's new drum major.

Other notable performances that year included a trip to Newark, New Jersey, to play Rutgers University and perform a halftime show "centering around the music," as Jim Dunlop put it. It was getting dark early by this time in November, so the band began practicing for this show and the one for Pitt the next week under the lights of Beaver Field. The traditional Thanksgiving Pittsburgh game for the band centered more on the field maneuvers. The band formed the word "PITT" during its pregame show, and at halftime it formed a pilgrim's hat, a turkey on a platter, and a football, all in tribute to the week's holiday and to the end of the gridiron season.

Some fans complained to the Blue Band about the halftime shows. The consensus, according to Dwight Tothero '53, was that the simple formations, like class numbers and halftime scores, were boring to the general public. Dunlop did not believe that to be the case, however, and assumed the complaints were isolated incidents. He changed his mind after listening to a Blue Band member who expressed his own dissatisfaction that the shows

SPOTLIGHT

Band Day

One of the most anticipated football games at Penn State through the 1950s, 1960s, and early 1970s was Band Day. Band Day was created by Jim Dunlop and Hum Fishburn as an entertaining and exciting recruiting tool. The first Band Day, November 11, 1950, had nine Centre County high schools participating. These students watched the Blue Band perform its halftime show from the sidelines. The next year young musicians from some twenty-four high schools were invited to perform on the field with the Blue Band. Each of the twenty-four high school band directors was a Penn State graduate, and many of them were themselves former Blue Band members.

Over the years Band Day grew to a production by 6,000 musicians representing sixty high schools from all over Pennsylvania at its peak in the early 1960s. The trademark of were not challenging enough. Dunlop and Fishburn made a concerted effort to make the formations and the music selections as interesting as they could.

The following spring the Concert Blue Band began to perform and travel much more. Touring for two days in mid-March, Dunlop and his ninety-member band visited four Western Pennsylvania towns: Brookville, Sharon, Slippery Rock, and Brockway. It played the same program of fifteen marches and other special selections locally on March 20 in Schwab Auditorium. Two more out-of-town shows were scheduled in April for Montgomery and Burnham. David Fishburn, Hummel Fishburn's son, was the featured soloist on the trombone that season.

The band continued its Sunday concerts, sometimes playing at Schwab and, on nice days, on the steps of Pattee Library. There was even a concert in Rec Hall on April 26, when Penn State hosted the final Olympic gymnastics tryouts and the National AAU Gymnastics Championship. This season marked the greatest number of Concert Blue Band concerts, with ten appearances.

About that time Fishburn decided to change the fanfare that started the pregame show, which he himself had written. The new fanfare was very fast and the perfect starting point for the band to take off down the field at 180 beats per minute. When asked how he created the fanfare, he replied, "It's taken from the first phrase of the Alma Mater, done

every Band Day was the formation of a huge PSC (later PSU) on the field spelled with thousands of musicians. The tradition of Band Day ended on November 16, 1974, when the last PSU was formed and dispersed after halftime. Penn State's Athletic Department decided it could no longer afford the thousands of tickets needed to seat the visiting high school bands.

Dr. Ned C. Deihl, Director of Bands at Penn State, succeeded in reviving Band Day in 1984 by holding it in April during the Blue and White Game, Penn State's scrimmage held in Beaver Stadium where the offensive and defensive squads square off for next season. Because this game in April was never sold out, Band Day again provided an opportunity for potential Nittany Lions to perform at a collegiate level. Band Day was short-lived, however. Retired again after 1988, Band Day had trouble convincing high schools

to send their bands in April, when most of the bands had finished their season, packed up their uniforms, and relinquished their practice fields to spring sports.

Band Day was just another example of the innovative spirit of the Penn State Blue Band and its staff. The powerful performance of 6,000 band musicians is but a memory now, but it is a memory

For the first few years, the high schools spelled "P-S-C" because Penn State was a college, not a university, at the time.

that will remain for a lifetime with the almost 100,000 Pennsylvania musicians who participated in its twenty-five-year run, not to mention the almost one million who witnessed Band Day live at the stadium over those years. ⇥

The 1952 Drum Major George Black.

in fast time." Fishburn, who originated this quick pace when he first started as director of the Blue Band, believed that the band was the fastest full-step marching band in the United States. Today the band still plays its trademark rapid-pace pregame show at approximately the same tempo.

The Blue Band traveled in October 1952 to an interesting event arranged by the Penn State Club of Harrisburg. The band was invited, for the second year in a row, to the Pennsylvania Horse Show at the Farm Complex in Harrisburg. Successful the previous year, the show again held a "Penn State Night" to honor the state's leading agricultural institution. The band performed in the huge arena, playing "Horses, Horses, Horses," which was quite popular with the people attending. Split in two, the band entered the arena from either side. According to Dunlop, it was difficult to perform without yard lines or hash marks.

In spring 1953 band musicians at Penn State began to branch out into basketball. On February 11 the first Basketball Pep Band gave its first performance in Recreation Hall as Penn State battled American University. Even though the members of the basketball band were from the Blue Band, it was organized by the Air Force ROTC, to which all the members of the pep band also belonged. The idea for a basketball band was floated many times over the years but was finally implemented by Major John McHugh, Assistant Professor of Air Science and Tactics. Major McHugh was adviser to the band, while Staff Sergeant Robert Campbell, another Air Force instructor, conducted the band. According to Allan McChesney, head cheerleader, the band showed promise as an aid to infusing spirit that had been sorely lacking at recent games.

The Blue Band's directors kept busy that spring as well. Jim Dunlop was guest conductor at the Delaware and the West Virginia All-State Band Festivals. He also served as a judge at numerous regional band competitions in West Virginia and Pennsylvania. Hummel Fishburn was honored by having the 1953 college yearbook *La Vie* dedicated to him at the annual yearbook dinner. Both directors during the summer, along with Frank Gullo, taught and conducted band classes at the Band, Orchestra, and Chorus School on campus.

The 1953 football season found the Blue Band as busy as usual, with its two away games at Franklin Field and Forbes Field. The game in Philadelphia was not without some controversy. On October 3, while attending the Penn game, the Blue Band was given rather poor seating. According to Blue Band President Don Lambert, the band was located low behind the goalposts, which meant the music could not be heard across the stadium and that half its members could not see the field.

Bands are not supposed to play during the play of the game, so not being able to see the field put the band at a severe disadvantage. Ernest McCoy, Penn State's Athletics dean, whose organization arranged the seating, agreed with the band and promised to rectify the situation. "I am sorry when any group is hurt [by our actions]," he stated later. "If there is anything we can do to satisfy the band, the students, the alumni, and the College's friends, we'll do it."

Ten days after that game the Blue Band traveled again, this time to Hershey, Pennsylvania, to help celebrate the birthday of President Dwight D. Eisenhower. The celebration was conducted at Hershey Stadium and Arena with the help of the Blue Band and four other marching units: the Temple Owls Band, the Archer Eppler Drum Corps of Philadelphia, the Valley Forge Military Academy Band, and the William Penn High School Band of York, Pennsylvania. The five bands played "The Star Spangled Banner" as the President entered the stadium. The bands then performed individually, with the Blue Band having the honor

"The Fireman's Song"

M y Father was a Fireman,
He … puts out … Fires.
Hummmmmmm.

My Mother was a Fireman,
She … puts out … Fires.
Hummmmmmm.

My Brother was a Fireman,
He … puts out … Fires.
Hummmmmmm.

My Sister was a Fireman,
She … puts out. …
Hummmmmmm.

This amusing little "drinking song" was a Blue Band tradition well before 1960. During the 1960s the band, an all-male organization at the time, sang this song on bus trips and similar occasions to lighten the serious mood before and after performances. From the early 1970s through the mid-1990s, this song became part of a Blue Band ritual at Beaver Stadium. Fans sitting in the bleachers above the football team and the Blue Band's tunnel entrance might barely have heard the band sing this song in four-part barber-shop harmony, its grave and reverent tones incongruous with the humorous punchline at the end. The song was led by a senior member of the band, known as "the fireman," who conducted the band with an unusual object for a baton, such as a "rubber ducky" or a yellow rubber mallet.

The song had the same purpose it did in earlier years. As the Blue Band was about to enter the field for its exciting pregame entrance, the tension of waiting for the moment when the drums began their cadence was palpable. The song helped break the tension and loosen up the band

for a better performance.

The song came under fire (no pun intended) in 1995 when a stadium ticketbooth worker found the song offensive and complained to the Blue Band staff. To appease the politically correct, the band moved the singing of "The Fireman's Song" away from the stadium and to the Blue Band's trailers at the practice field instead. But as one band member put it, the song under those circumstances no longer provided the psychological boost it once did.

In 1996, when "TailGreat" started, the song was sung anew at the Bryce Jordan Center across from the stadium. But in 1997, when some members of the Blue Band began to find the lyrics offensive, the tradition of singing "The Fireman's Song" ended.

of being first. From his seat at the head table in the end-zone, Eisenhower watched the band concerts. Later, inside during dinner, Fred Waring, Penn State Trustee and famous bandleader, was in charge of the music for the celebration. The bands performed again that evening, as did the Waring orchestra.

The band had the opportunity to perform before both Presidents Eisenhower in June 1955. Milton Eisenhower, his brother's closest adviser, invited Dwight to speak at the June Commencement. The Blue Band was on hand with the music.

Providing the music for campus events, especially those involving sports, was a Blue Band specialty. On October 8, 1954, the Blue Band led a pep rally on the lawn of Old Main attended by more than 2,500 students, faculty, fans, and the football team itself, encouraging the team to hopeful victory in the University of Virginia game the next day. The Nittany Lion Mascot, Alfred Klimke, made his first suited appearance as the Lion at this event. That Saturday the Blue Band performed the music of Stephen Foster, composer of "Swanee River" and "My Old Kentucky Home." Foster's music was a logical choice, said Dunlop about the show. Foster, a native Pennsylvanian, was better known as a composer of songs with a Southern flavor, which was perfect for honoring the visiting Cavaliers. Because it was the first day of Pennsylvania Week, Foster's music was appropriate too because he was a native son of the Keystone State.

The band played the same show the next year for the Virginia game, this time at Richmond. Entering the field with "Nittany Lion," the Blue Band formed "U OF V" and began to play "Dixie" and "Carry Me Back to Old Virginie." The band formed such things as a cabin and a banjo and played "My Old Kentucky Home," "O Susanna," "Camptown Races," and "Swanee River"—all Foster songs. While in Richmond the band also had the opportunity to play in the seventh annual Tobacco Festival Parade.

Another popular halftime show was presented by the Blue Band for the Penn game on October 29. The theme was television commercials and the band came up with such formations as a pack of cigarettes, to the "Lucky Strike Theme"; a can of Ajax cleanser, accompanied by its theme jingle; a car, to "See the U.S.A. in a Chevrolet," and a can of Pabst Blue Ribbon beer. The most difficult formation to make was the famous smoking cigar from the Muriel cigar commercial. Part of the band formed the cigar while the rest of the band made smoke that resolved into the letter "M." Although not really "politically correct" for today's band, the show was entirely appropriate for 1955 and quite successful, answering many of the critics who had been saying that the routines were boring.

After decades of away games, Penn State finally played the University of Pittsburgh at Beaver Field. Because the occasion was part of the centennial celebrations of the founding of Penn State, the Pitt Band played a show commemorating this event. The Blue Band's halftime show, on the other hand, was full of holiday-theme music, such as "White Christmas," "Auld Lang Syne," "Funny Valentine," and "When Irish Eyes Are Smilin'." The Pitt Band members were guests of the Blue Band at lunch before the game and for dinner afterward.

The football season of 1956 saw the Blue Band perform at Michie Stadium, the home of West Point's cadets. In order to get to West Point, New York, the Blue Band took buses

to Lewistown (thirty miles from State College), then a train from there that stopped in Harrisburg, Philadelphia, and finally New York City. After checking into the Hotel New Yorker, the band finally was bused to the Academy. The show presented by the band, "A Day in the Life of a Cadet at the U.S. Military Academy," had been revamped from the previous decade and was greeted with great appreciation from the spectators. Brigadier General John Throckmorton, commandant of cadets at the Academy, wrote a letter to Jim Dunlop after the game stating: "The skit your band presented during halftime was one of the most entertaining and skillfully done band presentations we have ever had the pleasure to watch in Michie Stadium." An elderly spectator approached Dunlop after the game and confirmed that. After coming to the games for more than thirty years, he said, this Blue Band was the best band he had ever heard on the field.

Such accolades were short-lived for some freshmen in the Blue Band the next morning. Supposedly a group of first-year students slept in too long and missed the bus back to State College. Missing transportation back home was treated by the band staff the same way it is treated today: students must find their own way back. According to Ron Reinhart, a freshman Blue Band member in 1956 who did make the bus, "train schedules waited for no man, and neither did Jim Dunlop."

At the homecoming game against Holy Cross on October 13 of that year, the Blue Band planned another interesting halftime show based on different types of bands in the world, including circus, Dixieland, military, and German bands. Although the band marched

The Blue Band used to march at "6 to 5" (six steps for every five yards) for pregame, until it was changed to "8 to 5" in 1965.

One of the most anticipated football games each year was the game designated as Band Day.

during the show, the music could not be heard at Beaver Field because a bright-yellow helicopter hired by the university's Young Republican Club was flying over Beaver Field carrying a banner that read "Young GOP says a Happy Birthday Ike." The stunt was supposed to take place after the game, as spectators filed out, but the pilot misunderstood and for thirty minutes during the entire halftime period he hovered over and near the field, effectively drowning out the Blue Band. University officials and the Young Republicans apologized afterward to the band and spectators for what had happened. After landing, the pilot was interrogated by state police and an investigation by aeronautics authorities began, because the university felt that the stunt was potentially dangerous to the spectators and the Blue Band.

The 1957 Concert Blue Band opened its spring season playing at the annual convention of the American Bandmasters' Association in Pittsburgh. The Blue Band was one of only two collegiate bands appearing at the convention, the other being Carnegie Tech's. Also providing entertainment was the U.S. Army Band and the U.S. Air Force Band. Membership in the prestigious convention was by invitation only. Jim Dunlop and Hummel Fishburn were two of the six Pennsylvania members.

The 1957 marching band returned Pitt's favor of three years earlier, of paying homage to an opponent's hometown, when the Blue Band performed a show with an operatic theme in tribute to Pittsburgh's cultural center. Besides the Wedding March from *Lohengrin*, "Wandering Minstrel" from the *Mikado*, and the William Tell Overture, the band played what was described as a little-known opera titled *Ernio Kovackski*, which

was the theme from Ernie Kovacs' television show.

The Blue Band honored its traditional foe again in 1958, ending its football season by traveling to Forbes Field to help celebrate the University of Pittsburgh's bicentennial. The Blue Band presented its traditional "number" routines, forming "1758" for Pitt's foundation, "1855" for Penn State's foundation, "1958," and then the number "200" while playing "Nittany Lion" and Penn State's Alma Mater.

Then, forming the routes of Pittsburgh's three rivers, the band played "Old Man River" and "Beautiful Ohio." The rivers eventually became a steam engine to the tune of "I've Been Workin' on the Railroad" and, finally, a submarine was formed to "Anchors Aweigh," honoring the creation of the first atomic submarine, *Nautilus*, whose propulsion system was built in Pittsburgh. The Pitt fans were once again appreciative to have the Blue Band at their stadium and voiced their approval loud and long after the band's performance.

Earlier, during its first Beaver Field appearance of the season at the homecoming game in October, the Blue Band provided another entertaining halftime show based on popular television shows. The band played the theme to the "$64,000 Question" while forming the game show's famous isolation booth, as well as a Colt 45 to the theme from "Gunsmoke." One of the most intricate designs was that of an automobile driving down the field to the theme of the show "Highway Patrol." The Blue Band ended its performance to the "Mickey Mouse Club" theme as it formed Mickey Mouse ears on the field.

The year 1959 was busy for the Blue Band, the Concert Blue Band, and Jim Dunlop

During homecoming in 1956, the Blue Band could not be heard over the noise from a low-flying helicopter. The band did look sharp in their new uniforms though.

Dunlop was a stickler for punctuality, and Blue Band members like James Weisner used any means possible to arrive at practice on time.

as well. Between the beginning of January and the end of February, Dunlop conducted three different All-State Band Festivals, traveling to Tampa, Florida; West York, Pennsylvania; and Westminster, Maryland, for each state's top high school musicians concerts. To be invited to conduct an All-State Band Festival was and is a great honor, and to have been invited to three in one year was unprecedented.

The Concert Band did a little traveling of its own that spring term. It was invited to perform at the Eastern Division National Music Education National Conference in Buffalo, New York, on January 23. Traveling by bus, the band arrived at the Statler Hilton Hotel, where the conference was being held. As the buses pulled away, the band managers realized they had left all the music on the buses. Dunlop could not rehearse the band and was prepared to receive totally different music from the conference, confident that the band would sight-read the music and still perform excellently. Fortunately, the band received the music just before the performance and by all accounts played its best concert of the year.

The Marching Blue Band also had a memorable season. Traveling to Cleveland with the football team, the band marched with the University of Illinois in late October 1959. During pregame the Blue Band formed the letters "US" while the Marching Illini Band surrounded it, forming a shield. Both bands then proceeded with the National Anthem. The Blue Band presented a halftime show with an abridged "television theme" version.

At home, at the Holy Cross game in mid-November the band celebrated its sixtieth anniversary and the growth of the athletic fields at the last game ever played on Beaver Field. The halftime show traced the history of old Beaver Field to the current new Beaver Field. In order to celebrate the growth of the fields, the band had groups of different sizes detach from the band and march down the field. Starting with a six-man drum and bugle corps representing 1899, the band eventually split twenty-two members away, representing the band that played at the first game at new Beaver Field in 1909. A sixty-four-piece "military style" band pulled away for 1920, when Beaver Field was expanded, and then an eighty-piece band re-formed a routine that was popular in 1942, of an airplane crushing a Nazi swastika celebrating the progress made in both the band and its field during World War II. Finally, to end the show all 108 members of the band formed a recent routine of a typewriter with moving parts.

The band celebrated the history of Beaver Field at this game because its bleachers were scheduled to be torn down afterward and moved to its present location, becoming Beaver Stadium with the addition of 16,000 more seats.

The Blue Band did not end its season in 1959 as usual, in Pittsburgh. Instead, the football team was invited to play the University of Alabama in the first annual Liberty Bowl in Philadelphia, and the band went along for its first ever bowl trip. The band practiced field maneuvers inside for the first time. Laying tape down on the floor of Rec Hall to represent yard lines, Jim Dunlop hoped the weather would clear so the band could practice at its golf course field.

The Blue Band members themselves voted on which routines they wanted to perform, representing the best of the year's offerings. However, many of the television-theme shows they chose from earlier in the season were vetoed because they represented programs televised on networks other than the one broadcasting the Liberty Bowl. Jim Burden, a Penn State Professor of Music and Blue Band song-arranger, provided extra music to honor Alabama, which would be treated as the away team and therefore as Penn State's guests. This did not mean, however, that the Blue Band still did not want to outperform Alabama's famous "Million Dollar Band." A picture of an Alabama band member was hung on the Blue Band Office bulletin board with a sign: "Your Competition for the Liberty Bowl."

Beaver Field

The home of Penn State football for more than seventy-six years, Beaver Field was originally located approximately where present-day Whitmore Laboratory now stands. "Old" Beaver Field, named after Board of Trustees member and former Governor James Beaver, saw its first Penn State football game in 1893 after the grandstand of 500 seats had been erected. The field was also the home field for the college baseball team, the track team, and the Cadet Band.

In 1909 Beaver Field was moved to a location adjacent to the Nittany Lion Inn on the north side of campus on what is today the site of Kern Building and the Nittany Parking Deck. In 1943 the famous Nittany Lion Shrine, sculpted by Heinrich "Heinz" Warneke, was placed at its entrance. Enlarged over the years to as much as 30,000 seats, "new" Beaver Field saw half a century of Nittany Lion football, baseball, lacrosse, soccer, and track. In 1959 the stands surrounding Beaver Field were dismantled and reassembled at its current location at the eastern end of the campus. Enlarged to 46,000 seats that same year, the new football and marching band venue was rechristened "Beaver Stadium." ⌐╫╾

The original Beaver Field before 1909 with Old Main in the background.

The Liberty Bowl was an extremely successful showcase for Penn State, for the Crimson Tide, and for Philadelphia. The battle on the field was won by Penn State 7 to 0 against legendary coach Paul "Bear" Bryant and was Penn State Coach Rip Engle's one-hundredth football victory. Over the years the football team and the band traveled to dozens of bowl games, including many Liberty Bowls in Philadelphia.

The decade closed with an eye to the future for the Blue Band. Performances in the new stadium, and annual trips to bowl games in December, would become eagerly anticipated events. Traditions that started in the 1950s, such as Band Day and the Basketball Pep Band, were also to be continued and appreciated by the musicians in the Penn State bands, the sports fans, and the university. Other, new traditions awaited the band in the decade to come. In spite of the changes at Penn State—formerly "College," now "University" since 1953—one old Blue Band tradition remained then and remains today: the Blue Band's quest to be the best marching band in the nation.

THE BEGINNING OF THIS DECADE *was a new beginning*

for the Penn State football gridiron as well. New Beaver

Field, located in the northwestern corner of the university

since 1909, was moved to its current site on the eastern side

of campus, and the seating was augmented to accommodate

46,000 spectators. This made Beaver Stadium, as it was

now called, the largest all-steel collegiate stadium in the

United States at the time.

The new stadium was shaped like a horseshoe, with

the open southern end allowing a spectacular view of Mount

Nittany. The Blue Band at this time had fairly good seats in

the new stadium. Located between the 10- and 20-yard lines

on the east side (away from the west side press box) and low

to the field, the band had quite a good view of the football

Beaver Stadium

Beaver Stadium, the home of the Nittany Lions and the Blue Band, was opened on September 17, 1960. With 46,284 seats, it was approximately 16,000 seats larger than the previous football gridiron, Beaver Field, and was the largest all-steel college football stadium in the country. Shaped like a horseshoe, the south end was open to view Mount Nittany. An additional 2,000 seats were added in 1969, and another 9,000 in 1974. In 1976 bleachers were added beyond the south end-zone, enclosing the stadium on all sides and allowing 2,667 more patrons to sit and watch the games.

In 1978 another addition was erected, bringing the seating capacity to 76,639, permanently closing off the south end-zone, and shaping Beaver Stadium like a bowl. The seating was again increased in 1980 and 1991 to hold 93,803 spectators. When another expansion is completed in 2001, Beaver Stadium—with a seating capacity of about 103,000, will continue to be one of the largest football stadiums in the Big Ten and in the nation.

Two views of Beaver Stadium. Top: In the early 1970s, looking south. Bottom: In 1991, looking north.

games. The first game played, marking the first appearance of the Blue Band in the new stadium, was against Boston College on September 17, 1960. The Lions easily handled the Eagles that day, 20 to 0.

That year, like other years, had ups and downs for the Blue Band. One highlight of the season for the band was once again hosting Band Day on October 29 during the West Virginia game. Led by the State College High School band, sixty other high school bands from around Pennsylvania paraded that morning from the eastern parking lots on campus. The parade led the way through campus down Pollock Road, onto College Avenue, up Burrowes Road, and back to the starting point, which is approximately the same parade route used by the homecoming parade today. From there the high school band members were invited to Beaver Stadium to watch the Blue Band perform its pregame show, watch the Penn State football game, and participate in the halftime show. The Blue Band's pregame show included the traditional fanfare as well as some arrangements with a Halloween theme, such as "Dry Bones," "Peter, Peter, Pumpkin Eater," and "That Old Black Magic," accompanied by such formations as a skull and crossbones, a jack-o'-lantern, and a blue-and-white "black" cat. At halftime the Blue Band led the high school bands in forming a huge "PSU" on the field, stretching end-zone to end-zone, and playing "America the Beautiful," "Washington Post," and "Over the Rainbow," closing with the Penn State Alma Mater. Even though the high school band members did not see the music or know their places in the "PSU" formation until that very morning, and had only a few hours to practice, the performance was impressive.

A troubling incident occurred later that year, the Thursday before the last game of the season against traditional rival Pittsburgh at the "Pound Pitt" pep rally. Fiery Offensive Line Coach Sever "Tor" Toretti, while addressing the more than 500 football fans gathered, made inflammatory remarks about the Blue Band, which was absent from the rally. "I don't call Blue Band members Penn Staters if they can't get out and support a group of men who have represented us so well this year," Toretti shouted to the shocked crowd. He praised the Ying Yang Band, a pep band of die-hard Penn State fans from the Centre County region that did participate in the rally, and he referred to the Blue Band members who had not showed up as "lounge lizards." "I hope the *Collegian* is here so they can publish my words," the coach finished. Agreeing with this sentiment, the gathered mass of football fans gave the loudest cheer of the rally.

The *Collegian* indeed had reporters at the rally, and they most certainly published Toretti's spirited statements. Such a biting attack on the Penn State Blue Band was met the next day with a heated response from another fiery individual on campus, Band Director Jim Dunlop. "If 16,000 students [the total student population at the time] can't show their spirit by attending pep rallies, then the Blue Band certainly can't compensate for it," Dunlop told a *Collegian* reporter. He stated that the Blue Band had been unable to perform at the pep rally because most of its members were attending accredited choir and symphony classes, and continued: "We never appear for any performance unless all 108 of our members are present and we can bill ourselves as the 'Penn State Blue Band,' just as the football team would not play a game with just ten players."

The director further defended the Blue Band. The band had always met the football team when returning from away games and led victory parades for it, he said, but he could not recall a time when the Blue Band had ever played for a pep rally when there was a conflict with classes.

Although the coach's remarks were inflammatory, Dr. Dunlop was not angry with him and assumed that Toretti's statements stemmed from his not realizing that most of the Blue Band members were at classes at that time. Dunlop called Toretti on Friday morning, and the two men cleared up the misunderstanding when their passions had died down concerning the situation. Some band members, however, were not so forgiving of Toretti, or of the rally supporters who agreed with his statements. After the incident, Blue Band

The first Alumni Band performance was in 1963. The traditional "Alums" formation has always been a part of it.

Originally, the Alumni Band sat with the Blue Band for homecoming, instead of in the north end-zone, where they now sit.

President Carl Sipe said to a *Collegian* reporter: "[The Blue Band's] spirit is not a reflection of the football players' attitude. The Band is purely voluntary. We don't get paid for our participation, nor do we receive scholarships." Another disgruntled and anonymous Blue Band member said he was going to root for Pitt "just for spite."

As it turned out, the Lions won the Pitt game 14 to 3, and with a 7–3 record received a second Liberty Bowl bid. Any bad blood between the usually supportive football team and the Blue Band was forgotten as the two groups traveled east to meet and then defeat the University of Oregon in Philadelphia that December.

The pep rally crowd's reaction to the absence of the Blue Band was not surprising. The popularity of the Blue Band with many sports fans is attributable only in part to the skill of its members and staff. Without competent marchers, talented musicians, graceful majorettes, precision flag drillers, and a hardworking staff of directors, music arrangers, and administrative support, the Blue Band would not be the outstanding organization it has been for 100 years. But even with its high level of performance, the Blue Band is still Penn State's Blue Band, and many of the fans and alumni who love the university and its sports teams love the Blue Band just because it exemplifies the spirit of their university. Part of the reason for the emotions stirred up in those who listen to the Penn State school songs is that they evoke fond memories of past times at State College. This is true whether those songs are performed by the Blue Band or by any of the university's numerous musical organizations. Every memory of past football victories has Penn State fight songs in the background.

By 1961 many students and alumni had requested that a recording of favorite school songs be produced by the Concert Blue Band and the Glee Club. With the music of the two organizations so much in demand, the two groups teamed together and recorded "Penn State in Hi-Fi," an album of ten Blue Band selections and eleven Glee Club arrangements of school songs. Recorded on May 7 at the auditorium of State College High School, the record went on sale the next semester in September through the Alumni Association. This was the first time an album of school songs performed by either group had been made available. Profits from the sale of this popular album were used for music scholarships.

An excellent musical performance at Beaver Stadium was presented by the Blue Band and clarinet artist Robert Lowry during halftime at the University of Southern California game in late October 1961. The show, "The 'Licorice-Stick' Story," featured Lowry playing pieces made famous by Benny Goodman, Ted Lewis, Artie Shaw, and Woody Herman. Lowry was a member of the Sioux City, Iowa, Symphony Orchestra and concertmaster of the All-American Bandmasters' Band whenever it appeared in the Chicago region. Devoting most of his time to being a clarinet clinician, Lowry held many clarinet camps and clinics at high schools and colleges in the Midwest. He got to know Jim Dunlop while they were members of the College Band Directors' Association. By all accounts, the show was a big success, displaying the broad talent of Lowry and of course the Blue Band, which accompanied him during the program.

"The 'Licorice-Stick' Story" was not the only interesting performance the Blue Band gave that year. Other halftime performances by the Blue Band in 1961 included a Civil War Centennial show and a "Salute to the Four-Term System" (which may have the reader wondering what music is appropriate for saluting the four-term system).

Another bowl controversy occurred in late November, with a happy ending for the Blue Band. Lack of funds was again the reason the university was not planning to send the Blue Band or cheerleaders to the Gator Bowl in Jacksonville, Florida, which bid the Nittany Lion football team had earned earlier that month. Because it had been decided that the band would not be there, the entertainment committee of the Gator Bowl planned the halftime show without the Blue Band. That made arguments to send the band south much harder to make. In spite of these setbacks, Blue Band President Carl Sipe met with University President Eric Walker to plead his group's case. Sipe argued that he and the other 107 members of his band wanted to go to the game to support the university and the team, considering how few students and other Penn State fans would be able to make the 2,400-mile trek. Sympathetic to the Blue Band's cause, President Walker told Sipe that he would do as much as he could to arrange for the estimated $9,000 it would take to send the band to the bowl game.

The *Collegian* was also in support of sending the band south. "The diligent members of the band are entitled, we think, to share in the sunny spoils," the editorial opinion read in the November 30 edition. "They are so entitled because of their daily practices in the traditional Nittany Valley rain and mud and their unflagging allegiance to the team." The editorial also suggested

The Blue Band received new uniforms in 1963, and then was used by the Ostwald Company as an advertisement.

that the Blue Band was due a warm-weather trip after having suffered through the icy winds of the past two Liberty Bowls in Philadelphia to provide support for the football players when the mere 16,000 people who attended the last Liberty Bowl game could not.

President Walker and the Athletic Department found the resources to send the band by train to Jacksonville in early December. Influencing the decision, according to Ernest McCoy, the university's Director of Athletics, were the Blue Band's "contributions to the intercollegiate athletic program." Another factor in the decision was the fact that the Gator Bowl committee was able to provide five minutes at pregame for the Blue Band to perform and play the National Anthem before the nationwide television audience. Because of plans already made, however, the Georgia Tech band was the sole entertainment at the halftime show. As is usually the case when the Blue Band is present to cheer them on, the Nittany Lions beat Georgia Tech 30 to 15 at the Gator Bowl.

Besides being a spirit-boosting organization for the football team, the Blue Band also represents the spirit of the university. The Blue Band understands its role as a representative of the university better than almost any other group affiliated with Penn State. Just as music often evokes emotions at a visceral and subconscious level, hearing and seeing the Blue Band play the Penn State school songs for many fans triggers memories of victories at Beaver Field and Beaver Stadium even more than seeing Penn State's football players can. As the Blue Band performs for much more than just football games, it further cements the image of band members as the embodiment of Penn State's character.

This kind of recognition by the Penn State fans is treated with respect by the Blue Band. Consciously or not, band members know that while in uniform they must act in ways that represent what's best about Penn State and curb themselves from engaging in even slightly improper behavior. With the discipline and the love of the alma mater that is necessary to practice grueling hours in any weather for the university's marching band, most band members are predisposed to conducting themselves with class no matter what the occasion.

Examples are too numerous to list, but what happened during the West Virginia game at Beaver Stadium on November 10, 1962, is a case in point. The West Virginia Mountaineer Marching Band visited Penn State for the game and performed during halftime, and many students attending the game became rowdy and began throwing eggs, mud, paper, and other objects at the WVU band as it prepared to take the field. The Blue Band is never involved in that type of activity. Its members understand the dedication that it takes to be in a collegiate band, and respect was and still is always there for opponents' bands when

Though no longer the Director of the Blue Band, Hum Fishburn continued to chart shows as well as to be the announcer for the Blue Band during the 1960s.

they come to visit. A letter to the *Daily Athenaeum*, West Virginia University's student newspaper, from a WVU band member attests to that:

> I, as a member of the [West Virginia] University Marching Band, would like to thank the Penn State Blue Band for the very warm reception and the refreshments that the band gave us at Beaver Stadium on November 10. We, as a band, were treated "great" by the Penn State band, but the reception given us by the student body was somewhat different. It is very disheartening to a band to be booed and to have numerous objects thrown at it when it is performing or preparing to do so.

The year 1963 marked the debut of a tradition that continues today: the Alumni Marching Blue Band. Celebrating his eighteenth season with the university bands program, Jim Dunlop got in touch with more than 100 former Blue Band members whom he had directed at Penn State since 1947 to participate in the homecoming game halftime show on October 3. The result was that 115 former Blue Band members (including nine former Blue Band presidents) came from ten different states and the District of Columbia that homecoming Saturday, including Glenn Stumpff '54, who made his way back to his alma mater from California. Because many of the alumni musicians had not picked up their

The Blue Band formed the letters "U-S-A" on the field of the Gator Bowl in 1967. This photograph was used as the cover of the 1968 Jacksonville Telephone Directory.

The Alumni Blue Band

I f there is a group of individuals more appreciated on football Saturdays than the Blue Band, it is the Blue Band alumni who return every homecoming to participate in the Alumni Blue Band. The almost 400 members who march at the game are highly respected by the current Blue Band, the university, and the fans who love to watch them perform. Much of that respect stems from watching these men and women, some of whom are in their eighties, march onto the field playing the Penn State school songs with as much vigor and enthusiasm as the younger, student band.

The Alumni Blue Band Association (ABBA), made up of nearly 1,000 members, is the largest Affiliated Program Group (APG) at the Pennsylvania State University. APGs are groups of alumni and friends who are affiliated with a Penn State college or constituent organization because of their academic backgrounds or interest in an extra-curricular activity. Membership is open to anyone who was a member of the Penn State Marching Blue Band or other university bands program who has completed one semester of participation. ⇥

instruments since they had graduated, the pieces chosen for the alumni to perform were all Penn State fight songs, which Blue Band alumni could easily play without music, the fingerings indelibly etched in their minds. During halftime the final figure formed on the field by the alumni and student Blue Bands was much like the drill for Band Day, where both bands created a large "PSU," the alumni forming the letter "s" in the middle.

Although the clouds threatened rain all day, the Alumni Band and the Blue Band entertained spectators with enthusiasm, and for most of the alumni attending the game, the combined performance was the highlight of the Blue Band's year. That homecoming was such a success for the alumni of the band that they have returned to play every year since 1963, including members who were in the Blue Band both before and after Jim Dunlop's first season.

The Blue Band sported uniforms in a new style in 1963. Quite different from the military style of previous uniforms, the new suits featured a white overlay vest placed over the blue suit jacket, with a large "s" on the front and a picture of the Nittany Lion shrine on the back. The uniforms also included blue trousers, spats, white gloves, and a white hat. During the Concert Band season the band members wore only the blue trousers and jacket, adding a dress shirt and bow tie for a more formal symphonic look. The women of the Concert Band still wore navy-blue dresses.

The new uniforms were impressive on the field. From the highest level of the stadium, the white overlays were more easily seen than just the blue jackets. The heavy vinyl overlay also helped keep band members warm during the windy winter days. For these reasons and others, the basic Blue Band uniform has not changed much since 1963. Band members currently wear the same style of jackets, trousers, spats, gloves, hats, and overlay. The only noticeable difference is in the figures featured on the overlay: the letter "P" has been added to the "s" on the front and the words "Nittany Lions" have replaced the lion shrine.

Hummel Fishburn, longtime director of the Blue Band and head of the Music and Music Education Departments since 1943, retired from the university with professor emeritus status on July 1, 1965. His involvement with Penn State lasted for more than forty years. As a student in the early 1920s, Fishburn was a member of the Blue Band and the Thespians, writing music and lyrics for the latter organization on four separate occasions. After graduating, Fishburn served as assistant to the dean of men, Dr. Warnock, and as an assistant in the Department of Music. Later, as Professor of Music, he again served a dual role by

When the temperature drops,
members of the Blue Band don
their topcoats before the game.

Before marching
rehearsals, band
members always
warm up with
stretching and
calisthenics.

The Blue Band
Silks practice as
the sun goes
down and the
lights come on.

Because intramural
sports teams and
the Blue Band
must share the
same practice
field, conditions
deteriorate quickly
over a season.

The Blue Band
Majorettes on
the practice field.

practice

A view of the
tunnel entrance,
from the field.

PHOTO BY GREG GRIECO

pregame

Singing the "Fireman's Song" in the tunnel was one of the longest traditions of the Blue Band.

OPPOSITE PAGE

TOP The Blue Band does its impressive "high-step."

BOTTOM School-purchased sousaphones, mellophones, and baritones shine on the field during the 1997 Ohio State game.

The drum major flips …

… lands …

… and jumps into a split.

PHOTOS BY PRISM PHOTOGRAPHIC,
J. A. LAWRENCE JR.

The Blue Band in
one of its trademark
formations.
PHOTO BY TOM MAIRS

The Blue Band Silks in
the 1992–97 uniforms.

Dr. Deihl with a future Blue Bander.

Drum Major Greg Stock, the longest-reigning drum major (1982–86).

A view from the Blue Band seats in 1986, before the move to the south end-zone.

During pregame, the band explodes from the tunnel …

… and forms a block band.

LEFT Fans in the Lions' Loft cheer the band and the drum major as the drum major completes yet another flip.
PHOTO BY TOM MAIRS

The first thing the football team sees as they rush onto the field to start a game is the Blue Band.

A member of the Blue Band Silks at the 1990 Blockbuster Bowl.

halftime

Feature Twirler Christine Wolfe, the only feature twirler to remain in that position for five continuous years.

Two "Touch of Blue" members perform during a halftime show.
PHOTO BY PRISM PHOTOGRAPHIC, J. A. LAWRENCE JR.

OVERLEAF

TOP LEFT Since they were introduced into the Blue Band in 1973, women have become an integral part of the band.

BOTTOM LEFT The band performing in concert formation as the drum major conducts.

TOP RIGHT Band members celebrate the 1987 Fiesta Bowl win.

BOTTOM RIGHT The Blue Band performing in one of its many complex formations.

corner concert

TOP One of the most enjoyable postgame events is the "Corner Concert" by the Penn State drum line.

BOTTOM The drum line puts an exclamation point on the postgame Corner Concert performance.

OPPOSITE The Penn State drum line, under the direction of Dave Buzminsky, has always been considered one of the best collegiate drum lines in the country.

Every year, hundreds of Blue Band alumni return for home-coming. Former band managers make sure school instruments are available for them.

The Alumni Band on the field.

One Alumni Band tradition is to march into the "ALUMS" formation.

No one leaves during the alumni halftime performance at homecoming.

OVERLEAF **Former Drum Major Wes Burns directs the 1997 Alumni Band in the south end-zone during the homecoming game.**
PHOTO BY GREG GRIECO

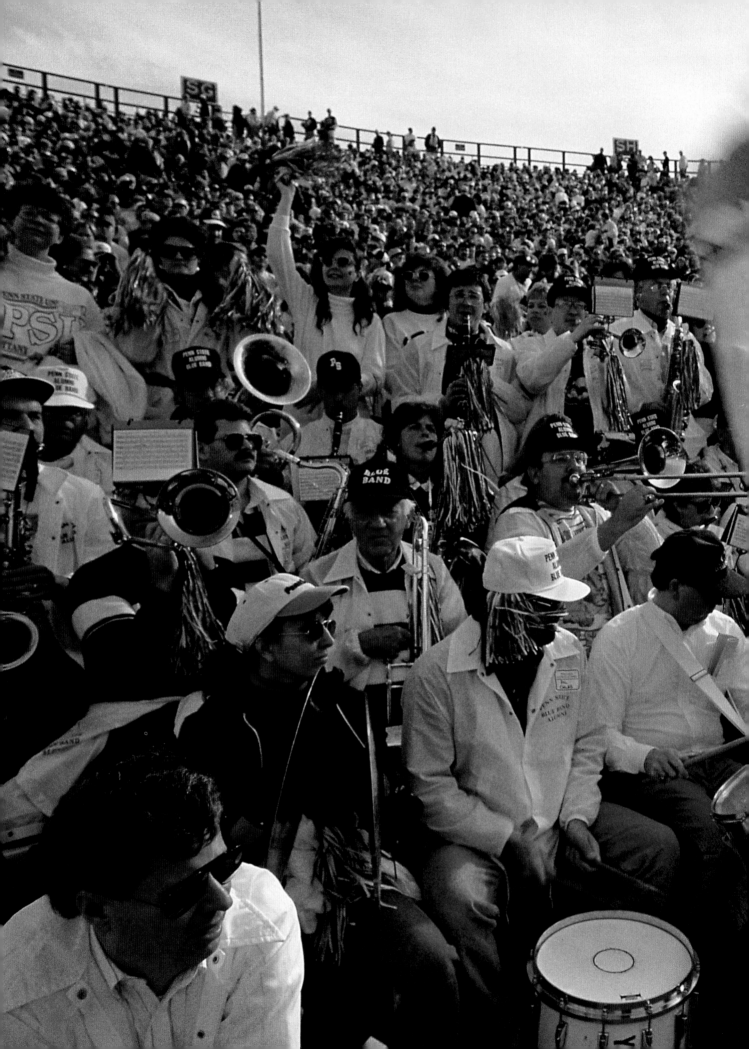

Two days before the 1987 Fiesta Bowl,
Dick Bundy panics.

The Nittany Lion is always a welcome
friend of the Blue Band.

The Blue Band practices in all types of weather,
even in snow at the Buffalo Bills stadium.

Every so often the Blue Band yells "We want the Lion!" the loudest.

The Touch of Blue at the 1988 Citrus Bowl.

At Bandorama, the Blue Band wears the uniform minus hat and gloves.

OVERLEAF Because of their instrument's size, sousaphone players are among the most noticeable band members on the field.

becoming department head for both music and music education in the 1940s. Taking the baton from "Tommy" Thompson in 1939, Hum was the Director of the Blue Band from 1939 until 1947, when he passed the leadership of the Concert Blue Band and the Marching Blue Band to Jim Dunlop.

As a salute to his many years of service to the university, and especially to the band programs, the Blue Band dedicated its October 23 homecoming halftime show to Fishburn. Performing many of Fishburn's favorite pieces on the field, the Blue Band spelled "Hum" in the formation.

Fishburn's association with the Blue Band did not end in 1965. Although he stopped writing the drills and formations for the halftime shows, he became the Blue Band's announcer at the games, introducing the band at pregame and halftime until 1975. The creation of the halftime formations was taken over by Assistant Band Director Ned C. Deihl, who later became only the fourth Director of the Blue Band in seventy-five years.

A major portion of Dr. Deihl's mark on the Blue Band occurred in 1965 when he originated and implemented a new pregame show. The halftime performances were different every week and generally had a theme. The pregame show, however, was and is essentially the same, game after game, and is based on the school fight songs and the Alma Mater. When Deihl came to Penn State he decided to create a new pregame show that was not so lackluster. Instead of having the band start from the end-zone, as it did before, he had the band rush at a high tempo from the team's entrance under the stadium, known to the Blue Band as "The Tunnel."

In addition to the tunnel entrance, Deihl created another innovative drill for the pregame show just after the singing of the Alma Mater. This routine became known as the "Floating Lions" drill. "I had seen a band once march into letters from the end-zone like a revolving Times Square sign," Deihl said, "but I never saw one pull letters from both directions. This is what I wanted to do." The difficult "Times Square" drill had been attempted twenty years earlier by Hummel Fishburn as he had the band spell "Pennsylvania is a Great State" during Pennsylvania Week. Locking himself in a hotel room, Fishburn wrote the drill in two grueling days. Pulling the letters first from one side and then from the other was even more difficult.

Performed for this show for the first time on Forbes Field at the Pittsburgh game on November 20, 1965, the Floating Lions drill had the band spell "Lions" while marching downfield from a block formation. Eventually, the band changed the form to spell "Lions" to the other side of the stadium while marching, or, as it appears, "floating," downfield in the other direction. The entire pregame show with the tunnel entrance and the Floating Lions became so popular with the spectators that it remains the Blue Band's trademark today.

An interesting if only slightly frustrating event took place in 1965 at the football game at the University of Maryland toward the end of the season. The Blue Band, in a rare third away trip, was scheduled to perform on national television and had been preparing for this game for a month, even though most halftime shows only received a week's worth

The Pregame Show

The Penn State Blue Band's pregame show is one of the most intricate, challenging, and exciting drills in the college band world. To Blue Band members, it is the thrill of a lifetime. "There's nothing like it. The rush you feel when you come out of the tunnel makes all the hard work you put into practicing worth it," said Drew Yingling '92, former Blue Band trombone player.

The pregame show starts with the drum major and the percussion section high-stepping (chair-stepping) from the end-zone and stopping at the 10-yard line. The drum major blows his whistle four times rapidly, and the drums begin their pregame cadence at more than 180 beats per minute. The rest of the band bursts onto the field from a tunnel under the stadium, forms a large block surrounding the percussionists, and

marches in place at the blistering pace the percussionists set. The Blue Band Silks are introduced, acknowledging the spectators with a crisp flag salute. The Blue Band's majorettes, known as the Touch of Blue, and the feature twirler, known as the Blue Sapphire, march between and through the band's ranks down the field and salute the crowd with high baton tosses.

Another whistle from the drum major signals the members of the band, now facing inward, to face downfield starting with the center ranks and working outward, creating a ripple effect. A quick drum "roll off" signals the musicians to begin the pregame fanfare, which is based on the Penn State fight song "Nittany Lion." As the fanfare concludes, the drum major is introduced. As the first strains of

"Nittany Lion" begin and the band high-steps downfield, the drum major races from the center of the band, struts to the 50-yard line, and does his famous front flip, ending in a split and a salute. It is said that if he "makes" the flip Penn State is ensured a win that day. The loud cheer from the fans that follows a successful flip is testament to the belief in that superstition.

Reaching midfield, the band concludes "Nittany Lion" and begins a cheer: "Go! State! Beat! [Today's opponent]!" The band then begins a series of "to the rear" turns, alternately facing the west and east sides of the stadium, while playing what Blue Band members refer to as "The Big Ending" of "Nittany Lion." Afterward, the percussion section signals a halt. The band stops marching and snaps to attention facing the American flag flying high above Beaver Stadium. In this position the band plays "The Star Spangled Banner."

Finishing the National Anthem, the Blue Band performs a complicated series of maneuvers to form a large "PSU" to an abbreviated version of "Fight On, State." In this position the band plays the Alma Maters of the opposing team and of Penn State.

Next comes the Blue Band's famous "Floating Lions" routine, one of the most complicated routines performed by a collegiate marching band. The band forms a block again, sideline to sideline in width, and marches south back toward the tunnel from which it entered as it plays the famous Bilik arrangement of "Nittany Lion." Almost immediately, the trombone rank does an about-face and marches in a collision course with the rest of the band. At perfectly timed intervals, each rank shifts just in time to avoid the northbound trombone rank and the rest of the ranks that follow them. The effect is to spell the word "Lions," letter by letter, from the center of a crisscrossing block of musicians, reminding one of a scrolling Times Square message. As the trombone rank, which makes up the "L," reaches the 50-yard line, they point their slides skyward at a 45-degree angle just as the word "Hail" is reached in the chorus of the fight song. The word "Lions" finally emerges from the block, visible to the press box side of the field, and "floats" downfield until the end of the fight song.

Without missing a beat, the band marches to a drum cadence to re-form the word "Lions" upside down so that the east side of the stands can read the word. The band then steps off again in the opposite direction while playing "Fight On, State." At the end of the song, the drums begin another cadence as the band forms a large aisle on either side of the tunnel and awaits the football team, which then rushes onto the field through the aisle while the band plays "Nittany Lion" once more.

Yingling describes the band members' feelings just before the pregame show starts: "When the drums come onto the field as you wait in the tunnel, the butterflies in your stomach are really bad. But once you are on the field and you hear the roar of the crowd, your adrenaline kicks in and you are all business." The spectators also feel the excitement the band produces during pregame. The pregame show has been so popular with those who go to the football games that it has remained virtually unchanged in thirty-five years. Dr. Deihl, creator of the pregame show, can attest to this fact. "Once, we tried to shorten the Alma Mater down to just one verse, but we received so many letters of complaint from the football fans that we had to put the other three verses back in for the next game."

The famous Penn State Blue Band pregame show is one of the most proud traditions at the university. As long as there are football Saturdays at Beaver Stadium, the Blue Band will pour into the stadium from the tunnel, thrilling the almost 100,000 spectators and instilling them with the pride and spirit that is Penn State.

The original Floating Lions drill ...

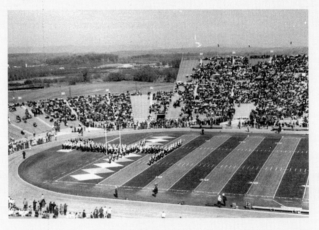

... had the Blue Band's tunnel entrance ...

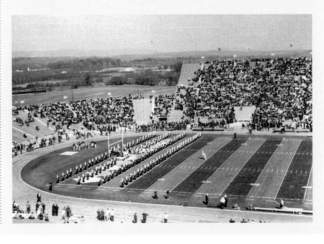

... from the north end-zone.

of preparation. Unfortunately for the Blue Band, the game was scheduled for the same day one of the Gemini space capsules was to be launched. During the first half of the game the network split the screen to show both the launch preparations and the Lions and the Terrapins battle on the gridiron. By halftime, however, the Blue Band was preempted for the launch.

The remainder of 1965 was typical for the Blue Band. There were performances for home football games, pep rallies, and other away games at Syracuse University (which was also televised and did feature the band) and the University of Pittsburgh. At the end of the season some of the Blue Band members continued to perform with the Basketball Pep Band, sponsored by the University Student Government instead of the Air Force ROTC now, and with the Concert Blue Band. In early December, however, the Blue Band was in the midst of another controversy when Dr. Dunlop, who had conducted the Concert Blue Band for more than seventeen years, was replaced by a twenty-five-year-old director from Connecticut, Smith C. Toulson III.

When Dr. Hummel Fishburn retired from the university, the last administrative connection between the Department of Music Education in the College of Education and the Department of Music in the College of Arts and Architecture was severed. The university elevated Professor Frances W. Andrews to head the Department of Music Education and hired Robert W. Baisley, assistant dean of Yale University's School of Music, to head the Department of Music.

The Concert Blue Band, or "Music 78" as it was officially known at the College of Arts and Architecture, was a one-credit course offered by the Department of Music. Dr. Fishburn had permitted Dr. Dunlop, a professor in the Department of Music Education, to cross departments and teach Music 78, but after Dr. Fishburn retired, discussions about the separate goals and roles of the two colleges led to the decision to end that arrangement. Instead, Smith C. Toulson III, an assistant conductor for Yale's concert band program, was hired by the Music Department to teach Music 78. Toulson, although only twenty-five years old, was a highly regarded clarinetist and director who had had professional experience with the New Haven Symphony Orchestra and the New Haven Youth Symphony as conductor, and with recording groups in New York City as a studio musician for record albums and films. In addition to conducting the Concert Blue Band, Toulson was also responsible for teaching woodwind classes and various ensemble groups. The marching band was to remain in the Department of Music Education. Marching Blue Band was not considered a course per se, but rather an extracurricular activity, although it could be credited as part of a student's physical education requirement. Dr. Dunlop remained head of the Blue Band on the field.

Dunlop directed the Concert Band program for more than seventeen years, was past president of both the Pennsylvania Music Educators' Association and the Pennsylvania College Bandmasters' Association, and had an outstanding reputation in music education circles around the nation. How could such a man be replaced by someone half his age and without those credentials? asked Dunlop's incredulous supporters. Dr. Jules Heller, dean

In 1965 pregame was changed by then graduate assistant Ned C. Deihl. The Blue Band started to perform the "Floating Lions" drill.

of the College of Arts and Architecture, stated that the decision was made to "expand the opportunity of the students . . . [by] making another teacher available to them." Heller also said that Dunlop was not removed as a "personal attack on his professional ability." Rather, in the reorganization of the two music departments, Dr. Baisley had stated: "It was decided by the faculty [of the Departments of Music and Music Education] last summer [1965] and later fully implemented that a professor listed under one department could not teach a class in the other department." Baisley contended that each faculty member was free to choose his or her own department and that "it was Mr. Dunlop's own decision. He had to make his choice between the two departments, and he chose Music Education."

Dr. Dunlop disagreed with some of the facts stated by Dr. Baisley in a January 21, 1966, *Collegian* article concerning his dismissal. "I was never . . . offered an opportunity to become a member of the Music faculty by [Dr. Baisley] or any other person on this campus." In response to the interdepartmental ruling preventing instructors to cross departmental boundaries to teach courses, he replied: "Three members of Mr. Baisley's Music Department have taught and are presently scheduled to teach music education courses [during the summer semester]. One assistant professor of German is also teaching Music courses at the present time."

When Dunlop learned that Toulson had been hired October 1965, he was at the University of Connecticut guest-conducting the Connecticut All-State High School Band while on sabbatical leave. He made an offer to Dean Heller and later to Dr. Baisley to cut short his six-month leave and return as the Concert Blue Band director—at no cost to them, because Dunlop's salary was paid for by the Department of Music Education. Because Toulson was already on staff, however, Dunlop's offer was denied.

President Walker supported the decision by Baisley and Heller, in that it was within the "academic prerogatives" of the faculty and the Music Department to make that decision. The Music Department faculty also supported Toulson's appointment. However,

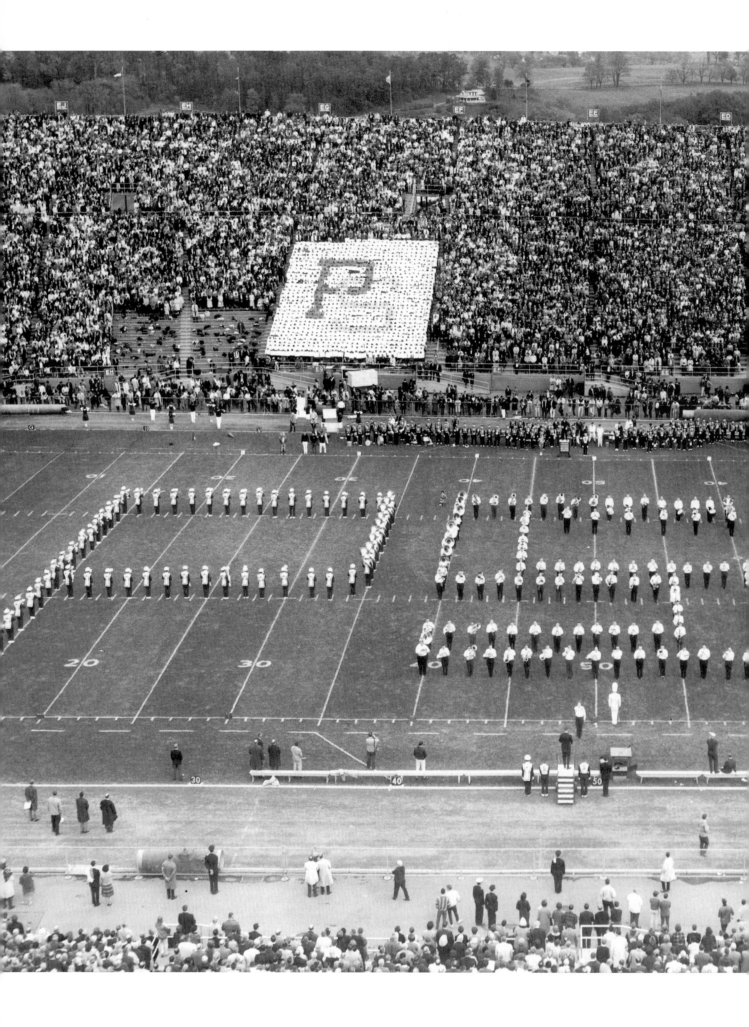

Usually at the end of any Alumni Band performance the Blue Band combines with the Alumni to form a huge "PSU."

the decision to replace Dunlop on an apparent technicality was met with heated protest by the members of the Concert Blue Band, the student body, and alumni. More than 200 letters of protest from former band members made their way to President Walker concerning this situation. In a boycott more than 100 Concert Band members chose not to return during the winter term. According to Arnold Alexander, the Blue Band's equipment manager, the boycott was spontaneous and no pressure was put on other band members to quit. Most of those who did not rejoin felt that without Dunlop there was no point in being in the Concert Blue Band.

A lot of pressure was placed on Smith Toulson. That semester there were approximately twenty-five Concert Blue Band members, down from well over 100 the year before. Most of those in the new band were first-time members. Besides being the focus of intense dislike from those loyal to Dunlop—quite unfairly, according to Ned C. Deihl in a 1998 interview—he had to rebuild a band that had been run successfully by a Penn State legend for almost twenty years.

Toulson did the best he could under the circumstances. After two years, however, his Music 78 course was changed to a wind ensemble and Dr. Dunlop was rehired as the Concert Blue Band Director when it became a Music Education course. Given Dunlop's experience and skill, his return was a practical decision that far outweighed following the strict letter of the rule. Professor Toulson still teaches at Penn State as a woodwind instructor and conductor of the Symphonic Wind Ensemble and is a highly respected member of the Department of Music faculty.

Although the spring semester was a low point in the band's history, better times were seen the next fall. The Pennsylvania State University Board of Trustees generously allocated more than $12,000 from undesignated Alumni Fund monies to the Marching Blue Band to purchase thirty new instruments. These additional funds allowed Dr. Dunlop to expand the band from 114 members to 134 and to fill in sections of the band that were weak on instrumentation, especially drums and sousaphones. This was quite a boon to the band, since with the growth in membership the band could fill the ever-expanding stadium with sound even better. More members also meant that formations on the field would be easier to create and that the Blue Band could compare itself more favorably with other big college bands.

The first football game of the year was also Band Day, but for the first time ever it did not feature the new Blue Band. The Blue Band members had not yet returned to campus because, although Penn State and the University of Maryland were scheduled to play on September 17, to meet the college football schedules, the academic year at Penn State did not begin until September 25. Taking the Blue Band's place as featured band was State College High School, whom Jim Dunlop directed along with fifty-eight other high school bands. Ironically, the debut of one composition that day, "Big Blue," written in salute to the Blue Band by famed composer and arranger Paul Yoder, was performed instead by the thousands of high school musicians participating in Band Day.

One memorable halftime performance that showed off the bigger, better band was

the "Salute to Pennsylvania" show. The band formed a keystone, the state's symbol and nickname, while the drums gave cadence and then formed a coal car while playing "Clementine" and "Sixteen Tons." The coal car turned into a horse and buggy to the tune of "Thanks for the Buggy Ride." Later in the show, the band performed drill movements to Revolutionary War medleys and finally formed the Liberty Bell while playing "God Bless America." According to many in the band, it was the best show of the year, with interesting formations, well-arranged music, and a more robust sound from the improved Blue Band.

The Blue Band had to prepare for the opening game of the next season quite early. Usually, band members have only a short time between auditioning for a position and performing the first show of the season on the football field, sometimes as short as one week. The year 1967 was such a year. Students began arriving on campus before the beginning of the semester on Sunday, September 17. Dunlop and Deihl spent the first three days of the week auditioning the new potential band members. After making the cut, the

A promotion photograph from 1968, used in some Beaver Stadium pictorials, showing the trombone rank and the drum major, Stanley "Chip" Willis.

newly selected members began working with the returning Blue Banders on marching and music morning, afternoon, and evening during "Band Camp," where the members spent up to twelve hours preparing for the first performance that Saturday. In order to save time, the entire band registered for classes as a group that Thursday.

When the final rehearsal was over on Friday, the new Blue Band loaded instruments, uniforms, overnight bags, and other equipment onto buses and headed for the Naval Academy at Annapolis, Maryland, to perform its first show during the Penn State–Navy game. The halftime show, "Salute to the Armed Forces," was well received at the Academy. Starting with "America," the band marched downfield and then made different maneuvers while playing the "Marine Hymn." Forming an anchor, the band played "Anchors Away" and then moved to become a figure of a jet during "Beyond the Blue Horizon." Finally the band created a shield to the tune of the "Battle Hymn of the Republic." The show was later performed at Beaver Stadium for the next game and revamped for the Gator Bowl that December.

The Nittany Lions did well that year, and the team received a bid to play Florida State in the Gator Bowl in Jacksonville, Florida. The band was invited to perform in the bowl too. The show it performed, "Salute to the Armed Forces," was one of the best of the college band performances of the bowl season. Dr. William J. Moody, Director of Bands at the University of Texas, stated that the Blue Band was "the finest marching band on television over the holiday period." Another director from a southern university wrote: "The Penn State Band show [at the Gator Bowl] was one of the most original I witnessed over the long bowl holiday." At one point in the show, the letters "USA" were formed. The aerial photograph of the Gator Bowl with the band in that formation was used as the cover of the 1968 Jacksonville telephone directory.

In spite of protests of the Vietnam War raging across the United States at the time, the Blue Band once again chose to support its armed forces. The Blue Band received many letters of appreciation from all over the nation from those who saw the Gator Bowl show on television. One woman, a Mrs. H. L. Slaton from California, wrote a particularly kind letter to the band:

> I am the wife of a Marine. At the moment, he is in a hospital [in Vietnam], wounded. We have suffered great abuse at the hands of a lot of people. At times, it has been pretty rough.
>
> Therefore, you can imagine what a pleasure it was to see your half-time presentation at the Gator Bowl. In my biased opinion, "Salute to the Armed Forces" was well deserved. And extremely well presented.
>
> On behalf of all the wives and families who wait, thank you. I only wish I could express in writing how much you have enhanced a difficult season. Holidays are very difficult.
>
> Thank you. God bless you.

The first game of the 1968 season at Penn State was against Navy. Owing to a

Auditioning and Band Camp

Auditioning for the Blue Band begins at "Band Camp," a week-long training session that starts just before the beginning of the fall semester, usually during orientation week. Hopeful prospective musicians, silks, and majorettes try out for the Blue Band on the first and second days of the camp. The auditions start with music, which includes performing individually a prepared piece, scales, and sight-reading. On the second day, specially selected veteran band members teach the potential band members the Blue Band's "high-step" style of marching. On the second day, students who were Blue Band members the previous year audition for their rank positions and then combine with the rookie hopefuls for the rest of the camp. Final cuts are made at the end of Band Camp, and the newest Blue Band begins practicing that very evening for the first football game show.

As part of the audition, each potential band member must memorize the pregame music and high-step march down the field playing the music by himself or herself in front of the entire camp, sometimes more than once. This part of the audition is not for the faint of heart or the less than completely confident. Band Camp is designed to weed out those who are not qualified musicians or performers. It leaves only the best musicians and marchers with the toughest constitutions and most dedicated spirits. In most years more than half of those who audition for the band do not make the block. And returnees do not get a free ride either.

The Band Camp schedule is incredibly grueling. Because the fall semester at the university begins in late August, it is generally more than 90 degrees outside, and the camp is held outdoors on the practice field. The days start at 9:00 A.M. and do not end until 8:00 P.M. on most evenings. All told, the camp is approximately 30 to 35 hours of marching and performing in the sweltering heat. Added to this physical stress is the mental stress of memorizing music and routines and the uncertainty of making the final cut.

When the camp is over, those who make the band are treated to a Labor Day picnic near the practice field sponsored by the Blue Band student officers. The hard work of camp is only temporarily suspended at the picnic though. Knowing that the first football game is just around the corner, the musicians, the silks, and the majorettes must learn their pregame and halftime routines and music quickly, performing flawlessly before they arrive at Beaver Stadium.

miscommunication between the band's equipment managers and the dry-cleaning service the band used for the uniforms, the uniforms did not make it back to the band by this game. Therefore, the band was forced to wear white shirts, dark ties, and dress trousers to perform at Beaver Stadium, the first time it had ever played at a game without uniforms.

This didn't stop the Blue Band from making the rest of the season one of its best. The main factor in its success was the band members' dedication to the university and to the football team. The extent of its dedication was demonstrated when it performed at the airport at 4:00 A.M. to welcome the football team back from victory at UCLA; when it went on an overnight trip to the West Virginia game and put in long hours practicing, performing, and traveling; and when it practiced in subfreezing weather for hours in preparation for the Syracuse game. One factor in the band's high performance level that year was certainly the good fortune of the Nittany Lions on the gridiron. The team went undefeated and was invited to play the University of Kansas at the Orange Bowl on New Year's Day. After a full season of dedicated service, the Blue Band welcomed the opportunity to perform in Florida before millions of television viewers.

The band performed four times while in Miami. The first was leading the Orange Bowl parade before an estimated 500,000 spectators along the parade route and many times more watching from home. Then the band appeared on the NBC program "Billboard." Then came a pep rally concert in the lobby of the band's hotel, the Deauville. Finally, the band performed at the game itself, but not without drawing some negative comments from a small minority of individuals on campus about the band's state of preparedness and level of support.

The Blue Band Silks

The Blue Band Silks can trace their history to 1968, when alternates were asked to carry flags on the field and to carry the Blue Band banner during parades. This all-male flag corps acted as a color guard only, though; they did not perform routines as the current silk squad does. The flag corps wore regular-issue Blue Band uniforms because they could take an absent musician's spot as an alternate at a moment's notice. The original flag corps had thirteen individuals.

Not until the late 1970s did the Blue Band Silks begin doing flag-swinging routines during the football shows. The silk squad no longer consisted of Blue Band alternates, but rather some of the finest college flag-twirlers in the nation. Because the silks still wore the band uniform, swinging a flag with the uniform's hats was difficult. The silk squad

therefore began wearing its own uniform, consisting of the same band trousers, a white blouse with blue collar and cuffs, and a beret to replace the awkward hat. The new uniform was complemented by a blue cummerbund and sash.

In 1988 the Silk uniforms were modified to include a light-blue diagonal stripe across the blouse, and in 1993 the silk squad traded in its band trousers for fitted slacks tailored especially for them. The current Silk uniform is more military in style, with a solid blue top that has buttons running diagonally from both shoulders in the front of the shirt. This new look made its debut in 1998.

The Blue Band Silks consists of approximately thirty individuals, and the squad has its own alternates. One duty of a Silk alternate at Big Ten Conference football games is to carry the opposing team's banner and run it across the field while the Blue Band plays the opponent's fight song during pregame. The alternates also place replacement flags and pick up dropped flags during the field performances.

More than thirty years old today, the Blue Band Silks are considered one of the finest flag squads in the collegiate world.

In a *Collegian* editorial, the president of the Penn State Jazz Club, Clark Arrington, accused the band of being "unprepared" and "uninterested" and having a "demoralized attitude," compared with the Kansas Jayhawk band, which was clearly more animated at the game, according to Arrington. Blue Band President Ned Trautman offered a rebuttal in a letter to the *Collegian*'s editor, stating that the Kansas band "merely kept up a continuous banging of cymbals and rolling of drums [after the halftime show]. … The Penn State Blue Band was there to make music, not cheer for the football team [in this fashion]." An agreement was made between the two bands at the game, Trautman explained, that each band would take turns playing during the game. "This is only band courtesy. However, Kansas did not uphold this agreement during the second half."

Those that understood the Blue Band's style better enjoyed the performance much more. The band received many letters of appreciation from people who were at the game and who watched at home. Dr. Dunlop was clearly impressed. When the next football season came early in 1969, Dunlop informed the band during the August band camp: "It is physically impossible to audition all old and new men, so we will accept you [returnees] on the basis of your Orange Bowl performance."

The Blue Band had a more contemporary repertoire under Hummel Fishburn and Jim Dunlop than it did under W. O. Thompson, and that was evident in 1969. During the homecoming game against Ohio University, the band performed "Sounds of 1969." The musical selections included marching downfield to the theme from "Hawaii Five-O," a new song that year by Blood, Sweat, and Tears called "Spinning Wheel," "Aquarius" from the Broadway production of "Hair," and, finally, "Up, Up, and Away" by the Fifth Dimension.

The show turned out so well that Dunlop decided to use it for the halftime show at the Orange Bowl, which invited Penn State for a second year in a row. The Blue Band was again praised for its skill on the field and during the parade, but it also received praise for being gentlemen off the field. The manager of Schraft's Motor Lodge, where the band stayed for the Orange Bowl, wrote to Jim Dunlop concerning the band's conduct: "One usually looks upon the arrival of 150 college boys with trepidation. However, there was not a single problem or incident during the entire time your men were here."

The 1960s was a time of student activism and social revolution in the nation at large. At Penn State this was not as evident as it was at some West Coast universities, but the students did stick up for what they believed was right. This was the case with the Blue Band as well. The 1960s was also a decade of tremendous growth at the university, both physically and academically. Part of that growth was reflected in the sheer number of Blue Band members, from just over 100 in 1960 to more than 140 as the decade closed. At the beginning of the 1970s that growth slowed for the university but picked up steam for the Blue Band, as it continued to evolve into the Big Ten style that so many Penn State fans are familiar with today.

THE 1970S WAS A DECADE OF TRANSITION *for the university, and the Blue Band, as it often had, reflected that. Band membership was continuing to increase, primarily through the efforts of Dr. Ned Deihl. A holder of two Big Ten university diplomas at the time, Deihl was accustomed to the marching style employed by the large, brass-dominated Big Ten marching bands and felt that Penn State's band was similar enough to embrace the Big Ten style fully. By embracing this style twenty-five years before Penn State actually joined the Big Ten Conference, the Blue Band played a role in the other Big Ten Conference universities' acceptance of Penn State as a good "fit" in 1993.*

The Blue Band in 1970 continued to do theme-based halftime shows. One of the most memorable of the year was

Before the drum major flip in 1971, the drum major could perform any special routine he wanted to during pregame.

presented at the game between Penn State and Army at West Point in October. The presentation, "Sounds on Campus," played "Fight On, State," "Halls of Ivy," "Varsity Drag," and other similar selections. One piece, "Make Me Smile," featured a solo by jazz drummer Roy Burns. Burns had performed in the orchestras of such music legends as Benny Goodman, Duke Ellington, Count Basie, and Peter Nero and was at the time a member of the NBC orchestra.

Another memorable performance during the twenty-first annual Band Day featured a piece written by a Penn State Professor Emeritus of Animal Nutrition. Dr. Raymond Swift, who wrote the "Intervention March" as a high school student in Boston in 1916, was on hand to witness the performance by more than sixty bands.

The 1970 season ended with the football team, with only a 7–3 record, declining the invitation to play at the Peach Bowl, so the band was home in snowy Pennsylvania for Christmas. Although disappointed then, the band had cause to be proud in March 1971 when Dr. Dunlop was elected president of the American Bandmasters' Association, the elite group of band directors with membership by invitation only. In April, Dunlop took the Concert Blue Band on a "Pennsylvania Tour," a three-city concert tour to Erie, Grove City, and St. Mary's. This was the precursor for the band's first concert on campus at Schwab Auditorium. Later in the semester the Concert Band was on hand to perform for Commencement, where the new university president, John W. Oswald, was inaugurated.

In 1971 the 150-member Marching Blue Band started its football season on October 2, when Penn State played Air Force at Beaver Stadium. The show it performed, "Season 71," featured school songs of the Nittany Lion opponents that year. The Blue Band made its debut garbed in new uniforms purchased with funds made available from the College of Health, Physical Education, and Recreation as well as the Associated Student Activities. The new-style uniforms were similar to those purchased seven years earlier, the only large difference being the designs on the overlays. Replacing the Nittany Lion Shrine on the back of the overlay were the words "Nittany Lions" in block letters. The large letters on the front were changed to "PS," and on both front and back the blue "lightning bolts" that ran along the edge of the overlay were removed.

A Blue Band tradition was begun at Band Day in 1971 and became a Blue Band trademark at pregame: the Drum Major Flip. Drum Major Jeff Robertson, dissatisfied with his pregame entrance and introduction to the spectators at Beaver Stadium during the first two games of the 1971 season, decided to try something new. In his pregame introduction, Robertson ran to the middle of the field through the center of the band as usual, but then performed a back flip instead of tossing his baton. Robertson recounts the story behind why he did that:

> [When I auditioned to be Penn State's drum major] I was a bit apprehensive because my high school's drum majors did not twirl a baton at all where I was from, and I had never tossed a baton in my life. The first home game, I was planning to do the [baton] toss. Never having seen [last year's drum major and successful baton-tosser] Chip Willis perform, I also did not think of the necessity for wearing cleats. During pregame, I broke the formation, strutted like crazy, and tried to stop to make the toss. Unfortunately, my feet kept going, landing me on my rear end. The crowd was sympathetic the first time. The second home game wasn't much better than the first. I slipped but didn't fall, and I lost the plume from my hat. The crowd was not amused.
>
> I had been in gymnastics as a young person and into high school. By the third home game, I was getting desperate. I didn't want to fall again, and I had no confidence in my baton toss. It was Band Day, and there were hundreds of high school students there on top of the normal crowd. I thought of doing a front flip [instead of a baton toss], but couldn't figure out how to make it smooth from the strut, so I decided to try a back flip from a roundoff.
>
> When it came time for pregame that day, I took the normal ribbing from the band members [for my first two pregame performances]. But I had my cleats so I wouldn't slip and I put a football helmet chin strap on my hat to keep it in place. When I broke through the block, everything went silent. I did the flip and actually landed on my feet, although I swung my arms down to stay balanced. The crowd at first wasn't sure if I had slipped again, but I was on my feet and there was some applause. I guess some of them figured out what I did.
>
> Sometime after that Band Day but before the next game, Dr. Dunlop came up to me and asked if I intended to continue doing the flip. When I told him I did, all he said was, "All right, but don't screw it up."

As popular as the flip was to the fans watching, Robertson performed it every game thereafter. "I had no intention of creating a tradition," Robertson said. "I was just surviving with the skills I had." Over the years the flip has evolved into a mid-air front somersault. The tradition of the flip continues today with a superstition attached to it: "If the drum major makes the flip and lands on his feet, the Nittany Lions are sure to win the football game."

The newly attired band traveled that season to two away games, both late in the season. The first was to the home of its traditional foe, the University of Pittsburgh, on November 20. The second trip was to Knoxville, Tennessee, to play the University of Tennessee Volunteers. The game was on December 4, and in front of a national television audience. The Blue Band ended its marching season almost four weeks later with a trip to the Cotton Bowl in Dallas, Texas, on December 31. The band cheered the Nittany Lions to victory against the University of Texas, 30 to 6.

The Concert Band in 1972 had memorable trips as well, the farthest journey being to Atlanta, Georgia, in mid-March. But even as the Concert Band was receiving accolades in the local papers that spring term, the Marching Blue Band was being criticized for discriminating against women. One critic wrote to the editor of the *Collegian* on February 4, 1972: "Traditions are good, generally, but when they only serve to perpetuate an injustice, they need to be ended. The Marching Blue Band, always an all-male group, is an example of such an unreasonable tradition." The debate focused on whether women had the stamina to be in the Blue Band raged in the student newspaper for the remainder of the spring and summer. But even before the debate started in February, Dr. Dunlop had been making preparations to add at least one woman to the band.

Judy Shearer, a sophomore who had attended the Schuylkill branch campus the year before, contacted Dunlop in the late fall regarding twirling baton for the Blue Band. Shearer, a professional baton-twirler with Atlantic City's Steel Pier, believed she could be an asset to the band and asked Dunlop to consider auditioning her. He agreed, and the audition took place on January 14, 1972, in the basement of the Department of Education building, Chambers. "The ceiling was so low I had to twirl the baton on my knees. Otherwise I couldn't toss it at all," Shearer recalled. Impressed with her skill and determination, Dunlop agreed to use her for some of the halftime shows. Later that spring he decided that a full rank of majorettes could accent the band well (and possibly relieve the growing pressure to integrate the band), and he asked Shearer to help with the auditions.

During the years 1943–45, World War II shipped many American men from college campuses to Europe and the Pacific. As a result, there was a dearth of male students at all colleges, including Penn State. Hummel Fishburn, the Blue Band Director at the time, allowed women to play in the Blue Band to fill the holes in instrumentation. It was always implicit that this was a temporary situation—a "sacrifice," like so many during the war, that would be remedied once the war was over. And such was the case in the fall season of 1946, when Fishburn split the band into the spring-term Concert Blue Band, which allowed coeds, and the Marching Blue Band, once again a men-only organization.

Arguments concerning the inequality of the Marching Band were numerous on both sides. Those in favor of allowing women argued that high schools across the nation and many fine college bands, such as the USC Trojan Band and Pittsburgh, had women in the ranks and that the physical strain of being in the Blue Band, although strenuous, did not preclude all women. Those who were against integrating females into the band, although few among the students, took the position that the Blue Band tradition and its military roots made it somehow not "right" to include women and that the band was fine just the way it was. There were still many bands in the Midwest that were all-male, it was argued, and they were also some of the finest bands in the nation.

Hoping to comply with the sentiments of many on campus without actually adding women as musicians to the rank and file, Dunlop introduced the first Blue Band majorettes, led by Judy Shearer: Charlotte Behm, Leanne Czekaj, Marie DiRinoldo, Darcy Fishell, Jere Fiyalko, Janese Hillings, Susan Jeffords, Nancy Mark, Lynann Stevenson, Debra Valencic, and Mary Wilchek. This group of twelve was selected from a field of sixty applicants during the previous spring term. The first performance of the majorettes was on Saturday, September 30, 1972, during the Penn State game with Iowa at Beaver Stadium.

In spite of the new majorette squad, the Blue Band still was being criticized for gender inequality in the ranks of musicians. Two university groups paying close attention to the subject were the Association of Women's Studies and the Associated Student Activities (ASA) Budget Committee. The ASA, formerly a part of the All-College Cabinet, traditionally funded one of the away football games each season, but this practice came under scrutiny by budget members. One particularly outspoken member, Undergraduate Student Vice-President Fern Itzkowitz, stated that because the Blue Band excluded females the ASA was unable to fund them. "According to federal law," she explained in a February 1973 *Collegian* article, "we can't give money to an organization which discriminates on the basis of sex." The law she cited was Title 9 of the Higher Education Act, which became effective in June 1972 and stated that no person shall be excluded on the basis of sex from participating in any activity at universities receiving federal grants or contracts.

To be fair to Jim Dunlop, the reason for

In 1971 the Blue Band acquired new uniforms with slightly different overlays. The new overlays had tassels on the shoulders as well as the words "Nittany Lions" on the back, instead of the Nittany Lion Shrine.

excluding women was not sexism on his part (he had worked with female musicians in the Concert Blue Band for twenty-five years and had featured many as soloists), but rather his stubbornness about having an outside group dictate whom he could and could not admit to his band. Dunlop submitted a rebuttal to the *Collegian*: "Women have never been denied auditions for the band, but since it has always been traditionally male, none have auditioned. I've said all along that women can try out." He did not gain many supporters, however, because later in the article he made the unfortunate statement "I'm not saying that women can't play horns or march. We have a good thing going. Why change it?"

After months of debate about whether women should audition for the Marching Band, Dr. Dunlop finally acquiesced, but said: "We're not going to let women into the band just to satisfy women's lib. If they make it, they will have to make it on their own as musicians."

The Touch of Blue

The majorette uniform has changed often since the first majorettes in 1972.

On January 14, 1972, Judy Shearer auditioned to be the first majorette in the Penn State Blue Band. Band Director James Dunlop was so impressed with her that he decided to add a full rank of twelve baton twirlers to the Blue Band. After auditioning sixty applicants, Shearer and Dunlop chose the eleven others who joined Shearer for the first fall season.

In 1978 the majorette uniforms were changed to an almost all white body suit with "just a touch" of blue highlighting. After that, the majorette squad was known as the "Touch of Blue."

Since 1972 many talented women have had the distinction of being in the Touch of Blue, which has twenty members today. The squad practices the same hours as the Blue Band, but usually not with them, practicing with a tape of the music for the next show. Membership in the "Touch of Blue" requires talent in baton twirling and dancing and being generally physically uniform with the rest of the squad, but, above all, lots of hard work and dedication. Many members of the majorette squad have gone on to be professional cheerleaders in the National Football League and professional majorette instructors at high schools and colleges around the nation, thanks to the experience they received as one of the elite Touch of Blue.

For the first time since 1945, female musicians were accepted as members of the Blue Band in August 1973. Eight women auditioned during Band Camp, the week-long tryout and practice session that starts the Blue Band's season. Of the eight, five made the final cut: Linda Hall, clarinet; Kathryn Murphey, trumpet; Carol Gabler, French horn; Susan Nowlin, percussion; and Debbie Frisbie auditioned on baritone horn but found a place as a flag bearer. These women were the first of many over the years to join the Blue Band, which in 1999 contained a female membership of approximately 120, nearly 40 percent of the musicians.

Even though majorettes had been in the band for more than a year, and talented female musicians marched side by side with male musicians, the women did not feel truly accepted until later in the season. Judy Shearer tells about the moment when the Blue Band was truly integrated:

> It was 1973 and the band had gone to Annapolis for the Penn State game versus Navy. When the Midshipmen saw girls on their campus and eating in their dining hall, they all wanted to talk to us. The friendlier the Navy guys got, the more protective our guys became. From that time on, it seemed we girls were just part of the Blue Band gang.

In the spring semester of 1974 more criticism of Penn State's athletic bands appeared in the pages of the *Collegian*. The Basketball Pep Band was accused of playing too loudly at the games in Rec Hall. It was argued that the players were having difficulty concentrating when the music was so loud, which seems absurd considering the noise level of the cheering fans and that the band was forbidden to play during the actual play of the game. The complaint had come from a student who was not on the basketball team, and when the team was approached about the subject, it was quick to dismiss the charge that it was bothersome. Indeed, some said, the loudness of the pep band help spur the team to play harder.

The Concert Band concerned itself that spring with happier thoughts. Lawrence Marynak and Kathleen Brown, both graduating members of the band, became the first Blue Band couple to marry each other. Later that summer they moved to Colorado, where they were members of the U.S. Air Force Academy Band. Not only were they the first married couple in the Air Force Band, but Kathleen Brown was the first female member of the Academy's band.

The 1974 fall season marked the end of an era for the Blue Band and for Penn State. On November 16, 1974, unbeknownst to the spectators, the Blue Band, or even the sixty high school bands participating, the last Band Day took place during a regular season game. In the spring of 1975 the Athletic Department told Dr. Dunlop that Band Day would have to be retired. The reason was not lack of interest or participation, but simply financial. Athletics could no longer afford to donate almost 6,000 tickets to the Blue Band to seat high school students when many times that number paying sports fans were clamoring to get tickets.

The Blue Band traveled often in 1974, playing Army at West Point in early October, and Pittsburgh on Thanksgiving in late November. A small pep band of fifty members attended the North Carolina game in Chapel Hill as well. The final event of the season was the Cotton Bowl in Dallas, where the Blue Band performed its routines and witnessed Penn State's victory over Baylor 41 to 20.

Tragedy struck the Blue Band the next summer, 1975. On August 7, Jim Dunlop, Director of the Blue Band for more than twenty-five years, died suddenly of a heart attack at the age of sixty-four while attending a summer music camp at the University of Utah in Salt Lake City. Ned Deihl, his assistant director, received the sad news while vacationing in Indiana. "It was really a shock to me," Deihl said. "He had been in such good health. But I hardly had time to grieve. Being August, we had already started preparing for the next season, and the first game was in Philadelphia before classes even started."

The first game was taxing on Deihl, who was now acting director. "I didn't have an assistant and the show was coming up right away. The only concession I had to make was to allow the returning band members back without an audition." With the game only three days after the start of orientation, the band had to learn its show fast. That game was considered a home appearance for the Nittany Lions, even though it was in the opponent's home town of Philadelphia against the Temple Owls.

The rest of the season was challenging for the Blue Band. It appeared in Columbus, Ohio, for the Ohio State game, where it matched its musical skill with the famous Ohio State Marching Band, long considered the benchmark standard for all collegiate band programs. The drum major that year, Eric Felack, became quite unpopular with the football fans. He chose not to do the flip that Jeff Robertson had made so popular for the past four years, and opted instead to toss a mace as his opening stunt for pregame. This was met with a cool reception at Beaver Stadium. "One of the worst experiences of my life was dropping that baton at the Stanford game [the first game at Beaver Stadium in 1975]," Felack said. "I wasn't expecting a negative crowd reaction for not doing the flip, and when I heard the booing it really threw my concentration off."

A saving grace for the 1975 season was homecoming. The Alumni Band returned to campus for the October 4 game, ready to honor the memory of former Band Director Dr. Dunlop with the student Blue Band. In a field formation spelling "Jim," the combined bands performed a salute to Dunlop, performing his favorite march, "Stars and Stripes Forever." Forming the letters "PSU," the bands played a medley of Penn State fight songs, ending the touching tribute.

Tragic news reached the band again, on April 19, 1976. Hummel Fishburn, former Blue Band Director and head of the two music departments at Penn State for many years, passed away. He had charted formations for the band until 1962, and then was the band's home game announcer until 1975.

Ned Deihl had been placed in command of the Blue Band until a nationwide search could be conducted for a permanent replacement for Dunlop. After interviewing four candidates in addition to Deihl, the Music Department decided that with Deihl's twelve years of experience with the Blue Band, and his many accomplishments, Deihl should be

appeared director. On July 1, 1976, Dr. Ned C. Deihl became only the fourth band director in the Blue Band's seventy-seven-year history, succeeding Thompson, Fishburn, and Dunlop.

A new band president was elected that year as well, and another first occurred. Carol Gabler, one of the original five women musicians in the marching Blue Band in 1973, was elected by the members at the beginning of the football season. Since that time, many Blue Band officers have been women.

Eric Felack, the drum major, began his second year. Even though the crowd was now supportive of his high-toss baton routine, the previous year had left him disheartened, and this was his last season as drum major. Of the fans, Felack said to the *Centre Daily Times*: "They were spoiled for the flip. I was doing the best I could and they booed me. Even then, I was proud of what I was doing, but that's when my attitude started changing."

Deihl, with the mandate from the Department of Music, began to transform the band according to his own vision. One of the first changes he made was to purchase "high steppers"

The 1973 Blue Band drum line posing in front of the Nittany Lion Shrine. Susan Nowlin (third from left, standing) was one of the first five permanent female members of the Blue Band.

NED C. DEIHL

Ned C. Deihl, born in 1931, grew up in the rural community of Hamilton, near Mansfield, Ohio. "Being a music director was about the only thing I ever wanted to do, right from high school," Deihl remarked. "Our county high school was so small we didn't have a band director one year when I was a student, so I filled in instead." Dr. Deihl remained at the podium ever since. Enrolling at Miami University of Ohio after high school, Deihl transferred to Indiana University in Bloomington, Indiana, during his sophomore year and earned a bachelor's degree in music education in 1954. "Indiana University had a large, famous music school and a good band program at the time," Deihl recalls.

After receiving his degree, he taught high school music in Spencer, Indiana, for a semester before being drafted into the army in 1954. Deihl spent his basic training at Fort Knox, Kentucky, and then was shipped out to Fort Ord, California, to participate in the band training school there. From there he was sent to Germany to play clarinet in the 7th Army Symphony Orchestra and lead the 9th Division band and choir. The years in the army were "fun," Deihl recalls. "I spent two years in the army. I was fortunate: I got to see much of Europe and perform while many of those at Fort Ord were shipped to Korea for the war."

After his tour of duty was over in 1956 he came back to the United States and earned his master's in music in one year from the University of Michigan, studying under the legendary William Revelli. From there he taught high school music again in Petersburg, Michigan, and South Bend, Indiana, for four years. In 1961 Ned married Janette Martin, a high school English teacher, and eventually had two sons and a daughter, Randall, Mark, and Laura, all of whom are Penn State graduates.

Deihl came to Penn State in 1961 originally planning to earn his doctorate and move on, but he never left. He said that a friend at the University of Michigan went to Penn State for doctoral work and recommended it to him. "Part of my attraction to Penn State was the band assistantship program they had for graduate students. Besides, I had been to the big band programs at Indiana and Michigan and wanted to try a smaller school [of music]."

Dr. Dunlop was instrumental in hiring Deihl as Assistant Director after he got his doctorate in 1962. "Jim knew I had a Big Ten background and wanted to promote that style in the Blue Band. He was more of a conduc-

tor and knew my experience would help modernize the band." For as excellent an organization as the Blue Band was, Deihl was surprised to see how underdeveloped in many ways the Blue Band was when compared with Michigan and Indiana. "For example, Hum Fishburn would write the drill for the halftime show and tack it up on the door of the Armory. The students would write down where their positions were on the field for the practice. So when I came into the band, I started making charts for everybody."

Dr. Deihl started making the drill more sophisticated too. Instead of scatter drills, where the band members simply run from one spot to another to spell words or make pictures, Deihl started charting organized movements from formation to formation, making much more elaborate configurations. As Band Director he changed the marching step from a military six-steps-to-five-yards to eight steps per five yards, which lends itself better to the four-beats-per-measure music and the fast marching tempo. "Marching was not as big a concern in the old days under Jim Dunlop and Hum Fishburn," Deihl said of the changes he made. "When I became the director we started including marching as part of the auditions for the potential Blue Band members."

One of the most visible innovations that Dr. Deihl created for the Blue Band was the "Floating Lions" pregame show in 1965, a Blue Band trademark that has remained virtually unchanged in almost thirty-five years. This pregame show also featured the band marching in a new style: the "high-step," or "chair-step." Another innovation attributable to Deihl that continues today was the start of Bandorama in 1978.

From the time he came to Penn State, Ned Deihl went about turning its "smaller" band program into one of the larger and most respected programs in the United States. During his first year at Penn State in 1961 the Blue Band had 108 members. In 1975, when Dr. Deihl became Penn State's Director of Bands, the Marching Blue Band grew to 166 members. By the time he retired in 1996, Dr. Deihl's band program had grown to a 275-student marching band. To explain increasing the size of the Blue Band, Deihl said: "A larger band is easier to chart than a smaller band. You can do more things with them. Also, Beaver Stadium grew rather large in my days, and we had to be able to fill the place with sound." Deihl also created two basketball pep bands that played for both the women's and the men's games; the Concert White Band for student musicians who had neither the time nor the desire to be in the Blue Band; the Nittany Lion Band, for more students who wanted to participate in a band; and various other ensembles and groups. To Dr. Deihl it was important for all who wanted to participate in a band at Penn State to have the opportunity to do so.

This did not mean that unqualified students made the block in the Blue Band, however. As the university grew bigger, more and more quality musicians auditioned for a rank spot. Even though the band grew to 250 percent of the size it was before Deihl started, more than half the musicians

who attempted to make the Blue Band were cut, a situation that was not much different from before the days of the band's expansion. One former band member commenting on the size of the Blue Band said: "There were bands in the South with over 400 members but Dr. Deihl preferred to limit our numbers to bring out the better musicians. Musicianship always came first in Jim Dunlop's day, and it was that way when Ned Deihl directed the Blue Band too."

Dr. Deihl's accomplishments with the Blue Band and other organizations are extensive. He was named to the American Bandmasters' Association in 1972, served as president of the Eastern Division of the College Band Directors National Association, and served as judge and guest conductor for numerous youth band festivals in the United States and Rome, Italy. He was also involved as a life member with many honorary music fraternities, such as Phi Mu Alpha and Pi Kappa Lambda. In 1985 Dr. Deihl was awarded the Citation of Excellence by the National Bandmasters' Association, and in 1988 he guest-conducted the U.S. Army Band at the American Bandmasters' Association National Convention. He has written extensively on music education and was a pioneer in computer-aided learning for instrumental music, having two separate research projects funded by the U.S. Department of Education. He also co-directed university research involving concepts in music for young children.

Dr. Deihl is a quiet, reserved individual with a passion and strength of character just under his dignified demeanor. "I'm not a very charismatic person, probably

conservative. Not flamboyant," he described himself in a 1996 *Penn Stater* magazine interview. He chooses his words judiciously and expresses himself carefully, often with small hand gestures to punctuate a point. "He never needed to raise his voice to get you to do what he wanted," said another former Blue Band member. He is also known to his colleagues and former students for his dry wit, which often comes quickly and unexpectedly to those who do not know him well. Above all, he is a modest man who likes to draw attention not to himself but to the accomplishments of the Blue Band, which he "just happened to direct" for more than twenty years. In his almost thirty-five years with the Pennsylvania State University, he molded the Blue Band from merely a well-respected program to a top-notch, modern, Big Ten style band that was and still is years ahead of its time. This and his shaping of the other bands at Penn State were a major contribution to the university's reputation for having two of the best music and music education programs in the nation. 🐚

The Corner Concert

*D*uring a football game, fans
may hear the glorious tones
of the traveling trumpets, but after
the game most depart for their cars.
Only a few thousand fans, those
who stay to hear the Corner Concert,
actually receive all the Blue Band
has to offer. The postgame concert,
held by the Penn State drum line and
affectionately called the "Corner
Concert," is performed in the north-
west corner of Beaver Stadium after
every game.

The Corner Concert, by one of
the most prestigious collegiate drum
lines in America, consists of percussion practice drills, and the highlight
of this short but memorable concert is
the performance of the "Parade
Order." During the Parade Order the
percussion line gets to show off
talents that normally would not be
highlighted during the parade to the
stadium. As well as the precise
playing of the entire drum line, the
cymbal and quintuple players add
visual routines to this exciting
performance. For some spectators
and fans, a true Penn State football
game is not complete until they have
heard the Corner Concert by the Penn
State drum line.

for the drum line. This piece of hardware elevates the snare drums away
from the legs of the drummers and allows drummers to march high- step
(or "chair-step") with the rest of the band. The Blue Band, forming pictures and numbers for decades on the field, began to form more abstract
designs at halftime, not definite tangible objects as much as patterns.

During the 1977 season the Blue Band saw a huge increase in
its membership; membership jumped from 174 members to 210. The
largest increase was in the trumpet section, which grew from 38 musicians to 48, adding a new rank. The silks also increased in number, from
twelve to sixteen. The reason for the expansion of the band was not
totally due to the wealth of talented musicians who were enrolled at
Penn State in 1977. The size of Beaver Stadium was also a factor. As the
stadium expanded over the decade, the Blue Band had to expand too,
so that its shows could be seen and heard by everyone attending the
games. The stadium in 1977 was enlarged to seat 60,000, and by the 1978
season, it held 76,000. According to Dr. Deihl, as quoted in the *Centre
Daily Times*, the increase in membership did not water down the Blue
Band's quality: "The expansion has not affected the standard of the
individual player. In fact, I think the overall quality of the expanded
sections, man to man, is better than last year."

The new drum major for the 1977 season was Ron Louder, an
Altoona native who brought back the now famous Front Flip. Because
of the negative reaction from the fans at the football games to Eric
Felack's decision not to do a flip, Deihl required that potential drum
majors auditioning for the Blue Band perform the pregame flip. Louder,
in order to perfect his technique, joined the Penn State Gymnastics
Club.

The 1977 season was lackluster at home. Though the Blue Band
always practiced in the rain, it had no control over whether it would
be allowed to march at the game if it rained. As a marching band of
more than 200 individuals marches on a field, it can do terrific damage
to the field if it is wet, according to Penn State's Athletic Department.
At the first three home games at Beaver Stadium, it rained so badly that
the band was not allowed to march. Homecoming was almost as bad.
The student and alumni bands were allowed to walk onto the field at
halftime into one formation and play a standing concert. Of the seven
home appearances, the Blue Band actually marched in three.

It seemed that in order to present a field show, the Blue Band had
to travel. The band performed a show in Syracuse on October 15 and at
a nationally televised game at Pitt on November 26. Although the band
marched at the Fiesta Bowl game in Tempe, Arizona, on Christmas Day,

that too was a disappointment. The full Blue Band did not go to the game. Unable to afford sending the entire 210-member Blue Band, Athletics paid to send a fifty-member pep band to the bowl game. Most of those who attended were seniors, with some under-classmen balancing out the instrumentation. But at the game, some band members questioned why the Blue Band had even attended the game, since the pregame and halftime festivities allowed the band only thirty seconds on the field.

In spite of the disappointing fall season, the spring season gave Blue Band members more oppor-tunities to perform. During the basketball season of 1978 a graduate assistant in the Music Education Department, Larry Fisher, approached Dr. Deihl with the idea of reorganizing the pep band into a Jazz Blue Band to perform at the games. With Deihl's approval, Fisher auditioned sixty current Blue Band members and chose twenty-one. Ron Louder made

TOP Because the Blue Band has no indoor facilities, the band practices outside no matter what the weather.

BOTTOM The Blue Band grew during the 1970s, fielding thirteen ranks of twelve players in the block band.

the jazz band, but as saxophone, not as drum major. A music major, Louder explained that the experience might broaden his knowledge of music.

In 1978 Beaver Stadium was remodeled and the north end-zone removed. This forced the Blue Band, which had been making its entrance for its famous pregame show from the north tunnel, to enter from the south tunnel. Instead of having every member of the band learn a new spot, Ned Deihl decided to just change the order of the entrance of the band, the last being first and the first being last. This made the clarinet rank lead the band out of the tunnel and down the field instead of the trombone rank "the way God intended it," according to one former band trombonist. Because the band entered from the south, the band's seats were also moved, toward the south end-zone. For the next nine years, the Blue Band sat on the 30-yard line on the east side away from the press box, on the southern end of the field.

Another novel Blue Band event was inaugurated in mid-November and remains popular today. Dr. Deihl organized the first Blue Bandorama, a concert featuring the Marching Blue Band in a symphonic setting, in Eisenhower Auditorium. The band, which

The sousaphone rank forms the diagonal line in the letter "N" in the Floating Lions drill.

Bandorama is an indoor concert presented by the Marching Blue Band and the Symphonic Band every year, usually on the Friday before the last home football game of the year. The first Bandorama was held in Eisenhower Auditorium in 1978 the day before the Temple University game in mid-November. Since then, Bandorama has been attended every year by thousands of spirited Blue Band fans.

The Symphonic Band plays its concert first and then leaves the stage. After a short intermission, the drum major and the percussion line enter, stopping at the edge of the stage. The percussion line begins its pregame cadence, followed by an entrance by the rest of the Blue Band from the rear of the auditorium to the stage at its famous marching clip of 180 beats a minute down the aisles. Once on stage, the band begins to play the pregame show music. Afterward the band members take their seats and the concert continues with favorite stadium songs and the best selections from the year's halftime shows. The concert also features indoor routines by the Blue Band Silks, the Touch of Blue, the feature twirlers, and sometimes guest solo performances by professional musicians, accompanied by the band.

Bandorama was the brainchild of Dr. Ned C. Deihl, who wanted to present the Blue Band's musical football season to more than just those who attend the football games and to give the fans a chance to hear the Blue Band's musicians in a concert setting. Considering the number of Blue Band fans there are, it's no wonder that Bandorama is a sold-out event year after year.

consisted of only a portion of the full band to balance the indoor event, played selected favorites from the football season, including the pregame music. Geared toward true Blue Band fans, Bandorama was well attended with hundreds in the audience and is a tradition that continues today.

The big trip this season was to New Orleans for the Sugar Bowl against Alabama on New Year's Day. One of the largest bands in the nation, Alabama's Million Dollar Band was almost twice as large as Penn State's band. When they formed a large "USA" during the combined show at pregame, Alabama formed the "U" and the "A" while the Blue Band became the "S." By all accounts, the better band was Penn State's, whose halftime show was considered more entertaining and whose music was more controlled and balanced. Lori Bowers, the head majorette known as the "Blue Sapphire," did not remember the trip as being altogether pleasant. Upon arriving at the band's hotel, she discovered that a large portion of her trip money was either lost or stolen. At the game she almost fainted while performing her routines during halftime. When she returned home, a visit to a doctor revealed that she had a severe case of mononucleosis.

The off-season gave the band a new academic home. In a cost-cutting move the dean of the College of Education, Henry J. Hermanowicz, decided to "cast off" the Blue Band, music education, and art education majors. In an article in the January 19, 1979, issue of the *Collegian*, he explained his decision: "The organizational difference between art and

Past drum majors, as well as musicians, come back to Penn State for Alumni Band every year.

art education or music and music education is a luxury the University can no longer afford." He added: "If the Music Education Department cannot be absorbed, I will recommend that the University eliminate it over a period of a few years." Considering that Director Dr. Ned Deihl and Associate Director Dr. Darhyl Ramsey both were employed by the Department of Music Education, the outcome of this move was of great importance to the future of the Blue Band—not to mention that the course for the Blue Band was offered in music education. Fortunately, the dean of the College of Arts and Architecture, Walter H. Walters, agreed to absorb the two departments and the Blue Band. Since they were now in the School of Music, Blue Band members started to receive music credits for participation in the band. Previously, Blue Band was counted as a physical education credit and could be used to fulfill the physical education requirement for graduation.

The move to the College of Arts and Architecture was the Blue Band's last major change in the decade. The band retired many of its old traditions and ushered in new ones in the 1970s—more than any other ten-year period in its history. Many of the innovative features of the Blue Band that are so distinctive now were introduced during the decade, and many are so unique to the band that they have become trademarks today. The next decade saw the beginnings of a new maturing of the Blue Band's style, incorporating the new traditions and the old in a way that made them the Blue Band's own.

11 | Continuing the Excellence, 1980–1989

THE DECADE OF THE 1980S *for the Blue Band was a*

time of growth, though not as dramatic as in the 1970s, and

of increased national exposure. Band enrollment grew from

230 members at the start of the 1980 football season to a high

of 285 in 1987. The band formations, written by Dr. Ned C.

Deihl and then by his former assistant and current band

director, Dr. O. Richard Bundy, became even more elaborate

and sophisticated, using more curvilinear designs and less

marching straight down or across yard lines. The halftime

entrances, to capture the attention of the spectators better,

changed in 1980 from simply running into place from the

sidelines in an unorganized "scramble" to marching in place

to a drum cadence from both sidelines. The music performed

continued to feature a fairly even mix of traditional marching band pieces, familiar classical music, and modern rock and pop arrangements, as it does today.

Many of the halftime performances were thematic, much as they had been in the past. In 1981 for the Penn State game hosting Alabama early in the season, the Blue Band performed a show based on TV commercial jingles. TV music was not new for the band, which had performed a similar show in the early 1960s. The new version of this show featured the commercial jingle music of Pepsi, 7-Up, Coke, Mountain Dew, Budweiser, Ford Motors, Bell Telephone, and McDonald's. The band also performed music from the TV shows "Dallas" and "CHiPs," and a jazzy version of NBC's "Chimes Festival," featuring feature twirler Lori Bowers.

Central Pennsylvania was treated to a televised special about the Blue Band on Altoona's WTAJ-TV (Channel 10) on Tuesday, December 23. The show featured excerpts from the past season's pregame and halftime shows at the football games, as well as that year's Bandorama. Hosting the show was WTAJ commentator John Riley and Dr. Deihl, who was preparing the band for its final trip of the season to the Fiesta Bowl later that week, striving for musical supremacy against Ohio State.

The next year saw the band travel back to the Fiesta Bowl, this time matched up with another famous marching band university, USC. A bowl trip for a college band is extremely hectic, exhausting, and exciting all at the same time. While a lot of fun, it is also a lot of hard work.

The 1981 Fiesta Bowl trip was typical and provides a good example of what a band bowl trip schedule is like. With the men in coats and ties, and the ladies in dresses and business suits, the Blue Band started loading the buses at 5:00 A.M. on Wednesday, December 30, at the Music Building in State College. Making it to Harrisburg International Airport by 7:30 A.M., the band checked in and took off for Arizona by 9:00. Arriving at Phoenix Airport at 2:00 P.M. MST, the band checked into its hotel by 3:00, changed, and began practicing that afternoon. By 7:30 P.M. the students were on their own for the evening.

The 1981 Blue Band in Beaver Stadium.

The next day, New Year's Eve, started with the fully uniformed Blue Band at breakfast at 8:15 A.M. Leaving soon after for Arizona State University's Sun Devil Stadium, the home of the Fiesta Bowl, the band practiced until 10:45. Fifteen minutes later the band was traveling to Phoenix's Civic Plaza for the Bowl Game Kickoff Luncheon and entered playing fight songs. Returning to the hotel by 2:00 P.M., some volunteers left again to perform for a pep rally at Mountain Shadows resort. At 7:00 P.M. the full band practiced again for an hour. By 8:30 P.M. the students dressed for a New Year's Eve dinner and dance sponsored by the

Alumni Band members usually sit in the north end-zone during homecoming.

hotel. Although most stayed until midnight and beyond, some turned in early, exhausted from the schedule and knowing that morning would soon be upon them.

On game day, Friday, January 1, the band had a 7:45 A.M. wake-up call and was practicing again by 8:45. After practice, the band was on its way to Sun Devil Stadium by 9:30. When the buses were finally unloaded, the band lined up for pregame positions at 11:00. Kicking off at 11:30, the Fiesta Bowl witnessed the Blue Band perform its thoroughly practiced bowl show and other music throughout the game. After cheering the Nittany Lions to victory over USC, 26 to 10, the Blue Band loaded the instruments on the buses, which then headed directly to the airport. The band members themselves headed back to the hotel for one last dinner in Tempe and grabbed an overnight flight back to Harrisburg, eventually returning to State College in the early hours the next morning.

Is a bowl trip worth this whirlwind pace? Of course, said Greg Graham, a former saxophone player in the early 1980s. "Bowl trips keep the band going. They are good for [the Blue Band's] recruitment of new members as well as for the football team." Another former band member, Dave Arnoldi, a sousaphone player in the late 1980s, summed it up this way: "Besides the pregame show, a bowl game is about the most fun you can have in the band. Both are a lot of hard work, but in the end the excitement you feel from the fans makes up for all the effort you put in."

The Blue Band started the 1982 fall season on the wrong foot, literally. With four home games in a row in September, the brutal early season practice schedule took its toll on two members in key positions. Carol Wilt, the Blue Sapphire, broke her foot during practice in the preseason and was unable to perform for the first three games of the season. Tony Petroy, the new drum major, also injured himself badly enough to sit out until mid-October. While practicing the flip, Petroy landed on his hands, breaking his third finger on one hand and causing a spiral fracture in the other. Unlike Wilt, who did not have a backup, Petroy had his position filled in the interim by a freshman band member, Greg Stock. Stock was not free from injury either, however, wearing ace bandages on his sprained ankles during the early season, but he performed the flip flawlessly at the games until Petroy's return.

The football fans were especially rowdy that year. Expecting one of the greatest seasons ever on the gridiron for the Nittany Lions, the stadium crowd often became over-exuberant, even hooliganish. During the final seconds of the game against the University of Nebraska, spectators from Beaver Stadium's southern stands, mainly students, were preparing to rush the field and tear down the goalposts to celebrate the apparent victory. As the play was stopped, the top rows kept pushing downward as the bottom rows waited for the end of the regulation time period. As they came into the south end-zone at the end of the game, stadium security officers did what they could to prevent the fans from injuring themselves without stopping them forcibly from taking down the goalposts. It seemed inevitable that both goalposts would be destroyed.

Fortunately for Beaver Stadium and Penn State, the Blue Band was there. Tradition-ally, the band forms a large sideline-to-sideline block in the middle of the field after the game to perform a short postgame concert. The band formed, two and a half yards apart per musician, while the mob massed in the south end-zone. As the unruly mob encroached into the first few ranks of the band, the band held its ground, refusing to yield. Although the south goalpost was lost, the Blue Band's block formation effectively barred the onslaught of ravenous fans from rushing to the north goalpost, saving it from sure destruction.

Penn State's top law enforcement officer, Director of University Safety D. E. Stormer, was especially grateful to the Blue Band for its heroic effort. "Having confronted a number of crowds over the years," he wrote in a letter to Ned Deihl, "I can appreciate the courage and dedication these band members demonstrated in maintaining their individual positions in the face of an on-rushing crowd. Not only did they continue to play, but they formed an effective crowd barrier. Please convey my sincere appreciation to them for a job well done."

The crowd got worse as the Nittany Lions defeated team after team. At the last game of the regular season, their biggest rival, Pittsburgh, came to Beaver Stadium with the Pitt Band. The crowd was particularly nasty to the visitors, and especially to the Pitt Band, pelting them with marshmallows and verbally abusing them as they sat in the south end-zone stands. With twenty-three seconds remaining in the game, the crowd rushed the north goalpost and leveled it. As the game finished, the crowd charged the opposite goalpost when the Pitt Band tried to leave the stadium to avoid the madness. But the band was trapped by the crush of people. In the end, the Pitt Band director, Don Hower, was hit by the goalpost as it fell, although he escaped injury. Other Pitt Band personnel were not as lucky. The crowd began pummeling some of the musicians, ripping their uni-forms, trampling their instruments, punching a few, including one female member, and sending one to the hospital with a concussion from a blow from a metal pipe.

The Feature Twirlers

The Feature Twirler position was created in 1972 by Judy Shearer when she asked Blue Band Director Jim Dunlop for the opportunity to perform with the band. Originally the majorettes' captain, the feature twirler position eventually distin- *guished itself apart from the rest of the majorettes, being featured during one Blue Band song every halftime show. The position was named the "Blue Sapphire" at approximately the same time the majorettes came to be known as the "Touch of Blue." The name "Blue Sapphire" disappeared for a while during the late 1980s and early 1990s when two individuals were chosen as feature twirlers: Lori Branley and John Mitchell.*

Eleven individuals in the history of the Blue Band have been Penn State feature twirlers: Judy Shearer (1972–73), Lori Donaldson (1974–77), Lori Bowers (1978–81), Carol Wilt (1982), Jamie Ritenour (1983–84), Donna Wolter (1985–88), Lori Branley (1989–91), John Mitchell (1989–92), Cheryl Smith (1993), Jennifer Steward (1993), and Christine Wolfe (1994–99).

Auditions for this position are quite competitive, and previous feature twirler experience is no guarantee for keeping the position. In 1989 both Lori Branley and John Mitchell were so evenly matched that the Blue Band staff could not *choose—so the staff decided to accept them both.*

Since 1989 the feature twirler position has been coached by Judy Shearer-Lawrence, the first feature twirler. When asked for her opinion when the band staff could not choose between Lori Branley and John Mitchell, she was soon hired to coach them both. The feature twirler position today continues to improve under the experienced coaching of the first. ⊸

The Nittany Lion Mascot, Nick Indeglio, takes off his head and proposes to Feature Twirler Christine Wolfe at the last home game of the 1997 season.
PHOTO BY STEVE MANUEL

After that disgusting display, Penn State beefed up its security staff at the games. Once again, it was the Blue Band that was the island of dignity in a sea of hooliganism. Before the game, the Blue Band provided apples and other refreshments for the Pitt Band. In fact, the Blue Band members were the only Penn Staters that day who treated them with respect and courtesy—in the opinion of many Pitt Band members who wrote letters to local newspapers concerning the incidents.

The final game of the Penn State season was the National Championship game at the Sugar Bowl. Penn State captured its first championship under Head Coach Joe Paterno with a win over Georgia, 27 to 23, in spite of Heisman Trophy winner Herschel Walker. Adding to the excitement of the game was the Blue Band's halftime show, the theme of which was a salute to James Bond films and featuring such pieces as the themes to *Goldfinger, Live and Let Die,* and *For Your Eyes Only.* The show had been performed at a previous game that season and was considered so good that it was presented again before

The 1981 sousa-phone rank wearing the new overlays. (The white strip on the collar of the overlay is no longer part of the uniform.)

the national audience at the bowl game. The creator of the show, Dick Bundy, was in his first year as a graduate assistant to the band. "That show was one of my proudest moments with the band," Bundy said later.

Part of the James Bond show was performed again at the first home game of the next season against Alabama in a performance called "The Sugar Bowl Revisited." It was brought back again in 1987 for one performance.

Another opportunity to witness the band at its best took place in late November at the sixth annual Bandorama in Eisenhower Auditorium. Along with the traditional fight songs, the band performed halftime music from the past season. "[Bandorama] is an opportunity for people to hear the marching band in a good acoustical setting," Bundy said before the event. Many people did get to hear the band, at the sold-out auditorium and live on television on WPSX-TV, the university's public broadcasting station. It was the first time Bandorama was broadcast live on television.

The next season brought back Band Day. With the expansion of Beaver Stadium over the years to about 84,000 seats by 1984, pressure to secure tickets eased slightly. However, the expansion was not enough to provide the hundreds of seats needed for the high school band members during the regular season. Instead, the Blue Band decided to resurrect Band Day at the Blue and White Game in April. The Blue and White Game is a scrimmage that the football team conducts in Beaver Stadium to evaluate talent for the next year. The offensive team and the defensive team square off against one another in their blue-and-white jerseys, hence the name of the game. Since the game was usually not sold out, the Blue Band could afford to invite a number of Pennsylvania high school bands to the stadium. Although not as large as in previous years, Band Day was successful, and continued to be for about five years.

The charting of the shows became much easier with the purchase of a personal computer during the summer of 1984. Dick Bundy, now Associate Blue Band Director, manned the new device. The old method of charting a field show involved writing positions on grid paper made to look like a football field. Each position was numbered, and the students often worked out how to go from position to position on their own. With a computer, the chance of making errors while charting decreased, and the chore required less time. Each student could receive a personalized chart specifically showing his or her movements and cutting down on practice time too. As a result, the Blue Band was able to create more intricate maneuvers for the following seasons. "It's probably the wave of the future," Ned Deihl said. "There will be some rough waves before smooth sailing, but that's true with all new technology."

One of the intricate computer-aided shows in particular was performed in 1985 and proved to be a favorite with the fans and the Blue Band. The show was based on the music of the rock band "Chicago." The music consisted of arrangements of "Along Comes a Woman," "You're the Inspiration," and medleys of other songs from the Chicago II and Chicago III albums. The band members were especially excited about the show, because the majority of the music had been arranged by Dick Bundy himself. The show was popular enough to present it in part during the Orange Bowl at the end of that season in Miami.

A common thread through the history of the band, at least since the 1920s, was the mixing of popular music with more traditional march themes. That year was no exception. The theme of the first show was "A Remembrance: The 40th Anniversary of World War II," which featured marches and 1940s popular tunes like "Sing, Sing, Sing"; the second show was an unnamed potpourri show featuring such popular 1980s tunes as "Just a Gigolo/ Ain't Got Nobody" and "Axel F/Neutron Dance," and Tchaikovsky's "1812 Overture."

From the top of the Blue Band trailer, staff, alternates, and fans watch the Blue Band practice.

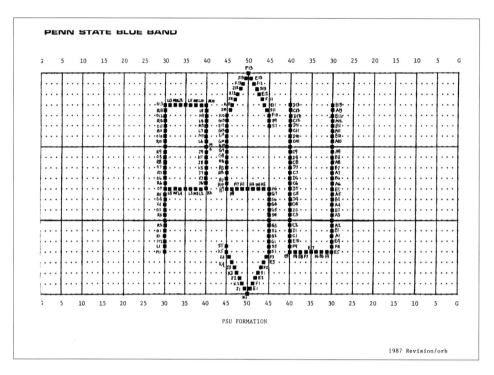

PENN STATE BLUE BAND

PSU FORMATION

1987 Revision/orb

The 1985 PSU chart, where every member of the block band receives a position denoted by a letter and a number. The bottom of the S is always a trumpet player.

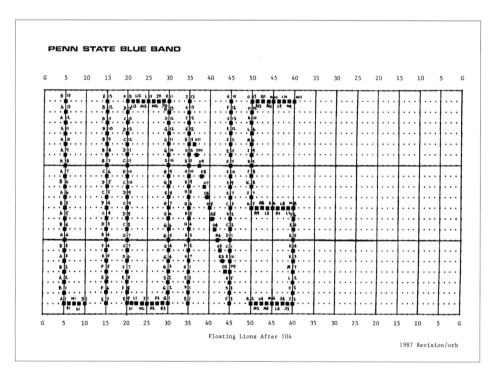

PENN STATE BLUE BAND

Floating Lions After 104

1987 Revision/orb

The Floating Lions drill was revised by Dr. Bundy in 1987 to include a new rank of marchers.

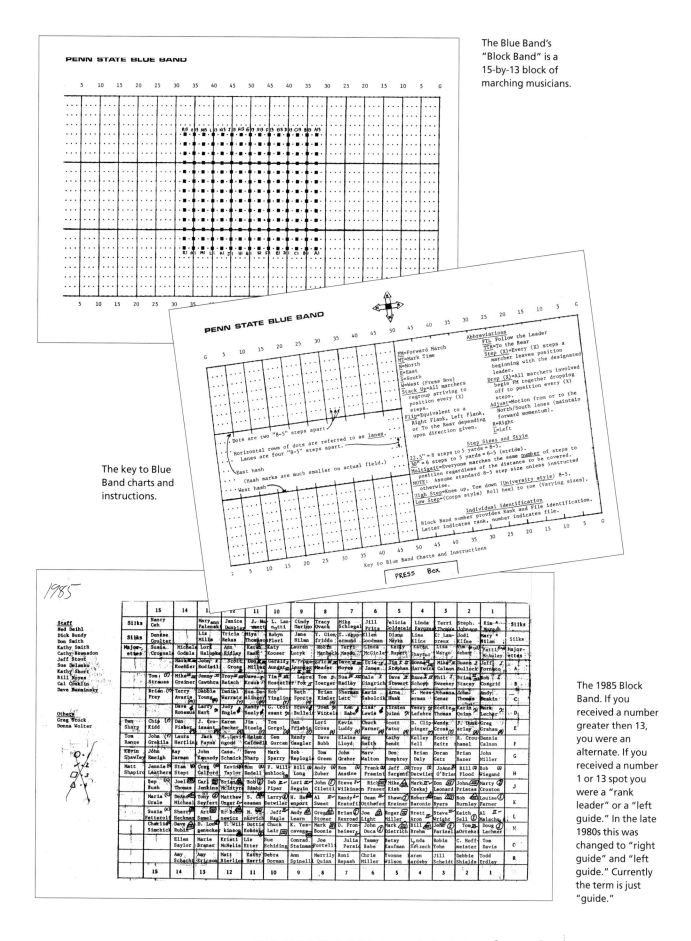

The Blue Band's "Block Band" is a 15-by-13 block of marching musicians.

The key to Blue Band charts and instructions.

The 1985 Block Band. If you received a number greater then 13, you were an alternate. If you received a number 1 or 13 spot you were a "rank leader" or a "left guide." In the late 1980s this was changed to "right guide" and "left guide." Currently the term is just "guide."

The Blue Band performed at the eighth annual Bandorama on November 15, 1985—the first time the entire band had participated in the event. Before, band members auditioned for about 100 spots, but on stage this time were 260 members, the largest Blue Band to date. The Marching Blue Band played American music by composers like Aaron Copland, Duke Ellington, and John Philip Sousa, among other highlights from the past season.

The band was not able to march for the last game of the season against Notre Dame. By the day of the game it had been raining for two weeks and the field at Beaver Stadium was a sloppy mess. The pounding of band members' feet would make things even worse, explained the Athletic Department. By tradition at the last game of the season, during the PSU formation in pregame as the music ended, all band members but the seniors dropped to one knee in tribute to their graduating compatriots. But this year the seniors in the Blue Band, looking forward to one last time out of the tunnel, did not march in their last Penn State game ever or receive the salute on the field. Notre Dame's band had expected to perform on the field too, but was also prevented by the field conditions. Having planned the trip weeks in advance, Notre Dame's band could not back out, so they sat in the stands.

The 1986 season was much more sunny, both for the Blue Band and for the football team. After a disappointing loss to Oklahoma in the Orange Bowl for the National Championship in 1985, the Nittany Lions were prepared to claim the title in 1986. The Blue Band was also in preparation for a memorable season, fielding as many as 275 of the best musicians, flag performers, and majorettes in the nation.

The year marked the 100th anniversary of the Penn State football program, and the Blue Band was on hand to kick off the celebration. The Blue Band's halftime show for the first game of the season was "A Salute to a Century of Excellence." Forming a large "100" in the middle of the field, the band played a special arrangement written for the occasion, "Century of Excellence." The show continued, with the band moving from formation to formation playing football-themed music such as "You Gotta Be a Football Hero" and "Mr. Touchdown." "Thanks for the Memories" and a medley of Penn State songs finished the evening's performance—which was the first night game played at Beaver Stadium, appropriately playing the Temple Owls.

The final performance of the season was at the Fiesta Bowl on January 2, 1987, where Penn State was vying for the National Championship against the University of Miami. The band selected three of its best pieces, which it performed in different shows that season: "Toccata and Fugue in D Minor," "Sing, Sing, Sing," and "Stars and Stripes Forever." Although the songs were not related to one another in any way, the music was a showcase for the powerful sound of the Blue Band. That day was not soon forgotten by anyone who witnessed the game or the halftime show, as both Penn State's football team and the Blue Band outshone the Miami Hurricanes in most dramatic fashion, not only capturing a National Championship in football but also reestablishing the marching band as one of the best in the nation.

Excellent performances by the Blue Band were not limited to the musicians. Greg

Stock, the band's drum major, ended his five-year career in that position at the bowl game. Stock fearlessly performed a successful game flip flawlessly for the thirty-second time during the Fiesta Bowl and, in keeping with the superstition, the football team was victorious. In fact, of the thirty-two games out of thirty-six in which Stock delivered successful flips, the team won thirty of those games. The four flips he missed resulted in three losses for the Nittany Lions. Greg Stock had the longest career of any of the "flipping" drum majors.

Performing for two national championship games in a row and with a talented freshman class, the band expanded again in 1987. Band membership grew to 285 people, making it the largest band in Penn State history. Unfortunately, rain-outs prevented the band from performing on the field at Beaver Stadium two weeks in a row in September. During one of those games, against Alabama, the Nittany Lions lost for the first time at home since 1984.

A rare non-sports-related appearance by the Blue Band took place in Philadelphia on September 17, 1987. The Blue Band led the "We the People 200" parade celebrating the Bicentennial of the United States Constitution and was given several minutes of television time on CBS. Invited by the event committee, Dr. Deihl said of the Blue Band: "We are excited about going. We are pleased that the University wants us to be there and represent the only land-grant college in the commonwealth." With large floats, many other

Because of game starting times, band members rarely had the opportunity to get lunch, so often they brought their own or had something delivered.

bands, and other entertainment, the Blue Band enjoyed performing before the estimated half-million spectators and was proud to attend what was billed as the largest parade in the history of the nation.

Controversy arose during the Syracuse game later that season. A twenty-member pep band from the Blue Band received permission to perform at the Carrier Dome for the game. Traveling at its own expense, the pep band was barred from entering the stadium with its instruments, even after confirming with Syracuse officials the previous day that they could perform inside the Dome. Stadium officials confiscated the instruments and locked them underneath the stadium for the duration of the game. Jerry McCormick, president of the Penn State Club of Greater Syracuse, stated that he was upset at the situation. "I think this is very improper of [Syracuse Athletic Director Jake] Crouthamel and his staff," McCormick was quoted as saying. Things went downhill for Penn State from there, as Syracuse upset Penn State by a huge margin.

The Blue Band was barred again that year, this time by Mother Nature, from being heard at Beaver Stadium at the Notre Dame game of November 21, 1987. The windchill

The Flipping Drum Majors

Since its inception in 1971 eleven individuals have successfully performed the drum major flip: Jeff Robertson (1971–74), Ron Louder (1977–79), Rich Gorodesky (1980–81), Tony Petroy (1982), Greg Stock (1982–86), Jay Dzigas (1987–89), Mike Harrell (1990–91), Tom Roberts (1992–93), Darren Bennett (1994–95), Derrick Ometz (1996), and Seth Walk (1997–98).

The first flip, introduced by Jeff Robertson in 1971, was a back flip, but after Ron Louder the flip evolved into a running front flip, or "Russian" flip. The flip is performed as the band finishes its "Nittany Lion" fanfare during pregame. Running from the center of the band, the drum major executes his flip on the 50-yard line, descends into a split, and salutes the west side stands. Subsequent drum majors have added more flips to their pregame routine, doing as many as three at separate times during the downfield block. After 1977 the flip became a requirement for drum major auditions.

While wearing the eighteen-inch-high hat, called a "shako," "sticking" the flip is no easy feat. The flipping drum majors have had their share of difficulties with their most famous task. While practicing the

flip in 1982, Tony Petroy landed awkwardly and fractured bones in both his hands. With his arms in casts, he was unable to perform the flip until after the homecoming game in mid-October. Fortunately, Freshman Greg Stock filled in for Petroy on the field while he conducted in the stands, making 1982 the only year the Blue Band had two drum majors.

Greg Stock also did not escape injury during a flip. He had fractured his ankle while auditioning again for drum major in 1983, but he kept his position and did not miss a game or an opportunity to flip that year. In 1990 Mike Harrell, during an away game at Boston College, was running out of the block of musicians in pregame when he heard a "pop" in his left leg. Feeling that "something" was wrong, Harrell attempted to complete the flip anyway. That decision proved disastrous, as he landed flat on his back. Getting up off the turf, he proceeded to the back of the band and off the field. After the pregame temperature that day was 30 degrees below zero, so it was the coldest Penn State game in living memory, and perhaps ever. The game was immediately referred to as the "Ice Bowl." "I can't ever remember being that cold," said Sue Marchetti, a Blue Band trumpet player who performed at the game. Because of the severe temperature, the oil that lubricated the moving parts of the brass instruments began to freeze. Managers of the band put glycerol, a sticky but nonfreezing substance at that temperature, on all the slides and valves, but when the glycerol began to wear off, the instruments started to freeze in place. But with two rainouts earlier in the season, the band was eager to march. "The wind had died down just before the half," said Dr. Bundy, "and we thought we would be okay. But as soon as we hit the field it picked back up again." Performing a show from the past, "James Bond," the band got quieter and quieter as instruments began to seize and cold-numbed lips blew through mouthpieces that seemed to squeeze smaller and smaller. By the end of the show, the only performers who could be heard were in the percussion section.

"Oh, it was cold," continued Bundy. "Some poor trombone player got his trombone frozen out in seventh position. After the half, many of the band members went into the

performance, members of the band found him unconscious on the sidelines. He was taken immediately to the hospital, where he learned that he had ligament damage in his left foot. Wearing the wrong shoes for Boston College's Astroturf field was the likely culprit, Harrell said later. Fortunately, the Blue Band was not going to perform at another game for three weeks, as the football team had two more away games. By the time the band was ready to perform again at Beaver Stadium, the ligament damage was mostly healed and Harrell finished the season without missing another flip.

With no alternates assigned to the drum major position, drum majors must perform no matter how they feel. In 1986 Greg Stock returned to do the flip even though he had undergone major arthroscopic knee surgery during the summer. In 1991 Mike Harrell contracted chicken pox but did not miss a game. In 1992, after directing Band Camp, performing at the Kickoff Classic, and then performing at three home

appearances in a row, Drum Major Tom Roberts was hospitalized for exhaustion. Fortunately, he recovered by his next scheduled appearance two weeks later.

As well as practicing daily with the band, most Penn State drum majors practice with the Gymnastics Club to help them perfect their flipping technique. Many potential drum majors have auditioned for the top band position since 1972, including Jen Croissant, the first woman to try out for drum major in 1990. In 1997 Greg Stock showed his appreciation of the Blue Band by endowing a scholarship for future drum majors. The Penn State Blue Band drum majors epitomize the dedication and talent each Blue Band member must have, and for that reason, above all others, they are all held in high esteem by the band and by Penn State fans everywhere. ⫞

TOP The only time there were two drum majors was in 1982.

BOTTOM After the flip, the drum major salutes the spectators.

John Mitchell

*J*ohn Mitchell served as one of
two feature twirlers from 1989
through 1992. He was both the first
African American feature twirler
for the Blue Band and the first male
baton twirler since 1940.

Penn State was not Mitchell's
first choice of colleges. In fact, he
spent his freshman year at the
University of Pittsburgh. At Pitt,
Mitchell auditioned as a baton
twirler with the Pitt Panther Band
but was told that only the drum
major twirls baton. He was offered
a position as a silk. The next fall
he transferred to Penn State and
accepted a co-feature-twirling
position with Lori Branley after the
Blue Band appointed them both.
When Branley graduated in 1992,
Mitchell became the sole feature
twirler for the 1992–93 season. In
1992 he and his coach Judy Shearer
Lawrence attended the National
Baton Twirling Association's World
Championship, held at Notre Dame.
Mitchell won the title as Men's
World Twirling Champion. ⚟

stadium restrooms and stayed there to get out of the wind and cold, like
many of the rest in the stadium."

Sean Smith, a manager with the Blue Band, remembers his experiences at the game. "I had been outside longer than the rest of the band,
taking care of instruments. After the halftime show, my fingers were so
numb I could barely move them. On the sideline the football players
had huge heat jets like giant blow-dryers. I, with about ten other band
members, huddled around one, but I got my hands too close. My white
uniform gloves began to melt on my fingers and finally burned the
fingertips out of them. My hands were so cold I didn't even feel it when
the heat melted the fingerprints right off my fingers."

Seating the band in the stadium came under discussion the next
semester. The band's seats, low to the field near the 10-yard line on the
east sideline, were changed in 1988 to the top seats in the south end-
zone. "Originally, Athletics planned to put us low in the end-zone, but
I protested," said Ned Deihl. "Acoustically, the band would never have
been heard from there." After several meetings with music faculty,
Athletics, and an acoustics expert, it was decided that the best place
for the band to be heard throughout the stadium was right underneath
the scoreboard. "Being near the scoreboard gives the band a lot more
television exposure," said L. Budd Thalman, Associate Athletic Director of Communications. The current band sits in those seats today, but
as Beaver Stadium expands it might have to move again.

In 1989 two feature twirlers were chosen for the Blue Band: John
Mitchell and Lori Branley. It had been a close competition, and the Blue
Band staff wanted to utilize the talents of both performers. Both had
an impressive resume of twirling successes. Branley had been a state
champion twirler in New Hampshire and a member of the World
Champion baton team, the Red Stars, in the 1980s, touring the Soviet
Union, Spain, and Denmark. Mitchell, a transfer student from the
University of Pittsburgh, had been a Pennsylvania State Boys Twirling
Champion four times, a Junior World Solo Twirling Champion, and a
Junior National Young Men's Twirling Champion. Dick Bundy said of
the two: "Blue Band history could not be made by a more dynamic duo.
They are mature, the best of friends, and just outstanding talents."

In addition to all the Penn State games the Blue Band performed
at that year, it was also invited to play at the game between the Buffalo
Bills and the Los Angeles Rams in Buffalo for the twentieth anniversary of "Monday Night Football," which took place soon after the
Syracuse game in mid-October. At the end of the football season the
band finally got to perform again at a bowl game. The previous year,

A close-up of some
trombone players.

A view from the Blue Band's perspective while waiting for the football team's entrance in the Team Aisle formation.

the Nittany Lions had five wins and six losses, the worst season ever under Joe Paterno, and as a result Penn State did not receive a bowl bid. With the invitation to the Holiday Bowl in San Diego, the Blue Band finally got to see a Penn State victory at a bowl game, the first since the National Championship season, when the Lions defeated Brigham Young University 50 to 39.

The Blue Band took an interesting side trip while in San Diego. It was invited to take a tour of the USS *Independence*, a huge Navy aircraft carrier, and to do a concert on deck. Soon after, when the *Independence* traveled to the Persian Gulf during the Gulf War, the band staff drew up a drill that spelled the ship's call letters, planning to send a photograph of the formation to the ship as a thank-you gift in return for the hospitality, and to show the band's support. However, a small but eloquent group of band members who did not believe the war was justified protested that forming such a figure was not in the best interests of the band, because not every band member supported American involvement in the Gulf. As a result, the formation was not performed.

The 1980s were a time of growth and national recognition for the Blue Band, which was seen on television frequently during the decade, at bowl games and other events. Often the fortunes of the football team drove the fortunes of the Blue Band. Adaptation to change in this decade was significant for the band, as it had always been. Constantly trying to find ways to better itself, the band started new traditions and improved on old ones. As the 1990s began, the Blue Band, well respected in marching band circles already, continued to earn the respect of other universities. Later in the 1990s, changes in the Athletic Department also brought about changes for the band, challenging the organization as never before. The band began to perform against other similar university marching programs, providing greater competition.

12 | Joining the Elite, 1990–1999

THE 1990S HAVE BEEN *an exciting time for the Blue Band.*
New challenges or old—the Blue Band continues to grow
and change in order to face them successfully. Usually the
challenges are triggered by events that begin from outside the
Blue Band, over which the band has no control. As a result,
the band adapts, and those adaptations are evident through-
out the decade, augmenting the Blue Band and improving it.
Sometimes the band anticipated the future and adapted or
made improvements even before something happened that
required change. An example of this is Penn State's induction
into the Big Ten Athletic Conference in 1993. Penn State's
athletic teams are a good fit with the Big Ten, and the
Blue Band is an even closer fit. It is comparable in style to
many of the other Big Ten college bands. It seems almost as

Mike Harrell, 1990–91 drum major.

OPPOSITE PAGE John Mitchell and Lori Branley, feature twirlers during the 1989, 1990, and 1991 seasons.

if the Blue Band had been preparing for the move, even if not consciously, for decades.

The band took other progressive actions throughout the decade, making history. The 1989–90 season saw the first African American man selected as a feature twirler in the Blue Band: John Mitchell. In 1990 the first African American man was featured in another prominent Blue Band role, that of the Blue Band's drum major. Many consider Drum Major Mike "Bull" Harrell one of the finest drum majors in the Blue Band's long history. When asked why Harrell was chosen as drum major, Dr. Ned Deihl replied, "Mike was selected for that position because of his outstanding leadership skills, athletic ability, and musical talent."

Mike Harrell was a commanding presence both on and off the field. Certainly one of the most athletic drum majors in history, he was able to make the famous drum major flip appear effortless. A former baritone horn player in the band, Harrell was and still is an excellent musician, capable of playing and conducting well. When asked about being the first African American drum major, Harrell shrugged and replied: "I am proud of being black, but I don't want people to focus on it. I want to be recognized because of my achievements." Harrell's first public appearance as drum major was on September 8, 1990, during the Penn State game with the University of Texas.

As drum major, Harrell was in command of a 274-piece band. When it was believed that the Blue Band was too large in 1987, the Blue Band cut back its membership the next year, from 285 to 265, but by 1990 it had grown back slightly, to 274. The band today remains approximately this size.

The band still suffered misfortunes owing to poor weather on game days. Always disappointed when it cannot march, band members are also embarrassed if a visiting marching band is banned from the field because of weather too. This happened in 1985, when Notre Dame's Fighting Irish Band came to Beaver Stadium, and it happened again in 1990. The Pride of the Orange, Syracuse's marching band, was on campus before it found out that it couldn't perform its halftime field formations because of inclement weather and current field conditions. This was quite unfortunate because Syracuse was released from Penn State's football schedule and this game was the last opportunity to see the Pride of the Orange perform in Happy Valley.

Other trouble awaited the 1991 season. It had been twenty years since the Blue Band had been under fire for sex discrimination. During the beginning of the 1991 fall season,

however, the band was forced into the debate again. The issue that year was the physical uniformity of the Touch of Blue.

To ensure uniformity, members of the majorette squad had "weigh-ins" twice weekly. The stated reason for the weigh-ins was the limited number of majorette uniforms. Selection of new squad members during auditions was contingent not only on the candidate's baton and dance skills but also on their physical relation to the rest of the squad. As Feature Twirler Coach Judy Shearer-Lawrence explained it, "If you have a seven-foot giant and the rest of the girls are five feet tall, who are you going to cut?" Of course, those who had a problem with the weigh-ins were not thinking of height discrimination.

A faculty member concerned about the weigh-ins, Michael Johnson, Associate Professor of Women's Studies and Sociology, wrote a letter to Dr. Deihl rebuking the Blue Band staff for such "antiquated practices." "The real issue is the extent of the focus on the women's bodies, and on the majorettes as not only skilled twirlers but objects of sexual interest," Johnson said in part. The letter was co-signed by two students after a female student complained about sexual discrimination in majorette tryouts. Deihl replied to Johnson that he would not object to a policy review concerning the Blue Band majorettes. After a brief correspondence between Deihl and Johnson, the situation was resolved to their mutual satisfaction. Although certain policies concerning the majorettes were made more lenient, some physical restrictions still apply for athletic, aesthetic, and practical reasons.

In 1991 the Blue Band members, whose immediate thoughts were on performing rather than controversy, played before the largest crowds in Beaver Stadium history to that date. The expansion of the stadium meant that approximately 94,000 spectators at every game saw and heard the pregame and halftime shows. The Blue Band also traveled more that year than in many previous years, starting the season with the Kickoff Classic in the Meadowlands near New York City against Georgia Tech. Another away game in Baltimore against the University of Maryland featured a performance by the Blue Band,

The Nittany Lion Mascot and the Blue Band drum major, two of the most recognizable icons on football Saturdays.

as did a professional football game in Buffalo, New York. The season ended with a trip to the Fiesta Bowl in Tempe, Arizona, to perform for Penn State fans and the opponents, the University of Tennessee.

With the start of the 1992 football season, Drum Major Mike Harrell retired and returned to playing baritone horn in the rank and file. Because of a small shattered bone in his right foot, he was cautioned not to perform the flip lest he aggravate the injury. With that, Harrell's flipping days were over. Harrell was replaced by Tom Roberts, another baritone horn player, who continued to play his horn during the spring basketball season in the Basketball Pep Band.

That year also saw the departure of Feature

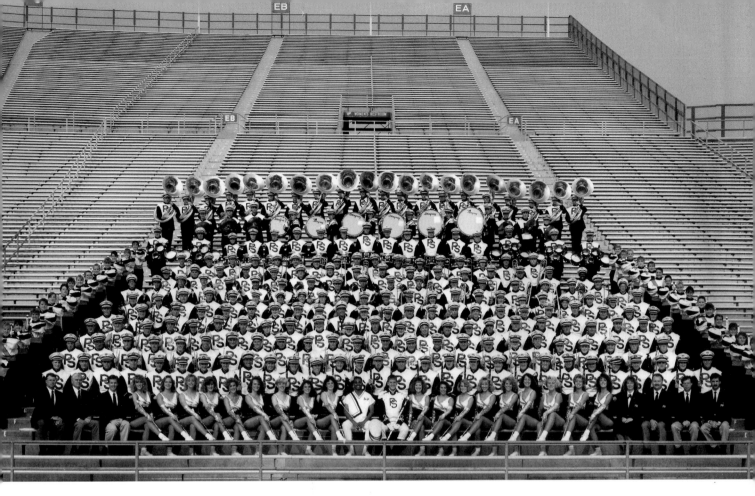

The 1992 Penn State Marching Blue Band.

Twirler Lori Branley, who graduated during the spring term of 1992. Her partner, John Mitchell, returned that fall to become the sole feature twirler. Other leadership positions were filled by new faces. Don Cramer, sousaphone player, was elected president of the Blue Band. As president, he brought back a tradition that had not been seen in many years. Band Director "Tommy" Thompson had always rewarded juniors and seniors with gifts, such as gold and silver medals, to show his gratitude for their years of faithful service. That tradition was lost during the years of World War II, but Cramer revived it by giving four-year members of the Blue Band stadium blankets with the "Penn State Blue Band" emblazoned on them. That tradition continues.

The band traveled to Miami for the Blockbuster Bowl during the Christmas–New Year's break, where Penn State lost to a surprisingly good Stanford team. This was Penn State's last game as an independent, nonconference football team. With the start of the 1993 season, Penn State joined the Big Ten Athletic Conference, becoming its eleventh team. Because of the obvious similarity of curriculums, history, and rural settings, Penn State University and its many programs and organizations are easily compared to those of the Big Ten universities. Although the Blue Band does not have as large a financial base as most of the other Big Ten bands, the marching precision and musical quality of the Blue Band made it one of the best bands in the country and one for other Big Ten bands to emulate, along with the benchmark bands of Michigan and Ohio State.

The Blue Band's first Big Ten performance away from home was a particularly important one for them, because it was at Ohio State in 1993. After traveling in seven buses in

The Big Ten

Penn State was officially voted into the Big Ten on June 4, 1990. Though Penn State could be integrated into the Big Ten in some sports quickly, it wasn't until 1993 that the football team started to carry a Big Ten schedule. So the Beast from the East finally met the teams of the Midwest.

The change in schedule was exciting from the Blue Band's perspective. Before the change, Penn State was declared an independent and could play any school, because it was not restricted by a conference schedule. The Blue Band would apparently have the opportunity to perform for many different band programs around the nation, although most of the time the band played at the Temple game, the Pittsburgh game, or every so often, if the money was available, at Boston College, Syracuse, Notre Dame, or some other university that wasn't too far away. Though all the above-mentioned schools have respectable college band programs, none could really compete with the size and quality of the Blue Band. (Since that time, though, Pittsburgh has increased the size of its band

immensely, and Temple currently has two former Blue Band members working on staff, one as the director and the other as silk coordinator.)

On the other hand, the Big Ten contained some of the most prestigious marching bands in the United States. Almost everyone had heard about the famous "Script Ohio" that the Ohio State Band performs, as well as the sheer power that the Michigan Band puts out at every home game. But all the marching bands of the Big Ten have quality programs. Since the creation of the Louis Sudler Intercollegiate Marching Band Trophy in 1982 to recognize a college marching band of exceptional merit, seven out of the eleven schools of the Big Ten have won this prestigious award. Michigan (1982), University of Illinois (1983), Ohio State (1984), Michigan State (1988), University of Iowa (1990), Northwestern (1992), and Purdue (1995) have all been recipients of the award. If it had not been a condition of the award that a school can win the award only once, the Big Ten could actually have had a monopoly on the award.

Will the Blue Band ever win the Louis Sudler Award? So far it has been overlooked, but certainly someday the Blue Band will receive this coveted award. When it comes to quality, the Blue Band compares favorably with the other schools of the Big Ten, but when it comes to financial support the Blue Band is sometimes lacking. The Blue Band is one of two Big Ten marching bands that does not have its own, nonshared, practice facility. The Blue Band is one of the few college bands that does not have an assistant director position, as well as two graduate positions. Some of the

Big Ten bands actually pay for five graduate assistants, while the Blue Band is fortunate to afford just one. The Blue Band is also one of the few bands of the Big Ten that has no indoor practice facility in case of poor weather. Several of the Big Ten schools compensate their student officers financially for the hours of work they do for the band, while the Blue Band does not.

This lack of funding does not lie solely with Penn State Athletics or the Penn State School of Music. Comparing the two with the other schools of the Big Ten, the percentage of monies made available to the Blue Band by Penn State is similar (but not in the league of the "Big Two" marching bands, Michigan and Ohio State). What the Blue Band does lack, however, is funding from donations. Most of the Big Ten schools have active fund-raising organizations for their bands, and it is hoped that the creation of the Floating Lions Club and the reorganization of the Alumni Blue Band Association will make it possible to get the additional funding the Blue Band needs to continue as one of the most elite collegiate marching bands in the United States.

Dr. O. Richard Bundy at an away game in Syracuse, New York.

snow and rain, the Blue Band did an exhibition at a local Columbus area high school the night before the game and spent the night with host families. The next morning the Blue Band participated in Ohio State's "Skull Session" before the game, which is comparable to Penn State's TailGreat. The famous Ohio State Marching Band performed for the many fans of its music and of Ohio State football. After the game the Blue Band was invited to a mixer at Ohio's band practice and storage rooms. Apparently, however, word of the mixer did not get around to the Buckeyes. The Blue Band arrived first, while the Ohio State band was performing the postgame show. When Ohio State did come to the practice room there seemed to be some confusion when they found Penn State's Blue Band there. Three-quarters of the Ohio State band members simply changed out of their uniforms, put away the instruments, and left, leaving many Blue Band members feeling snubbed.

During the last home game of the season, on November 13, against Illinois, the weather was once again dismal. The rain was so bad that Coach Joe Paterno decided not to have the Blue Band perform its pregame or halftime routines. A popular story has Drum Major Tom Roberts, graduating that year and performing in his last Beaver Stadium game, searching for Joe Paterno on the field before the game and asking if the band could perform. As the story goes, Roberts told Paterno, "You have never lost when I've made the flip. Let me do it one last time at Beaver Stadium." According to Roberts, that version of the tale is not quite correct. He says that the first person to ask Joe Paterno if the band could march was a drummer, Matt Kozsuch. Kozsuch and Roberts were by the south goalpost when they received word that the band would not be allowed to march because of field conditions. Kozsuch noticed Paterno nearby watching his team stretch and yelled over to him: "Mr. Paterno, it's our last game too, can we march on the field?" The coach did not hear Kozsuch, so Roberts repeated the question. Paterno approached the two young men, crossed his arms, looked up to the sky, and said, "Okay, go ahead." The Blue Band quickly got ready for pregame and began the last performance of the year. Three-quarters of the way through the pregame show, however, the sky opened up and it began to pour. Euphoric from the coach's decision, the band finished without noticing the rain at all.

After joining the Big Ten in 1993 the Blue Band was often compared to the two premier bands in the Conference. The Blue Band visited one of those band's universities that year: Ohio State. The other top Big Ten marching band, Michigan, received the Penn State Blue Band in mid-October 1994 at Michigan Stadium, competing for the accolades of the 100,000 people attending the game.

The trip to Ann Arbor from State College was a long one. The Blue Band rode on the buses for more than eight hours, passing the time by watching feature films and videos of past halftime performances. The night before the game, the band participated in an exhibition at a local high school and then went to the homes of their host families. The next day, at the "Big House," the Blue Band helped cheer the Nittany Lions to a crucial victory over the Wolverines, to continue the undefeated season. After the game, the Blue Band was invited to a mixer with the Michigan band in the practice room. Unlike the preceding year's trip to Ohio State, the Michigan band treated the visitors warmly and were appreciative that the Blue Band had made the trip. The evening ended with T-shirt swapping and a general feeling of camaraderie between the two bands.

On the trip back to State College the Blue Band stayed overnight at a hotel in Ohio, where some of the band members called their roommates back home to find out how the campus had reacted to Penn State's big win and certain Number One ranking. They were informed that, in celebration, a large group of students had broken in to Beaver Stadium and taken down one of the goalposts. Carrying the huge goalpost across campus, the students laid it on the front lawn of Coach Paterno's house, in tribute to his team's victory.

The Nittany Lions continued their unbeaten streak all the way to the Rose Bowl on January 2, 1995, to play and later defeat the University of Oregon Ducks. Although the football team had played in the Rose Bowl in 1923, the Blue Band was making its first appearance there. Feeling privileged to participate in the Tournament of Roses Parade in Pasadena, California, and in the bowl game, the Blue Band could now boast that it had performed in every major bowl game in existence to date.

In 1995, after two years of visiting other Big Ten schools, the Blue Band played host to two conference bands. These were the first visits by Big Ten marching units to Beaver Stadium

Members of the 1994–95 Blue Band say "Thank you" to all the supporters who contributed funds to acquire new uniforms.

since Penn State joined the Big Ten in 1993. The fans of Penn State had the opportunity to compare their Blue Band with two of the best bands in the nation: Ohio State and the University of Wisconsin.

Although the Blue Band has never traveled to all the away football games, in 1996 a pep band that would travel to all the games the full Blue Band cannot attend was formed. The group of approximately fourteen musicians, mostly upperclassmen, was composed of volunteers, typically six trumpets, two trombones, two mellophones, one sousaphone, one baritone, two percussionists, and either a graduate assistant or the drum major to conduct the ensemble. Although most universities usually welcome and even encourage an opponent's pep band, the home team's stadium administration has the final say as to whether to allow the musicians to bring instruments into the stadium.

During the spring semester of 1996, after twenty years as the Director of University Bands and more than thirty-five years as a Blue Band staff member, Dr. Ned C. Deihl decided to retire from Penn State. As Director of Bands, Dr. Deihl was responsible for the Marching Blue Band (although Dr. Bundy was conducting rehearsals), the Symphonic (Concert) Blue Band, the Concert White Band, and the Basketball Pep Band. After Deihl's retirement, the School of Music chose to reorganize the structure of the university bands.

The Blue Band became the center of attention at TailGreat in 1997.

Eliminating the position of Director of University Bands, Music created two more positions: Director of Athletic Bands, to which Dr. O. Richard Bundy was elevated at this time, and Director of Concert Bands, held now by Michigan graduate Dennis Glocke. This reorganization effectively split the sports-related bands and the purely symphonic bands.

Today, as Concert Bands Director, Glocke is responsible for the Symphonic Wind Ensemble, the Symphonic Band (formerly known as the Concert Blue Band), the Concert Band, and the Campus Band. Dr. Bundy, Athletic Bands Director, is responsible for the Marching Blue Band and "The Pride of the Lions" basketball band.

Dr. Deihl gave his farewell concert on April 14, 1996, in Eisenhower Auditorium. Many alumni from previous Concert Blue Bands were in attendance when he directed "Nittany Lion" for his last time and ended the concert with "Stars and Stripes Forever."

A piece of Blue Band history was discovered in 1996. The gold watch given to Wilfred Otto "Tommy" Thompson by the university in 1939 for his retirement was received by the Commonwealth of Pennsylvania under the provisions of the Unclaimed Property Act. Pennsylvania State Treasurer Barbara Hafer loaned the watch to Penn State for a centennial display of Blue Band memorabilia in the Penn State Room of Pattee Library from November 1998 through February 1999.

The fall semester of 1996 marks the first season with a new Band Director since 1975. Dr. O. Richard Bundy became only the fifth Director of Penn State's Marching Blue Band

ORRIN RICHARD BUNDY JR.

Orrin Richard Bundy Jr. was born on June 19, 1948, and grew up in Beaver, Pennsylvania, north of Pittsburgh. He had not always dreamed of being a band director. "Up until my senior year in high school, I wanted to do something in chemistry and had advance placement courses in it," Bundy recalls. Between his junior and senior year of high school, however, he attended the Band, Orchestra, and Chorus Summer School at Penn State in 1965. "I made first chair in the band, and it was then that I realized I might be a better trombone player than I thought," Bundy admitted. He studied under Matty Shiner, a guest instructor at the school and one of the top trombone teachers in the nation. After his experience with the summer band school, Bundy planned to enroll at Duquesne University, where Shiner taught, but he chose Penn State instead. "There was only one scholarship to Duquesne for trombone available, and I didn't get it," said Bundy. "Penn State was a logical choice after that. It was not nearly as expensive as Duquesne, and I had been impressed by Jim Dunlop, who conducted the summer school." That fall Dick Bundy enrolled at Penn State as a music education major and became a member of the Marching Blue Band, the only Blue Band Director to have played in it as an undergraduate. (Hummel Fishburn was in the Concert Band and Orchestra as an undergraduate, but not the Marching Band.)

Just before graduating from Penn State in the spring of 1970, Bundy applied for graduate school at the University of Michigan for that fall. That summer, however, he enlisted in the army instead. "It was imminent that I would be drafted before I could go to Michigan," he recalls, "so I enlisted in the army for a three-year commitment. I felt I could serve best by performing with one of the army bands, but there was no guarantee I would make it. If there wasn't an opening, it didn't matter how good a musician you were." After auditioning, Bundy was accepted into the Fiftieth Continental Army Command Band in Virginia, where he spent his entire tour of duty.

During his time in the military, Dick and his wife, Christine, had two children, Richard and Jennifer. Later, in 1976 and 1979, they had two more, Heather and Jeffrey. All four of the Bundy children became musicians of varying degrees, and all went to college at Penn State, although none was in the Marching Blue Band.

After his time in the service was finished, graduate school was put on hold so he could work for two years as band director at Iroquois High School in Erie, Pennsylvania. With the help of the G.I. Bill, Bundy began graduate school at Michigan in 1976, attending during the summers. At the time, according to Bundy, Michigan had a better trombone program and a much more developed school of music than Penn State. Bundy also was influenced by Jim Dunlop, also a Michigan graduate, to go to Michigan.

After learning about an opening for a band graduate assistant, Bundy came back to Penn State in 1980 to work on his doctorate, and he has been there ever since. In 1983 Assistant Director Dr. Darhyl Ramsey left to eventually become a music teacher at the University of North Texas, which gave Bundy the opportunity to become Dr. Deihl's new Assistant Director. In 1988 Bundy earned his doctorate and remained Assistant Director, which became a tenured position that year. After Dr. Deihl announced his retirement in 1996 Dr. Bundy became Penn State's Director of Athletic Bands.

Bundy's position as Director of Athletic Bands is slightly different from the Director of Bands position that Deihl had held. The Athletic Bands Director is responsible only for the Marching Blue Band, the basketball band (Pride of the Lions), and various courses in conducting and marching band methods for future band directors. The decision to change this position stemmed partly from a reorganization of the Schools of Music and Music Education and partly from the reality that with the growth of Penn State's music programs the Athletic Bands position had become a full-time job, with more than 250 separate performances by the athletic band students to coordinate each year.

Dick Bundy is a soft-spoken individual with a warm and approachable personality. Beneath that easygoing exterior is a deep commitment to his students. "One of the challenges the athletic bands face is how to hold the line on the preparation time the kids face, considering the increased amount of performance time we now have," says Bundy. "We must keep organized enough to give good performances that reflect well on the band and the university, which I feel we do." Part of the pride he felt as a former Blue Band member is reflected in how Bundy directs the Blue Band today. "I feel I have more of a vested interest personally in the Blue Band because I had been a member as well as its director." He is also a student of Blue Band history, writing often on the subject in magazines, newspapers, and once in a published university thesis.

His most indelible mark on the Blue Band as its Director may be yet to come, but already in his nearly twenty years of involvement with that organization Dick Bundy has left an impression in the minds of many who worked with him on the field and off. Art Miley, a 1991 graduate and former Blue Band president, recalls one moment that exemplified Bundy's dedication: "I had just made the band in late August of 1987. We had practiced the whole week, and that last day of band camp we had practiced morning, afternoon, and evening. I went to the wrong building that night around 10:30 P.M. to get fitted for my band uniform and made my way to the Blue Band office instead. There I saw Dr. Bundy, who had been directing us all day, in the office working on the field charts for the first game. Seeing him still there after fourteen hours inspired me to work as hard as I could to be the best."

Dick Bundy's commitment to the Blue Band has inspired hundreds of musicians at Penn State to be the best. As a legacy for the future, it's hard to top that. ≋

in its ninety-seven-year history. Although he had a new title, Dr. Bundy was not new to his position. He had led the Blue Band for a number of years in everything but name.

Dick Bundy worked not only during the football season with the student Blue Band, but also off the field with the Alumni Blue Band. A Blue Band alumnus from the late 1960s, Dr. Bundy believed that the Alumni Blue Band Association (ABBA) could take on a greater role in promoting and supporting the band, including financially. During October 1996 he asked for volunteers for a steering committee to establish long-range goals for ABBA. A twenty-five-member committee made up of many past Blue Band presidents, drum majors, graduate assistants, and other former Blue Band members was formed, and the group got together in December to define and establish the role of the ABBA in the future of the university and the Blue Band.

The season started at the typical fast and furious pace. The Kickoff Classic in the Meadowlands, in which Penn State was participating, took place only three days after the start of the semester. Because of this abbreviated schedule, Dr. Bundy decided to not have returnees audition for positions, a rare occurrence. The holes left by graduating seniors were filled by rookies.

A new tradition for home football games began with the start of "TailGreat," a joint "tailgate" party sponsored by AT&T, Walmart, the Nittany Lion Club, and the Alumni Association held at the Bryce Jordan Center. The Blue Band and the Penn State Cheerleaders performed while guests paid $10 to $15 for the entertainment and an all-you-can-eat buffet. The first "TailGreat" was not too successful. Some critics noted that the number of attendees was less than the number of Blue Band members performing for them.

In its second year, 1997, TailGreat was modified to stimulate more spectator participation. The admission fee was removed, and in place of a buffet the Bryce Jordan Center concession stands were open. With these changes, TailGreat became vastly more popular and is today a great way to enjoy the Blue Band and the Penn State Cheerleaders.

The Ohio State Marching Band came east in 1997 to support its football team at Beaver Stadium. Rivalry between Penn State and Ohio State that year almost matched Michigan's rivalry with the Buckeyes when the visiting band was announced. Although the Ohio State band was extremely talented, its slogan—"The Best Damn Band in the Land"—bristled the Beaver Stadium crowd. As the OSU band announcer introduced the visiting musicians and its slogan, Penn State fans booed loud and long, especially from the student section. Halfway through the visitors' halftime drill, the chant "We want the Blue Band" could be heard in pockets all over the stadium.

One week earlier, the Blue Band traveled to its farthest Big Ten opponent, the University of Illinois. It took eleven long hours on the buses to reach the university, and another eleven to return. To break up the trip, the band members slept overnight at host families both to and from the game.

Nike

During the 1995 football season, Penn State fans noticed a slight change in the football team's uniform. The uniforms still had no names on the backs, no little decals on the helmets to signify having made a "good play," but a small but noticeable decal did find its way onto the front of the uniforms: the Nike "Swoosh."

There was much criticism about advertising Nike on the quite conservative Penn State football jerseys, but no one can deny the many benefits the university has received from Nike. Nike has provided funding for most of the university's athletic teams, including the women's teams. It has been said that if the deal with Nike had not been achieved, some of the sports programs that both men and women enjoy at Penn State would not exist.

Nike also provided funding for sneakers: as part of the deal, most of the athletic teams receive footwear for their members. Fortunately for Blue Band members, the deal included the Blue Band.

Before 1996, Blue Band members had to provide their own shoes for games and performances, so style varied depending on where the students bought them. In 1996, the season after the "swoosh," the Blue Band began to wear black Nike sneakers for performances. Because part of the uniform was spats (foot coverings), the sneaker had to have a heel. If it didn't, the straps that hold the spats to the foot would rip and the football field would then be covered with spats.

The members of the Blue Band received new sneakers each year, and the style of the sneakers has also changed. The first season of wearing Nike sneakers was 1996–97, and the sneakers had high tops, making it difficult to point the toe. In 1997 the style changed to a "low-top" style. All the footwear was custom-colored black with a black Nike swoosh on it. According to Matt Kologi, a member of the Blue Band when it went Nike, "I can't imagine marching in anything else." When asked what the Blue Band members do with the sneakers after the season, Katy McDowell, president of the Blue Band during the 1998–99 season, replied, "Throw them out. After a season of marching, the sneakers are basically trashed."

During the Citrus Bowl, as the Nittany Lions were being handled easily by Florida, the men's and women's basketball teams were offering serious competition. Because Athletics wanted to have a pep band at all the home basketball games and the Blue Band was 1,000 miles away, members of the Alumni Blue Band Association graciously provided the music. The organizer of the Alumni Basketball Band was Dick Ammon, a member of the ABBA board of directors. The band became so popular that plans were made for other alumni pep band engagements.

An engagement of another kind occurred at the end of Penn State's 1997 season between two prominent Penn State figures at Beaver Stadium. Nick Indeglio, the Nittany Lion Mascot, proposed to Christine Wolfe, the Blue Band's Blue Sapphire, after the Blue Band's halftime show during the Wisconsin game. On bended knee, and with his Lion's head off, Indeglio produced an engagement ring before Wolfe, who accepted his proposal before the almost 100,000 cheering Penn State fans. Indeglio and Wolfe had met at a pep rally and had been dating for three years, and Nick thought that his last football game as the Penn State Mascot was the perfect time for him to propose. "You only get to be the Lion once," he said in a *Collegian* interview, "and I wanted to take advantage of that." After

Many members arrive at rehearsal early to practice their music.

During rehearsal, the Blue Band sometimes breaks up into smaller groups by instrument to practice their music.

clearing the event with Athletics in August, Indeglio had been planning the event for months. Wolfe, who suspected she'd get a proposal sometime that year, was taken by surprise by when and where it happened. "I was speechless," she said. "It was one of those things you don't think about, because time just flies by."

In 1998 the Blue Band was in its 100th season, but it was business as usual for the band members. Auditions for this anniversary season were quite competitive as usual, and in one case as many as fifteen individuals auditioned for two spots. After the final cuts were made, the new Blue Band had less than a week to prepare for the Penn State game with Southern Mississippi at Beaver Stadium on September 5, 1998.

The next week the Blue Band hosted the Bowling Green University band and cheered the Nittany Lions to Coach Joe Paterno's 300th career victory. Coincidentally, the Blue Band was present at Joe Paterno's 200th victory eleven years earlier, also defeating Bowling Green. After the game, the Blue Band formed the number "300" on the field and played two selections: the traditional postgame song, "Lion Special," and a special arrangement of "Ode to Joy," which the Blue Band referred to as "Ode to Joe."

The Blue Band and its alumni began celebrating the band's first century at a formal reception during the spring of 1999. This reception was the start of a year-long celebra-

tion honoring those who had been in the Blue Band in the past 100 years, with events planned for the fall of 1999 and spring of 2000.

The Blue Band in the 1990s adapted well to its challenges and changes, and in so doing it has become an agent of change itself. The band has helped Penn State adapt to a new athletic conference by being comparable to and competitive with the other conference bands. By providing its football team with its support and spirit, the band has also helped the Nittany Lions on the field and in the stands to adapt to the Big Ten. Embracing old traditions and introducing new ones, the Blue Band has played a part in helping the Big Ten's colleges adapt to Penn State as well. The precision maneuvers and excellent musical performances of the Blue Band have helped raise the standards of the Big Ten bands, thereby increasing the competitiveness of other marching band programs. Traditions that are new for Penn State, like TailGreat, in which the Blue Band plays a major role, have provided an atmosphere in which the Big Ten can welcome Penn State warmly. New challenges and opportunities await Penn State and the Blue Band in the twenty-first century, but there is no question that Penn State and the Blue Band will rise to the challenge, as they have always done.

Dr. Bundy looks on from the Director's Loft as the band practices.

13 : For the Future That We Wait: 1999 and Beyond

ON SEPTEMBER 17, 1999, *The Pennsylvania State University Marching Blue Band will celebrate its 100th birthday and begin another century of excellence. For 100 years, the Blue Band has provided inspiration for its sports teams, its alumni, and Penn State fans everywhere, and it will continue that tradition into the next century.*

The quality of Blue Band performances and the dedication of its members will continue to grow. The planned purchase of new band instruments not currently available will help the band take another step in its continuing quest for perfection by increasing the uniformity of the band's sound and appearance.

Another less-immediate step in the improvement of the Blue Band in the future will be a permanent practice

facility, although whether and when that goal will be realized is uncertain. With the blue-prints already drawn, the financing of a practice facility is the only thing standing in the way of the Blue Band's most sought-after goal.

Future Blue Band members will continue to meet the standards of excellence that have been exhibited throughout the band's history, demonstrating their talents with precision marching and music. As enrollment at Penn State increases and more talented high school musicians come to University Park, the Blue Band will be adding even more members. As long as the core values of dedication, musicianship, and precision remain, a larger Blue Band will continue its tradition of excellence.

In the years to come, Blue Band members will continue to be ambassadors of Penn State, performing at away football games, at off-campus celebrations, and at other away-from-home events. As always, the Blue Band will represent the positive aspects of Penn State, of collegiate athletics, and of Central Pennsylvania.

Many things have changed at Penn State from its beginnings as the Farmers' High School almost 150 years ago, but few organizations have been as consistent in its dedication to its alma mater as The Penn State Blue Band. As the university continues to grow and evolve, the Blue Band will remain as it always has: a reminder of past glory and tradition, a mirror of the current times, and an example of the bright future that awaits The Pennsylvania State University.

For the Glory of Old State,

For her Founders, Strong and Great,

For the Future that we wait,

Raise the Song, Raise the Song.

Afterword
by O. Richard Bundy

DIRECTOR, PENN STATE BLUE BAND

THE SMALL GROUP OF STUDENTS *who banded together a century ago to provide marching music for the student body at then fledgling Penn State College shared two important traits—a talent for music and a desire to contribute to their alma mater. As the Penn State Blue Band marches into a new century, and a new millennium, talent and desire still characterize the student membership of this proud organization.*

The outstanding talent of the student musicians has greatly contributed to the Blue Band's growth in prestige as a musical organization in its first century. For its members, past and present, the desire to contribute to their alma mater through involvement in the Blue Band has been a source of great pride and a vital connection to their university. Hundreds of thousands of Penn State fans, alumni, and friends have enjoyed the credit reflected upon Penn State by this respected student organization.

Much is owed to the leadership of past directors "Tommy" Thompson, Hum Fishburn, Jim Dunlop, and Ned Deihl, whose efforts laid the foundation of musical excellence and enthusiasm for Penn State that continues to guide the band program. And much is owed to the thousands of wonderful students who have passed through the ranks of the Blue Band over the years. Their musicianship and love of Penn State have made the band program a source of pride for all Penn Staters. Grounded in traditions from the past, the Blue Band looks forward to the challenges of an exciting future that will continue to raise the pride and spirit of a great university.

It is an exciting time for bands at Penn State. Whether on the marching field or in the concert hall, the University Bands program provides Penn State students with exceptional opportunities to excel as musicians and people. I can only imagine where the talents and desires of the next century's students will take us.

For the future that we wait …

Appendixes

At a Glance:

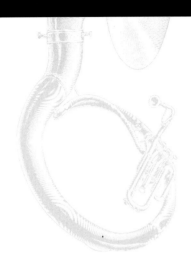

Many collegiate marching bands have similar timelines. Usually by the late 1800s or very early 1900s the student body decides it would like a marching band. In the late 1910s or early 1920s, a permanent band director is hired. If the band is any good, usually John Philip Sousa visits the campus in the 1920s. During World War II a shortage of men makes fielding a band impossible or forces the temporary use of women in the band. And then in the 1970s women become permanent members of the band.

When comparing the Penn State Blue Band with other collegiate bands, there are many factors to consider. Though the size and age of the band are important, probably the most important factor is marching style. Many bands incorporate a variety of styles during the season, but most marching bands can be placed in one of the following six categories.

Big Ten Style. This type of band usually performs "theme" halftime shows with at least one concert number. Intricate formations are used, with a mixture of linear and curvilinear forms. For the concert number, the band stays at attention while the color guard (the silks and majorettes) performs. A hallmark of this style is each band's "high-step," or "chair-step," used throughout the pregame performances and incorporated into halftime as well.

Ivy League Style. This type of band performs theme-based shows, but there is no marching from formation to formation. The band instead uses something that has been called a "scatter" drill, where the band members run to their spots in the next formation, usually screaming or yelling at the top of their lungs as they do. The instrumentation is also often nontraditional, with some bands fielding string instrumentalists and sometimes kazoos.

Drum Corps Style. This type of band emulates the style of contemporary drum and bugle corps. Generally, one halftime show is performed during the season, and the members continually strive to perfect their performance. Drills make use of asymmetrical formations and near constant movement. Very few Division IA colleges use this style.

Show Style. This type of band also performs theme-style shows and is quite similar to a Big Ten style of band. One major difference is the way the concert numbers are performed. Band members "dance" or move in various ways instead of just standing at attention and playing while the color guard performs. More often than not, props are used while performing.

Military Style. This is a marching band that has no silk squad or majorettes. Usually the band is primarily all brass, but sometimes some woodwinds might be included. This band is particularly proud of its precision marching. The emphasis is on straightforward parade-style marching in blocks with traditional music and little showmanship.

"Historically Black College" Style. These bands' repertoires draw heavily on popular music (rhythm and blues, soul, etc.). The emphasis is on showmanship, with a lot of dancing while playing and distinctive steps while marching.

Selected American College and University Marching Bands (BY CURRENT SIZE)

College or University	Name of Marching Band	Origin Year	Current Size	Current Director	Style
Princeton University	Princeton University Band	1919	63	Student run	Ivy
Yale University	Yale Precision Marching Band	1919	90	Thomas Duffy	Ivy
Rutgers University	The Rutgers Band	1915	150	William Kellerman	Big Ten
Syracuse University	Pride of the Orange	1900	200	Bradley Ethington	Big Ten
Ohio State University	Ohio State University Marching Band	1878	225	Jon Woods	Big Ten
UCLA	The Bruin Marching Band	1925	240	Gordon Henderson	Big Ten / Drum Corps
University of Wisconsin	University of Wisconsin Band	1885	240	Mike Leckrone	Big Ten
University of Pittsburgh	Pitt Band	1911	250	Jack Anderson	Big Ten
Michigan State University	Spartan Marching Band	1870	255	John T. Madden	Big Ten
Pennsylvania State University	Blue Band	1899	275	O. Richard Bundy	Big Ten
University of Southern California	The Trojan Marching Band	1880	275	Arthur C. Bartner	Show
University of Michigan	Michigan Marching Band	1896	276	Kevin Sedotole	Big Ten
University of Minnesota	University of Minnesota Marching Band	1892	285	Jerry Luckhardt	Big Ten
University of Notre Dame	Band of the Fighting Irish	1887	300	Luther Snavely	Show / Big Ten
Indiana University	Marching 100	1896	300	David Woodley	Big Ten
Florida A&M University	The Marching 100	1892	330	Julian White	"Historically Black College"
West Virginia University	Mountaineer Marching Band	1901	330	Don Wilcox	Big Ten / Drum Corps
University of Illinois	Marching Illini	1890	352	James F. Keene	Big Ten / Show
University of Texas	Longhorne Band	1900	360	Paula A. Crider	Show
Purdue University	All-American Marching Band	1886	360	David Leppla	Big Ten
Texas A&M University	Fightin' Texas Aggie Band	1894	400	Lt. Colonel Ray Toler	Military

How the Band Has Grown

Year	Name of Band	No. of Members	Bandmaster/ Director	President/ Student Leader	Drum Major	Feature Twirler
1899–1900	The Cadet Band	6	E. E. Godard	George Deike	None	—
1900–1901	The Cadet Band	23	E. E. Godard	George Deike	G. W. Dodge	—
1901–1902	The Cadet Band	28	E. E. Godard	George Deike	None	—
1902–1903	The Cadet Band	28	E. E. Godard	George Deike	None	—
1903–1904	The Cadet Band	26	E. B. Norris	R. W. Bowers	C. C. Wagner	—
1904–1905	The Cadet Band	29	E. E. Godard	F. A. R. Hoffeditz	C. H. Smith	—
1905–1906	The Cadet Band	35	E. E. Godard	Harry M. Jacobs	Charles M. Piper	—
1906–1907	The Cadet Band	43	R. J. Smith	B. A. Smith	W. R. Barlow	—
1907–1908	The Cadet Band	36	D. A. Isenberg	R. H. Allport	L. W. Arny	—
1908–1909	The Cadet Band	40	R. H. Allport	L. F. Meissner	C. W. Markham	—
1909–1910	The Cadet Band	35	L. R. Meissner	E. M. Frid	None	—
1910–1911	The Cadet Band	32	P. M. Snavely	R. B. Clapp	None	—
1911–1912	The Cadet Band	30	P. M. Snavely	None	None	—
1912–1913	The Cadet Band	29	W. A. Moyer	Samuel Redsacker	O. B. Gippel	—
1913–1914	The Cadet Band	33	George L. Sumner	Samuel Redsacker	None	—
1914–1915	The Cadet Band	60	Wilfred "Tommy" Thompson	W. B. Strickler	None	—
1915–1916	The Cadet Band	58	Wilfred "Tommy" Thompson	W. G. Powell	M. Dunbar	—
1916–1917	The Cadet Band	66	Wilfred "Tommy" Thompson	C. R. Snyder	None	—
1917–1918	The Cadet Band	71	Wilfred "Tommy" Thompson	Oscar B. Feldser	None	—
1918–1919	The College Military Band	88	Wilfred "Tommy" Thompson	Oscar B. Feldser	Gilson Felton	—
1919–1920	The College Military Band	107	Wilfred "Tommy" Thompson	George Carl / Ezra Reider	George Supplee	—
1920–1921	The College Military Band	99	Wilfred "Tommy" Thompson	Lewis Kimmel	George Supplee	—
1921–1922	The College Military Band	108	Wilfred "Tommy" Thompson	C. C. Gailey	G. B. Lane	—
1922–1923	The College Military Band	118	Wilfred "Tommy" Thompson	G. B. Lane	K. R. Dever	—
1923–1924	The Blue Band	50	Wilfred "Tommy" Thompson	A. F. Texter	E. S. Wetzel	—
1924–1925	The Blue Band	50	Wilfred "Tommy" Thompson	J. E. Greene	T. M. Schuchman	—
1925–1926	The Blue Band	75	Wilfred "Tommy" Thompson	W. B. Widenor	E. S. Wetzel	—
1926–1927	The Blue Band	75	Wilfred "Tommy" Thompson	E. P. Baker	E. S. Wetzel	—
1927–1928	The Blue Band	75	Wilfred "Tommy" Thompson	W. E. Biery	H. C. Williams	—
1928–1929	The Penn State Blue Band	75	Wilfred "Tommy" Thompson	H. C. Williams	H. C. Williams	—
1929–1930	The Penn State Blue Band	74	Wilfred "Tommy" Thompson	P. R. Kester	None	—
1930–1931	The Penn State Blue Band	75	Wilfred "Tommy" Thompson	F. C. Everitt	None	—
1931–1932	The Penn State Blue Band	75	Wilfred "Tommy" Thompson	Donald Shelley	Charles Brightbill	—
1932–1933	The Penn State Blue Band	75	Wilfred "Tommy" Thompson	Paul Filer	William Click	—
1933–1934	The Penn State Blue Band	78	Wilfred "Tommy" Thompson	C. E. Shappelle	A. M. Miley	—
1934–1935	The Penn State Blue Band	78	Wilfred "Tommy" Thompson	D. E. Nesbit	James Townsend	—
1935–1936	The Penn State Blue Band	86	Wilfred "Tommy" Thompson	F. W. Hunsicker	P. W. Longstreet	—
1936–1937	The Penn State Blue Band	78	Wilfred "Tommy" Thompson	K. L. Fritz	S. I. Booth	—
1937–1938	The Penn State Blue Band	78	Wilfred "Tommy" Thompson	A. P. Lyford	F. M. Anderson	—
1938–1939	The Penn State Blue Band	78	Wilfred "Tommy" Thompson	E. M. Treese	F. M. Anderson	—
1939–1940	The Penn State Blue Band	98	Hummel Fishburn	Bruce Garner	James Leyden	—
1940–1941	The Penn State Blue Band	86	Hummel Fishburn	J. P. Menham	James Leyden	—
1941–1942	The Penn State Blue Band	90	Hummel Fishburn	Walter James	James Leyden/ Jay H. Lucas	—
1942–1943	The Penn State Blue Band	79	Hummel Fishburn	Victor Dimeo / Edward Pollock / William Knutsen*	Wes Burns	—
1943–1944	The Penn State Blue Band	79	Hummel Fishburn	Joe Connon	None	—
1944–1945	The Penn State Blue Band	79	Hummel Fishburn	John Setar	None	—
1945–1946	The Penn State Blue Band	79	Hummel Fishburn	Glenn Orndorf	None	—
1946–1947	The Penn State Blue Band	84	Hummel Fishburn	William Keefauver	None	—
1947–1948	The Penn State Blue Band	79	James Dunlop	Frank Hess	P. Grove	—
1948–1949	The Penn State Blue Band	80	James Dunlop	William Laughlin	Jay H. Lucas	—

* Vic Dimeo was put on active duty during World War II and could not finish his term as Band President, so Pollock and Knutsen shared the responsibility and finished the term.

Year	Name of Band	No. of Members	Bandmaster/ Director	President/ Student Leader	Drum Major	Feature Twirler
1949–1950	The Penn State Blue Band	81	James Dunlop	Allen Baker	Jay H. Lucas	—
1950–1951	The Marching Blue Band	96	James Dunlop	Raymond Dombrowski	Jay H. Lucas	—
1951–1952	The Marching Blue Band	101	James Dunlop	Charles Brouse	Carrol Chapman	—
1952–1953	The Marching Blue Band	113	James Dunlop	Thomas Hahn	George Black	—
1953–1954	The Marching Blue Band	99	James Dunlop	Don Lambert	Francis Taylor	—
1954–1955	The Marching Blue Band	105	James Dunlop	George Black	George Black	—
1955–1956	The Marching Blue Band	105	James Dunlop	Roger Staub	Francis Taylor	—
1956–1957	The Marching Blue Band	102	James Dunlop	David Andre	Don Fought	—
1957–1958	The Marching Blue Band	99	James Dunlop	Jere Fridy	Don Fought	—
1958–1959	The Marching Blue Band	108	James Dunlop	James Ressler	Gary Glenn	—
1959–1960	The Marching Blue Band	108	James Dunlop	Floyd Frisbie	Don Fought	—
1960–1961	The Marching Blue Band	117	James Dunlop	Carl Sipe	Rob Fought	—
1961–1962	The Marching Blue Band	113	James Dunlop	Carl Sipe	Rob Fought	—
1962–1963	The Marching Blue Band	113	James Dunlop	Malcolm Andre	Rob Fought	—
1963–1964	The Marching Blue Band	111	James Dunlop	Richard Ammon	Maynard Barley	—
1964–1965	The Marching Blue Band	111	James Dunlop	Maxwell Mascia	Charles Rosebrock	—
1965–1966	The Marching Blue Band	114	James Dunlop	John Prendergast	Charles Rosebrock	—
1966–1967	The Marching Blue Band	134	James Dunlop	Bernard Keisling	Charles Rosebrock	—
1967–1968	The Marching Blue Band	134	James Dunlop	Charles Cahn	Charles Rosebrock	—
1968–1969	The Marching Blue Band	139	James Dunlop	Ned Trautman	Stanley "Chip" Willis	—
1969–1970	The Marching Blue Band	145	James Dunlop	Daryl Shadle	Stanley "Chip" Willis	—
1970–1971	The Marching Blue Band	140	James Dunlop	John Kovalchik	Stanley "Chip" Willis	—
1971–1972	The Marching Blue Band	149	James Dunlop	Thomas Little	Jeff Robertson	—
1972–1973	The Marching Blue Band	155	James Dunlop	Gerald F. Lowman	Jeff Robertson	Judy Shearer
1973–1974	The Marching Blue Band	161	James Dunlop	Richard Fries	Jeff Robertson	Judy Shearer
1974–1975	The Marching Blue Band	170	James Dunlop	William Gregory	Jeff Robertson	Lori Donaldson
1975–1976	The Marching Blue Band	166	Ned C. Deihl	Robert Trout	Eric Felack	Lori Donaldson
1976–1977	The Marching Blue Band	174	Ned C. Deihl	Carol Gabler	Eric Felack	Lori Donaldson
1977–1978	The Marching Blue Band	210	Ned C. Deihl	Ed Ober	Ron Louder	Lori Donaldson
1978–1979	The Marching Blue Band	210	Ned C. Deihl	Greg Spangler	Ron Louder	Lori Bowers
1979–1980	The Marching Blue Band	210	Ned C. Deihl	Phil Loewen	Ron Louder	Lori Bowers
1980–1981	The Marching Blue Band	230	Ned C. Deihl	Jeni Lindsey	Rich Gorodesky	Lori Bowers
1981–1982	The Marching Blue Band	231	Ned C. Deihl	Dave Uhazie	Rich Gorodesky	Lori Bowers
1982–1983	The Marching Blue Band	230	Ned C. Deihl	Mike Jacisin	Tony Petroy/ Greg Stock	Carol Wilt
1983–1984	The Marching Blue Band	230	Ned C. Deihl	Brad Townsend	Greg Stock	Jamie Ritenour
1984–1985	The Marching Blue Band	242	Ned C. Deihl	Rosemary Gillis	Greg Stock	Jamie Ritenour
1985–1986	The Marching Blue Band	256	Ned C. Deihl	Marty Croxton	Greg Stock	Donna Wolter
1986–1987	The Marching Blue Band	275	Ned C. Deihl	Amy Smith	Greg Stock	Donna Wolter
1987–1988	The Marching Blue Band	285	Ned C. Deihl	Andy Zuber	Jay Dzigas	Donna Wolter
1988–1989	The Marching Blue Band	265	Ned C. Deihl	Thomas Range	Jay Dzigas	Donna Wolter
1989–1990	The Marching Blue Band	265	Ned C. Deihl	Randy Seely	Jay Dzigas	Lori Branley and John Mitchell
1990–1991	The Marching Blue Band	274	Ned C. Deihl	Scott Woomer	Mike Harrell	Lori Branley and John Mitchell
1991–1992	The Marching Blue Band	275	Ned C. Deihl	Art Miley	Mike Harrell	Lori Branley and John Mitchell
1992–1993	The Marching Blue Band	275	Ned C. Deihl	Don Cramer	Tom Roberts	John Mitchell
1993–1994	The Marching Blue Band	275	Ned C. Deihl	Sean Strine	Tom Roberts	Cheryl Smith and Jennifer Steward
1994–1995	The Marching Blue Band	275	Ned C. Deihl	Brian Tuckmantel	Darren Bennett	Christine Wolfe
1995–1996	The Marching Blue Band	275	Ned C. Deihl	Tom Frank	Darren Bennett	Christine Wolfe
1996–1997	The Marching Blue Band	275	O. Richard Bundy	David Wagenborg	Derrick Ometz	Christine Wolfe
1997–1998	The Marching Blue Band	275	O. Richard Bundy	Bryon Maddas	Seth Walk	Christine Wolfe
1998–1999	The Marching Blue Band	275	O. Richard Bundy	Katy McDowell	Seth Walk	Christine Wolfe

Index

"Aaronsburg Story," 84
Adelphia Quartet, 56
Affiliated Program Group, 112
Agricultural Building, 21
Agricultural College of Pennsylvania, 7
Ahrends, A. E., 28, 39
Alexander, Arnold, 16, 120
Alexander, Duane, 16
Alexander, Fred, 16
Alexander, Keith, 16
All-American Bandmasters' Band, 108
All-American Marching Band, 183
All-College Cabinet, 70, 80, 88, 89, 131
All-State Band Festivals, 94, 100
Allport, R. H., 184
Alma Mater (Penn State's), 53, 58, 93, 113
"Along Comes a Woman," 149
Alpha Fire Company, 67
alternates, band, 48
Alumni Association, 169
Alumni Band, 106, 108, 111, 112, 119, 134,
    142, 145, 169
Alumni Basketball Band, 171
Alumni Blue Band Association (ABBA), 112,
    164, 169, 171
Alumni Day, 25, 34
American Bandmasters' Association, 83,
    98, 128, 137
American Red Cross, 45, 90
American Telephone & Telegraph Company,
    49, 169
American University, 94
"America the Beautiful," 39, 105, 122
Ammon, Richard, 171, 185
"Anchors Aweigh," 99, 122
Anderson, F. M., 184
Anderson, Jack, 183
Andre, David, 185

Andre, Malcolm, 185
Andrews, Frances W., 116
"Aquarius," 125
Archer Eppler Drum Corps, 95
Armory, 10, 13, 20, 40, 73, 136
Armstrong, H. P., 24
Army football team, 133
Arnoldi, Dave, 145
Arny, L. W., 184
Arrington, Clark, 125
Arthur, Robert, 79
Associated Student Activities, 128, 131
Association of Women's Studies, 131
Astroturf field, 60
Atherton, George, 10–11, 13, 17, 21, 45
Atherton, Helen, 17, 24
Athletic Advisory Board, 67
Athletic Association, 49–50, 57, 70–71, 80,
    85
Athletic Bands position, 169
Athletic Department, 70, 90, 93, 133,
    138–39, 152, 158
"Auld Lang Syne," 96
Auman, W. R., 49
"Axel F/Neutron Dance," 149

Baisley, Robert W., 116, 117
Baker, Allen, 184
Baker, E. P., 184
Baker, Miss, 38
Baker, Newton D., 45
Band Camp, 122, 123, 133
Band Day, 83, 90, 91, 92, 93, 102, 104, 112,
    120, 128, 129, 133, 148
"Banddidntstrike," 38
Band of the Fighting Irish, 183
Bandorama, 137, 140–41, 144, 148, 152

Bands, college and university. *See also
    under names of individual bands and
    individual colleges and universities*
All-American Marching Band (Purdue),
    183
Band of the Fighting Irish, 183
Bruin Marching Band (UCLA), 183
Connecticut All-State High School
    Band, 117
Fightin' Texas Aggie Band, 183
Fighting Irish Band, 160
Georgia Tech Band, 109
Golden Tornado Marching Band, 47
Kansas Jayhawk Band, 125
Longhorne Band, 183
Marching 100 (Indiana), 183
Marching 100, The (Florida A&M), 183
Marching Illini (Illinois), 100, 183
Michigan Marching Band, 164, 183
Million Dollar Band (Alabama), 101, 141
Mountaineer Marching Band (West
    Virginia), 110
Ohio State Marching Band, 134, 164,
    165, 170, 183
Pride of the Orange (Syracuse), 55, 160,
    183
Princeton University Band, 183
Pittsburgh Panther (Pitt) Band, 76, 79,
    146–47, 183
Red Raider Band, 70
Rutgers Band, 183
Spartan Marching Band, 183
Temple Owls Band, 95
Trojan Marching Band, 183
U.S. Air Force Acadamy Band, 83, 98,
    133
U.S. Army Band, 98, 137
U.S. Marine Corps Band, 51

U.S. Navy Band, 83
University of Minnesota Marching
    Band, 183
University of Wisconsin Band, 183
USC Trojan Band, 130
Yale Precision Marching Band,
    183"Barber of Seville," 23
Barley, Maynard, 185
Barlow, W. R., 184
Bartner, Arthur C., 183
Basie, Count, 128
Basketball Pep Band, 58, 94, 102, 116, 133,
    162, 167
"Battle for Democracy," 56
"Battle Hymn of the Republic," 122
Baylies, James, 28, 39
Baylor University, 134
"Beautiful Ohio," 99
Beaver, James Addams, 10–11, 17, 53, 101
Beaver Field, 18, 24, 30, 31, 44, 61, 64, 74,
    75, 77, 79, 96, 97, 98, 99, 100–101, 103,
    110
"Beaver Field Pictorial," 81
Beaver Stadium, 34, 37, 46, 60, 93, 95, 101,
    103, 104, 108, 110, 111, 115, 123, 131,
    134, 137, 138, 140, 144, 146, 148, 152,
    153, 155, 156, 160, 162, 165, 166, 170,
    171, 172
Behm, Charlotte, 131
Bellevue-Stratford Hotel, 56
Bennett, Darren, 154, 185
"Beyond the Blue Horizon," 122
Bezdek, Hugo, 52
Biery, W. E., 184
"Big Blue," 120
Big Ten Athletic Conference, 35, 60, 124,
    125, 127, 136, 137, 159, 163, 164, 166,
    170, 173
Bilik, Jerry, 34
"Billboard" (NBC program), 124
Black, George, 94, 185
Blakely, David, 3
Block Band, 151
Blockbuster Bowl, 163
Blue and White Game, 93, 148
Blue Band Silks, 114, 124, 138, 141
Blue Key society, 76
Blue Sapphire, 114, 141, 145, 147, 171
Booth, S. I., 184
Boston College, 104, 154–55, 164
Boston Symphony Orchestra, 28
Boston University, 91
Bowers, Lori, 141, 144, 147, 185
Bowers, R. W., 15–16, 184
Bowling Green University, 172
Brandeis University, 84
Branley, John, 160–61
Branley, Lori, 147, 156, 160–61, 158, 163, 185
Brigham Young University, 158
Brightbill, Charles, 184
Brouse, Charles, 185
Brown, Kathleen, 133
Bruin Marching Band (UCLA), 183
Brumbaugh, Martin G., 30, 31, 39

Bryant, Paul ("Bear"), 102
Bryce Jordan Center, 46, 58, 169–70
Bucknell University, 59, 77
Buffalo Bills, 156
Buffalo (N.Y.) Civic Stadium, 70
Buffalo (N.Y.) Junior Chamber of
    Commerce, 70
Bunche, Ralph, 84
Bundy, Christine, 168
Bundy, O. Richard, 143, 148, 149, 155, 165,
    167, 168–69 (bio), 173, 185
Burden, James, 73, 101
Burns, Roy, 128
Burns, Wes, 184

Cahn, Charles, 185
Campbell, Robert, 94
"Camptown Races," 96
Campus Band, 78, 167
Carl, George, 184
Carlisle Indian School, 18, 20
Carnegie, Andrew, 11, 13, 17, 73
Carnegie Hall, 38, 73
Carnegie Library, 17
Carnegie Tech, 88–89, 98
"Carry Me Back to Old Virginie," 96
"Catharina Cormare," 35
CBS television, 153
Centre County Red Cross, 39
Centre Daily Times, 135, 138
"Century of Excellence," 152
chair step. See high step
Chambers Building, 130
Chapman, Carrol, 92, 185
Citrus Bowl, 171
Civil War, 49
Clapp, R. B., 184
"Clementine," 121
Click, William, 184
Clingerman, Becky, 66
Colgate University, 70–71
College Band Directors National Associa-
    tion, 137
College Choir, 80
College Chorus, 82
College Military Band, 40, 48
College of Arts and Architecture, 116–17,
    142
College of Education, 116, 141
College of Health, Physical Education, and
    Recreation, 128
College Orchestra, 17, 26
College Quartet, 29
Collegian, The, 18–19, 22, 24, 28, 30, 35, 36,
    44, 57, 64, 73, 81, 88, 105, 109, 117, 125,
    130, 131–32, 133, 141, 171
Concert Band, 167
Concert Blue Band, 77, 78, 116
Concert White Band, 78, 137, 167
Connecticut All-State High School Band, 117
Connon, Joe, 184
Copland, Aaron, 152
Cornell University, 10, 20
Corner Concert, 138

Cotton Bowl, 80, 130, 134
Craig, John Monroe, 10, 11
Cramer, Don, 163, 185
Crandell, John S., 26
Crider, Paula A., 183
Crimson Tide, 102
Croissant, Jen, 155
Crouthamel, Jake, 154
Croxton, Marty, 185
Cugini, Carmen, 83
Curtiss-Wright Corporation, 75
Czarnecki, S. J., 40
Czekaj, Leanne, 131

Dad's Day, 60–61, 64
Daily Athenaeum (WVU student news-
    paper), 111
Daughters of the American Revolution, 45
"Day in the Life of a Cadet," 97
"Day in the Life of a Soldier," 74
Deauville (Miami hotel), 124
Deihl, Ned C., 78, 83, 93, 113, 120, 121,
    127, 134–35, 136–37 (bio), 139, 140,
    141, 142, 143, 144, 146, 153, 156, 160,
    162, 167, 180, 185
Deike, George Herbert, 9–13, 12 (bio), 84,
    184
Department of Civil Engineering, 28
Department of Military Science and
    Tactics, 28, 31, 35, 39, 44, 56, 58
Department of Music, 22, 29, 31, 35, 36,
    45, 52, 57, 58, 66, 67, 68, 69–70, 73,
    76, 82, 84, 85, 88, 112, 116–17, 134,
    135, 164
Department of Music Education, 67, 68,
    82, 112, 116–17, 139, 142
Dever, K. R. ("Danny"), 50, 184
Dickinson College, 15, 16, 17
Dimeo, Victor, 73, 184
DiRinoldo, Marie, 131
"Dixie," 48, 96
Dodge, Fred P., 15
Dodge, George Washington, 10–11, 13, 15,
    184
Dombrowski, Raymond, 185
Donaldson, Lori, 147, 185
Donovan, William J., 84
Druids, 76
Drum Major Flip, 129, 154–55
"Dry Bones," 105
Duff, James H., 84
Duffy, Thomas, 183
Dunbar, M., 184
Dunlop, James, 78, 82–83 (bio), 84, 98,
    91–92, 97, 99, 105, 108, 116, 120, 121,
    125, 128, 131–32, 134, 135, 136, 137,
    147, 168, 180, 184–85
Duquesne University, 168
Dye, Bill, 28–29
Dye, Louise, 76
Dzigas, Jay, 154, 185

Edison, Thomas, 12
Edison movie company, 22

Edwards, Oliver Christmas ("Irish"), 10
Egolf, Ralph J., Jr., 89
"1812 Overture," 149
"Eight to Five," 46, 72, 136
Eisenhower, Dwight D., 88, 95–96
Eisenhower, Milton Stover, 87, 96
Eisenhower Auditorium, 140, 141, 148, 167
Elder, P. G., 16
Ellenberger, Richard, 62
Ellington, Duke, 128, 152
Engineers' Band, 47, 49
Engle, Rip, 102
"Ernio Kovackski," 98
Espenshade, A. Howry, 10–11, 56
Ethington, Bradley, 183
Everitt, F. C., 184

Farmers' High School, 6–7, 178
Farrell School District, 82
Feature Twirler, 147, 162–63
Felack, Eric, 134, 135, 138, 185
Feldser, Oscar B., 184
Felton, Gilson, 184
Field Day, 44
Fiesta Bowl, 138, 144–45, 152–53, 162
Fife and Drum Corps, 36
"Fight for Penn State's Rights," 39
Fighting Irish Band, 160
Fightin' Texas Aggie Band, 183
"Fight On, State," 34, 35, 45, 46, 115, 128
Filer, Paul, 184
"Fireman's Song," 95
Fishburn, David, 93
Fishburn, Hummel, 34–35, 52, 60–62, 64,
    65, 66 (bio) 68, 69, 72, 73, 74–75, 76,
    77, 79, 80, 82, 84, 91, 92, 94, 98, 112–
    13, 116, 125, 130, 134, 135, 136, 168,
    180, 184
Fishell, Darcy, 131
Fisher, Larry, 139
Fisher Plaza, 60
Fiyalko, Jere, 131
Flemming, Neil, 60
Flip, the. See Drum Major Flip
Floating Lions Club, 164
Floating Lions Drill, 35, 113, 136, 140, 150
Florida A&M University, 183
Florida State University, 122
Forbes Field, 94, 99, 113
Foster, Katherine, 24
Foster, Stephen, 96
Fought, Don, 185
Fought, Rob, 185
Frank, Tom, 185
Frankfurter, Felix, 84
Franklin Field, 56, 94
Fred Waring NBC Show, 80
Freelance, The, 13, 53
Friars society, 76
Frid, E. M., 184
Fridy, Jere, 185
Fries, Richard, 185
Frisbie, Debbie, 133
Frisbie, Floyd, 185

Fritz, K. L., 184
Froth, The, 62
Fundamentals of Music Appreciation
    (Fishburn), 67
funding, 90
"Funny Valentine," 96

Gabler, Carol, 133, 135, 185
Gailey, C. C., 184
Garbrick, Allen, 16
Garbrick, Barbara, 16
Garbrick, J. Henry, 16
Garner, Bruce, 184
Gator Bowl, 109, 111, 122
Georgia (Institute of Technology) Tech, 47,
    48, 52, 162
Georgia Tech Band, 109
G.I. Bill, 77
Gillis, Rosemary, 185
Gilmore, Patrick Sarsfield, 2, 4
Gippel, O. B., 26, 184
Glee Club, 25, 26, 29, 31, 36, 38, 55, 66, 67,
    80, 82, 108
Glenn, Gary, 185
Glocke, Dennis, 78, 167
Godard, Edgar Earle ("Paddy"), 10, 11, 13,
    15, 17, 184
"God Bless America," 121
Golden Tornado Marching Band, 47
Golla, Eugene, 81
Goodman, Benny, 108, 128
Gorodesky, Rich, 154, 185
Graham, Greg, 145
Graham, J. E., 26
Grand Army of the Republic, 15
"Grand Commander," 56
Grant, Richard, 35, 55, 58, 60, 73
Grant, T. E., 49
Gray, Alexander, III, 25
Great Depression, 59
Greene, J. E., 184
Gregory, William, 185
Grove, P., 76, 184
Gulf War, 158
Gullo, Frank, 67, 71, 82, 94

Hafer, Barbara, 167
Hahn, Thomas, 185
Hall, Linda, 133
"Halls of Ivy," 128
Hansen, Albert A., 34
Harmon, M. F., 16
Harrell, Mike, 154–55, 160, 162, 185
Harrisburg Alumni Association, 56
Haugh, Hubert H., 88
Hay, Commandant, 21
Heller, Jules, 116–17
Henderson, Gordon, 183
Henney, R. F., 40
Henrotte, Pierre, 70
Herman, Woody, 108
Hermanowicz, Henry J., 141
Hess, Frank, 184
Hetzel, Ralph Dorn, 56, 58, 77, 82

Higgins, Bob, 28
Higher Education Act, Title 9, 131
high step (chair step), 72, 114, 137, 138, 182
"high-steppers" (drum line equipment),
    135, 138
Hillings, Janese, 131
Hirsh Weintraub Company, 60
Hoffeditz, F. A. R., 184
Holiday Bowl, 158
Hollenback, William, 24
Holy Cross College, 97, 100
"Horses, Horses, Horses," 94
Hotel New Yorker, 97
Hotel Pennsylvania, 49
Hotel Schenley, 26
Hotel Washington, 15
Howard, George S., 69
Hower, Don, 146
"huddle," the, 46
Hunsicker, F. W., 184

Ice Bowl, 155
Indeglio, Nick, 147, 171–72
Indiana University, 136, 183
Infantry Band, 49
Institute of French Education, 55
Institute of Music Education, 55
Inter-Class Finance Board, 71, 89
Intercollegiate Band Festival, 88
Intercollegiate Marching Band Trophy,
    Louis Sudler, 164
"Intervention March," 128
Intramural Sports Fields, 60
Isenberg, D. A., 184
Itzkowitz, Fern, 131–32
"I've Been Working on the Railroad," 99

Jacisin, Mike, 185
Jacobs, Harry M., 184
James, Walter, 73, 184
Jazz Blue Band, 139
Jefferson, Thomas, 2
Jeffords, Susan, 131
Johnson, Michael, 162
"Just a Gigolo/Ain't Got Nobody," 149

Kansas Jayhawk Band, 125
Kansas State University, 88
Kappa Kappa Psi, 50
KDKA radio, 52, 55, 59
Keefauver, William, 80, 184
Keene, James F., 183
Keisling, Bernard, 185
Kellerman, William, 183
Kennedy, J. D. P., 16
Kennedy, J. B., 35
Kern Building, 60
Kester, P. R., 184
KFXX radio, 52
Khan, Mohammed Aly Zafrullah, 84
Kickoff Classic, 155, 162, 169
Kimmel, Lewis, 184
"King Pomp Pompous I," 66
Klimke, Alfred, 96

Knights Templar, 17, 56
Knoche, B. Frank, 7–8
Knutsen, William, 184
Kologi, Matt, 170
Kovalchik, John, 185
Kozsuch, Matt, 165–66

Ladies' Cottage, 26
Lafayette College, 59, 64
Lambert, Don, 94, 185
Lane, G. B., 184
Laughlin, William, 184
La Vie, 13, 17, 28, 29, 74, 94
Lawrence, David, 90
Lawton, Captain, 16
"Lead Me On," 53
Lebanon Valley State College, 31
Leckrone, Mike, 183
Leety, Harry E., 9
Lehigh College, 13, 30, 31, 35, 47
Lemoyne High School, 56
Leppla, David, 183
Levy, Aaron, 84
Lewis, Ted, 108
Lewis, Willard, 82
Leyden, Donald, 80
Leyden, James A., Sr., 31, 34, 49, 80
Leyden, James A., Jr., 34, 80, 184
Liberty Bowl, 101–2, 108, 109, 121
"Life's Lullaby," 25
Lincoln, Abraham, 7
Lindsey, Jeni, 185
"Lion Special," 172
Little, Thomas, 185
Loewen, Phil, 185
Logan, John A., 15
Longhorne Band, 183
Longstreet, P. W., 184
Los Angeles Rams, 156
Louder, Ron, 138, 139–40, 154, 185
Lowman, Gerald F., 185
Lowry, Robert, 108–9
Lubin Company, 22
Lucas, Jay, 18, 185
Luckhardt, Jerry, 183
Lyford, A. P., 184

Maddas, Bryon, 185
Madden, John T., 183
"Make Me Smile," 128
Mandolin Club, 17, 25, 26, 31, 38
Mansfield State College, 82
Marchetti, Sue, 155
Marching Illini (Illinois), 100, 183
Marching 100 (Indiana), 183
Marching 100, The (Florida A&M), 183
marching styles (Big Ten style, drum corps
   style, historically black college style,
   Ivy League style, military style, show
   style), 182–83
"Marine Hymn," 122
Mark, Nancy, 131
Markham, C. W., 184
Martin, Janette, 136

Marynak, Lawrence, 133
Mascia, Maxwell, 185
Mason, Harrison Denning ("Joe"), 12
McAllister Hall, 18, 24
McAlpin Hotel, 48
McChesney, Allan, 94
McCormick, Jerry, 154
McCoy, Ernest, 95, 109
McDermott, Tom, 81
McDowell, Katy, 170, 185
McHugh, John, 94
McKinley, William, 13
Meissner, L. R., 23, 184
Memorial Day 1920, 45
Menham, J. P., 184
Metropolitan Opera House, 70
Miami University of Ohio, 136
Michigan State University, 30, 79, 164, 183
Miley, A. M., 184
Miley, Art, 169, 185
Military Week, 56
Miller, Rich, 34
Million Dollar Band (Alabama), 101, 141
Mine Safety Appliances Company, 12
"Missouri Waltz," 79
Mitchell, H. Walton, 55
Mitchell, John, 147, 156, 160–61, 163, 185
"Monday Night Football," 156
Moody, William J., 122
Morrill, Justin S., 7
Morrill Land Grant Act, 7, 44
Mountaineer Marching Band (West
   Virginia), 183
Mount Jewett High School, 82
Mount Nittany Savings & Loan
   Association, 67
Moyer, W. A., 26, 184
"Mr. Touchdown," 152
Murphey, Kathryn, 133
Music Building, 144
Music Education Association, 100
Musser, Boyd, 56
"My Old Kentucky Home," 96

National Anthem, 76, 100, 109
National Association of College Band
   Directors, 83
National AUU Gymnastics Championship,
   93
National Baton Twirling World Champion-
   ship, 156
National Defense Act, of 1920, 44
"National Emblem," 64, 91
National Football League, 132
National Music Week, 56
Naval Academy, 47, 52, 65, 79, 122, 133
Navy Blue and Gold, 79
NBC Studios, 56
Nero, Peter, 128
Nesbit, D. E., 184
New Haven Symphony Orchestra, 116
New Haven Youth Symphony, 116
New York University, 56–57, 71
Nike, 170

"Nittany Lion" (fight song), 34, 45, 46, 96,
   99, 114, 154, 167
Nittany Lion Band, 78, 137
Nittany Lion Club, 169
Nittany Lion Inn, 101
Nittany Lion Mascot, 147, 162, 171
Nittany Lion Shrine, 36, 101, 128, 131, 135
Norris, Earle B., 15–16, 184
Norris, Edwin Ray, 10, 15–16
North Carolina State University, 83
Northwestern University, 164
Nowlin, Susan, 133, 135

Ober, Ed, 185
"Ode to Joy," 172
officers, band, 63
Ohio State University, 4, 21, 28, 36, 134,
   144, 163, 164, 165, 166, 167, 170, 183
Ohio University, 125
Old Main, 10, 21, 24, 25, 45, 60, 70, 73, 79,
   96, 101
"Old Man River," 99
Ometz, Derrick, 154, 185
Orange Bowl, 123–24, 125, 149, 152
Orndorf, Glenn, 184
Ostwald Company, 109
"O Susanna," 96
Oswald, John W., 128
"Over the Rainbow," 105

"Parade Order," 138
Parmi Nous society, 76
"Pas des Echarpes," 38
Pastime Theatre, 66
Paterno, Joe, 147, 165–66, 172
Pattee, Fred Lewis, 53
Pattee Library, 21, 73, 78, 93
Peach Bowl, 128
"Penn State" (march), 31, 40, 49
Penn State Alumni Association, 12
Penn State Athletics, 164
Penn State Club of Greater Syracuse, 154
Penn State Club of Harrisburg, 94
Penn State Gymnastics Club, 155
"Penn State in Hi-Fi," 108
Penn State Jazz Club, 125
Penn State Night, 55, 94
Penn State Thespians, 55, 80, 81
Pennsylvania College Bandmasters'
   Association, 116
Pennsylvania Day, 17, 20, 30, 38, 50
Pennsylvania Future Farmers of America, 83
Pennsylvania Horse Show, 94
Pennsylvania Music Educators'
   Association, 67, 116
Pennsylvania State Agricultural Society, 6
Pennsylvania Week, 84, 96, 113
Pennypacker, Samuel, 17
"Peter, Peter, Pumpkin Eater," 105
Petroy, Tony, 145–46, 154, 185
Phi Mu Alpha, 66, 80, 137
Pi Kappa Lambda, 137
Piper, Charles M., 184
Pittsburgher (hotel), 89

Pittsburgh Panther Band (Pitt Band), 76, 79, 146–47, 183
Pollock, Edward, 64, 68, 184
Polo Grounds, 47, 48
Pond, George Gilbert, 13, 26, 45, 63
Potter, George L., Jr., 7
Powell, W. G., 184
practice fields, 60
"Praise the Lord and Pass the Ammunition," 74
pregame show, 114
Prendergast, John, 185
Pride of the Lions, 58, 167, 168
Pride of the Orange, 55, 160, 183
Princeton University, 18, 183
Princeton University Band, 183
Purdue University, 164, 183
pushball scrap, 27

Radio City Music Hall, 73
Ramsey, Darhyl, 142, 168
Range, Thomas, II, 185
Read, William, 7, 8
Recreation Hall, 58, 60, 78, 93, 94, 101, 133
Red Raider Band, 70
Redsacker, Samuel, 184
Regimental Drum and Bugle Corps, 30
Reider, Ezra, 184
Reinhart, Ron, 97
Reserve Officer Training Corps (ROTC), 7, 39, 40, 44, 49, 50, 77
Ressler, James, 185
Revelli, William, 82, 83, 136
Riley, John, 144
Ritenour, Jamie, 147, 185
Ritenour, Joseph, 82
Roberts, Tom, 154, 155, 162, 165–66, 185
Robertson, Jeff, 129, 134, 154, 185
Robinson, Clarence, 29, 31, 45
Rockefeller Center, 73
Rookie Run, 46
Roosevelt, Theodore, 20
Rose Bowl, 166
Rosebrock, Charles, 185
Rutgers Band, 183
Rutgers University, 92, 183
Ryan, John, Sr., 12
Ryan, John, Jr., 60

"Saber and Spurs," 51
Sacher, Abram, 84
Salem College, 82
Sanders, Joseph, 35
"Schlop" Schlosser's Orchestra, 66
School Musician Director and Teacher (magazine), 83
School of Agricultural Science, 28
School of Arts and Architecture, 22, 90
School of Liberal Arts, 31
School of Music, 78, 142, 167, 168
School of Music Education, 168
Schraft's Motor Lodge, 125
Schuchman, T. M., 184
Schwab, Charles, 17

Schwab Auditorium, 17, 18, 21, 24, 25, 26, 31, 35, 40, 45, 51, 56, 66, 78, 79, 80, 93, 128
"Script Ohio," 164
"Second Regiment Connecticut National Guard," 35
Sedotole, Kevin, 183
Seely, Randy, 185
Selective Service Act, 44
Setar, John, 184
Shadle, Daryl, 185
Shappelle, Claude, 60, 184
Shaw, Artie, 108
Shearer (-Lawrence), Judy, 130–31, 132, 133, 147, 156, 162, 185
Shelley, Donald, 184
Shiner, Matty, 168
"Sing, Sing, Sing," 149, 152
Sioux City Symphany Orchestra, 108
Sipe, Carl, 108, 109, 185
"Sixteen Tons," 121
"six to five," 97, 136
Skull and Bones society, 76
Skull Session (Ohio State's), 165
Slaton, H. L., Mrs., 122
Smith, Amy, 185
Smith, B. A., 184
Smith, C. H., 184
Smith, Cheryl, 147, 185
Smith, Don, 73
Smith, R. J., 184
Smith, Sean, 156
Snavely, Luther, 183
Snavely, P. M., 24, 25, 184
Snoeberger, Percy Marvin, 11
Snyder, C. R., 184
Sousa, John Philip, 2–4, 22, 28, 50–51, 68, 152
Southern Methodist University, 80
Spangler, Greg, 185
Sparks, Edwin, 21, 28, 31, 35, 36, 39, 44, 45
Sparks, Mrs. Edwin, 38
Spartan Marching Band, 183
"Spectator, The," 18–19
"Spinning Wheel," 125
Sproul, William C., 40
Stanford University, 134, 163
Stark, Jacob, 60
"Stars and Stripes Forever," 134, 152, 167
"Star Spangled Banner," 39, 40, 70, 95, 114
State College High School, 75, 104, 108, 120
Statler Hilton Hotel, 100
Staub, Roger, 185
Stevenson, Lynann, 131
Steward, Jennifer, 147, 185
Stock, Greg, 152–53, 154, 155, 185
Stone, William A., 15
Stormer, D. E., 146
Strickler, W. B., 184
Strine, Sean, 185
Stuart, Edwin, 21
Student Army Training Corps, 40
Student Council, 50

Student Government, 116
Stumpff, Glenn, 111
Sudler, Louis. See Intercollegiate Marching Band Trophy
Sugar Bowl, 141, 147, 148
Sumner, G. L., 29
Sun Devil Stadium, 144–45
Supplee, George, 184
"Swanee River," 96
Swift, Raymond, 128
Symphonic Band, 78, 167
Symphonic Orchestra, 26, 29, 66, 77
Symphonic Wind Ensemble, 120, 167
Syracuse University, 55, 57, 116, 138, 154, 156, 160, 164, 165, 183

Taft, William Howard, 28
Tag Day, 47
TailGreat, 165, 167, 169–70, 173
Taliaferro, Thomas, 9–10
Tatgenhorst, John, 34
Taylor, Francis, 185
Team Aisle formation, 158
Temple Owls Band, 95
Temple University, 70, 73, 81, 134, 152, 164
Tener, John K., 30
Texas A&M University, 183
Texter, A. F., 51, 184
Thalman, L. Budd, 156
"Thanks for the Buggy Ride," 121
"That Old Black Magic," 105
"There Will Be a Hot Time in the Old Town Tonight," 64
Thespian Orchestra, 26
Thomas, John Martin, 52
Thompson, Wilfred Otto ("Tommy"), 23, bio 28–30, 34, 35, 36, 39, 40, 43, 45, 46, 47, 49, 50–51, 52, 58, 59, 60, 61, 62, 64, 65, 66, 67, 68, 73, 80, 84, 89, 113, 125, 135, 163, 167, 180, 184
Throckmorton, John, 97
Times, The (State College, Pa.), 13, 15
Title 9 of the Higher Education Act, 131
Tobacco Festival Parade, 96
"Toccata and Fugue in D Minor," 152
Toler, Ray, 183
Toretti, Sever ("Tor"), 105
"To the Colors," 70
Tothero, Dwight, 92
Touch of Blue, 114, 132, 141, 147, 162
Toulson, Smith C., III, 116–17, 120
Tournament of Roses Parade, 166
Townsend, Brad, 185
Townsend, James, 184
Trautman, Ned, 125, 185
Treese, E. M., 184
Trojan Marching Band (USC), 130, 183
Trout, Robert, 185
Truman, Harry S., 79
Tuckmantel, Brain, 185
Turner, Lois, 75

UCLA, 123, 183
Uhazie, Dave, 185

Uniforms, 36–37
U.S. Air Force Academy Band, 83, 98, 133
U.S. Army Band, 98, 137
U.S. Marine Corps Band, 51
United States Military Acadamy, 51
U.S. Navy Band, 83
University Faculty Senate, 67
University Inn, 20. *See also* Nittany Lion Inn
University of Alabama, 101, 141, 144, 148, 153
University of Connecticut, 117
University of Florida, 171
University of Georgia, 147
University of Illinois, 100, 164, 165, 170, 183
University of Iowa, 131, 164
University of Kansas, 123
University of Maryland, 63, 113, 120, 162
University of Miami, 152
University of Michigan, 4, 82, 83, 84, 136, 163, 166, 167, 168, 183
University of Minnesota, 183
University of Montreal, 66
University of Nebraska, 84, 146
University of New Mexico, 83
University of North Carolina, 134
University of North Texas, 168
University of Notre Dame, 152, 164, 183
University of Oklahoma, 152
University of Oregon, 108, 166
University of Pennsylvania, 31, 40–41, 47, 51, 55–56, 74, 76, 96
University of Pittsburgh, 25, 31, 35, 38, 39, 40, 47, 52, 55, 59, 70, 73, 74, 76, 79, 89, 92, 96, 99, 116, 130, 134, 146, 156, 164, 183
University of Southern California, 4, 108, 130, 144–45, 183
University of Southern Mississippi, 172
University of Tennessee, 130, 162
University of Texas, 4, 122, 130, 160, 183
University of Utah, 83, 134
University of Virginia, 96
University of Wisconsin, 44, 60, 167, 171, 183
"Up, Up, and Away," 125

Ursinus College, 56
USS *Independence*, 158

Valencic, Debra, 131
Valley Forge Military Academy Band, 95
"Varsity Drag," 128
Varsity Quartet, 31, 49, 52
"Victory," 31, 34, 45, 46
Victory Raffle, 76
Vietnam War, 122
Vitagraph, 22

Wagenborg, David, 185
Wagner, C. C., 184
Walk, Seth, 154, 185
Walker, Elton D., 28, 65
Walker, Eric A., 12, 109
Walker, Herschel, 147
Wallace, Tom, 34
Walmart, 169
"Wandering Minstrel," 98
Waring, Fred, 34, 80, 96
Warner, Glenn ("Pop"), 18
Warnock, Arthur R., 66, 112
war stamps, 76
Washington, George, 2
Washington Music Conservatory, 66
"Washington Post" (Sousa march), 51, 105
Washington State University, 80
Watts, Ralph L., 28, 65
WEAF (AT&T studio), 49
Weeks, John W., 44
Weisner, James, 100
Wells College, 66
Westinghouse Corporation, 52
West Point, 2, 28, 96, 133
West Virginia University, 50, 55, 91, 104, 110, 183
We the People 200 parade, 153
Wetzel, E. S., 184
"When Irish Eyes Are Smilin'," 96
White, H. V., 10
White, Julian, 183
"White Christmas," 96
White Oak High School, 80
Widenor, W. B., 184

Wilchek, Mary, 131
Wilcox, Don, 183
Wilde, Cornel, 84
Willard Building, 10
William and Jefferson College, 16
William Penn High School Band, 95
William Penn Hotel, 89
William Rowland Company, 50
William Tell Overture, 98
Williams, H. C., 184
Willis, Stanley ("Chip"), 121, 185
Wilt, Carol, 145–46, 147, 185
WIP radio, 56
WJZ radio, 56
Wolfe, Christine, 147, 171–72, 185
Wolfe, Silas, 8
Wolter, Donna, 147, 185
Women in the Blue Band, 74
Women's Chorus, 66
Women's Symphonic Orchestra, 66
Wood, Alan, 83
Woodley, David, 183
Woods, Jon, 183
Woomer, Scott, 185
World War I, 39, 40, 43, 44, 49, 56
World War II, 69, 73, 78, 130
World's Columbian Exposition, 28
WPSC radio, 56
WPSX-TV, 148
WTAJ-TV, 144

Yale Precision Marching Band, 183
Yale University, 26, 183
Yankee Stadium, 50, 71
Yingling, Drew, 114, 115
Ying Yang Band, 105
Yoder, Paul, 34, 120
"You Gotta Be a Football Hero," 152
Young Men's Christian Association (YMCA), 17, 26, 45
Young Republican Club, 98
"You're the Inspiration," 149

Zarney's Big Circus, 40
Zerby, A. B., 52
Zuber, Andy, 185